T0200515

Project Management Tools and Techniques for Success

PROJECT MANAGEMENT TITLES
FROM AUERBACH PUBLICATIONS AND CRC PRESS

Managing Web Projects
Edward B. Farkas
ISBN: 978-1-4398-0495-7

The Complete Project Management
Methodology and Toolkit
Gerard M. Hill
ISBN: 978-1-4398-0154-3

Implementing Program Management:
Templates and Forms Aligned with the
Standard for Program Management —
Second Edition (2008)
Ginger Levin and Allen M. Green
ISBN: 978-1-4398-1605-9

Project Management Recipes for Success
Guy L. De Furia
ISBN: 978-1-4200-7824-4

Project Management of Complex and
Embedded Systems: Ensuring Product
Integrity and Program Quality
Kim H. Pries and Jon Quigley
ISBN: 978-1-4200-7205-1

Leading IT Projects: The IT
Manager's Guide
Jessica Keyes
ISBN: 978-1-4200-7082-8

Building a Project Work Breakdown
Structure: Visualizing Objectives,
Deliverables, Activities, and Schedules
Dennis P. Miller
ISBN: 978-1-4200-6969-3

A Standard for Enterprise
Project Management
Michael S. Zambruski
ISBN: 978-1-4200-7245-7

Global Engineering Project Management
M. Kemal Atesmen
ISBN: 978-1-4200-7393-5

Effective Communications for
Project Management
Ralph L. Kliem
ISBN: 978-1-4200-6246-5

Managing Global Development Risk
James M. Hussey and Steven E. Hall
ISBN: 978-1-4200-5520-7

The Strategic Project Leader: Mastering
Service-Based Project Leadership
Jack Ferraro
ISBN: 978-0-8493-8794-4

Determining Project Requirements
Hans Jonasson
ISBN: 978-1-4200-4502-4

Practical Guide to Project Planning
Ricardo Viana Vargas
ISBN: 978-1-4200-4504-8

The Complete Project Management
Office Handbook, Second Edition
Gerard M. Hill
ISBN: 978-1-4200-4680-9

Staffing the Project Office for
Competitive Advantage
J. Kent Crawford
ISBN: 978-0-8247-5477-8

Project Management Maturity Model,
Second Edition
J. Kent Crawford
ISBN: 978-0-8493-7945-1

Optimizing Human Capital with
a Strategic Project Office: Select,
Train, Measure, and Reward People
for Organization Success
J. Kent Crawford and
Jeannette Cabanis-Brewin
ISBN: 978-0-8493-5410-6

Project Management Tools and Techniques for Success

Christine B. Tayntor

CRC Press
Taylor & Francis Group
Boca Raton London New York

CRC Press is an imprint of the
Taylor & Francis Group, an **informa** business
AN AUERBACH BOOK

CRC Press
Taylor & Francis Group
6000 Broken Sound Parkway NW, Suite 300
Boca Raton, FL 33487-2742

First issued in paperback 2019

© 2010 by Taylor and Francis Group, LLC
CRC Press is an imprint of Taylor & Francis Group, an Informa business

No claim to original U.S. Government works

ISBN: 978-1-4398-1630-1 (hbk)
ISBN: 978-0-367-38403-6 (pbk)

Library of Congress Cataloging-in-Publication Data

Tayntor, Christine B.
   Project management tools and techniques for success / Christine B. Tayntor.
     p. cm.
   Includes bibliographical references and index.
   ISBN 978-1-4398-1630-1 (pbk. : alk. paper)
    1. Information technology--Management. 2. Project management. 3. Six sigma (Quality control standard) I. Title.

T58.5.T372 2010
658.4'04--dc22
                                         2010010973

Visit the Taylor & Francis Web site at
http://www.taylorandfrancis.com

and the CRC Press Web site at
http://www.crcpress.com

For my niece,
Lindsay Tayntor Laskowski

Contents

SECTION I   INTRODUCTION TO PROJECT MANAGEMENT

SECTION II   THE INITIATION/DEFINITION PHASE

SECTION III THE PLANNING PHASE, PART 1: WHO IS INVOLVED?

SECTION VI THE EXECUTION AND CONTROL PHASE, PART II: MAKING IT HAPPEN

SECTION VII THE CLOSEOUT PHASE

SECTION VIII APPENDICES

List of Figures

List of Tables

Introduction

Managing a project is difficult. Unlike general management, which is centered on repetitive tasks and stable staff, project management focuses on delivering change. Each project is unique. It is also temporary, with a clearly defined end. The staff who comprise the project team are often temporary as well, brought together for this one endeavor. Many are on loan from other departments, sometimes unwillingly. Time constraints may be imposed without considering the scope of work. Customers may have unrealistic expectations. Even worse, they may change their requirements after the project has begun. If this makes successful project management sound like an impossible dream, read on.

Successful project management is challenging—there is no denying that—but this book can help. Utilizing a series of tools and techniques, some adapted from Six Sigma with its proven success in the manufacturing and service industries, it provides methods for surmounting the project management challenge and improving the probability of success.

The book is divided into eight sections. The first provides an introduction to project management, contrasting the stages of poor project management with the phases of formal management. Because change is inherent in any project, Section I outlines the human effects of change and suggests ways to mitigate them. It also discusses the ways in which Six Sigma precepts and tools can be used in making projects more successful. Section I concludes with an introduction to the case study that is used to illustrate techniques throughout the rest of the book.

Section II is devoted to the first phase of a well-managed project: Initiation and Definition. It introduces concepts that are critical for the entire project life cycle, including selection of the right people, definition and prioritization of requirements, management of expectations, and risk assessment. Section II concludes with the drafting of the preliminary business case.

Because planning is an essential but often short-changed part of any project, two sections are devoted to it. The first concentrates on the human aspects of planning, including the selection of leaders and the formation and motivation of the team. Section III includes discussions of team dynamics and provides guidance for sourcing alternatives. Section IV focuses on the "what" and "when" aspects of the project, explaining the creation of network diagrams and schedules, project specifications, and the final business case, including cost/benefit analysis.

Section V begins the discussion of the third project phase, Execution and Control, with chapters devoted to the creation of a rule book, the establishment of a change management process, and the development of a communication plan. The second section devoted to Execution and Control, Section VI, covers project monitoring, quality and control, and organizational readiness. It concludes with a chapter on possible pitfalls and ways to avoid them.

The shortest of the sections, Section VII describes the final phase of a project: Closeout; and the appendices in Section VIII provide detailed instructions on how to create four of the most important tools discussed in the book, along with a list of acronyms and suggested reading.

About the Author

Christine B. Tayntor has been an IT manager and frequent contributor to technical publications for more than thirty years. She worked in the insurance, banking, manufacturing, and consulting industries, most recently as the director of global applications sourcing for Honeywell International in Morristown, New Jersey, where she became a Six Sigma Black Belt and received her DFSS certification. She is currently a full-time writer and lecturer.

INTRODUCTION TO PROJECT MANAGEMENT

Although there are many books about project management, a surprising number of projects are still undertaken with unrealistic expectations and minimal understanding of the tasks needed to make them successful. Despite the fact that projects are abandoned and others are less successful than originally anticipated, the trend shows no sign of abating. This book is designed to help companies increase the probability of consistently delivering projects on schedule, within budget, and with full functionality.

As its name implies, the first section provides an introduction, creating the foundation for the rest of the book. Chapter 1 provides a brief definition of project management and contrasts the four phases of poor project management (wild enthusiasm, disillusionment, panic, punishment of the innocent and reward of nonparticipants) with those of formal project management. Because projects, by their very definition, are designed to implement change, it is important to understand how change impacts people. Chapter 2 discusses the human effects of change and outlines methods to make the changes that are inherent in a project successful.

One underlying theme of this book is "prior planning prevents poor performance." Chapter 3 describes classic project management failures and introduces Six Sigma as a technique for avoiding those pitfalls. Although at its most fundamental, Six Sigma is a measurement of quality, the term is now used to encompass concepts and tools, all of which are designed to help achieve the goal of nearly perfect processes. A number of the classic Six Sigma tools and those that form part of Design for Six Sigma (DFSS) can be used to increase the probability of successful projects.

The majority of this book utilizes a case study of a fictional company to illustrate the concepts, tools, and techniques being described. Chapter 4 provides an introduction to that case study.

Chapter 1

Defining Project Management

Horror stories abound about projects that have run amuck. Some are over budget, others are completed many months past their scheduled deadlines, while still others deliver only a fraction of the promised results. The objective of this book is to outline techniques that enable project teams to reduce the likelihood of serious problems and prevent project management disasters.

Since the first phase of project management is its definition, and since one cause of project failure is the lack of a common understanding, let us begin with a few definitions.

Definitions

- *Project*—A unique, finite set of multiple activities intended to accomplish a specific goal. It should be noted that the adjectives in this definition are critical, because they differentiate a project from other types of activities.
- *Unique*—Although there may have been other similar efforts, a true project is unique in at least one aspect. For example, a mother of three children may arrange birthday parties for each child every year. She may be an expert at planning, but each party will be unique, if only because it is being held on a different date with participants who are older than they were at the last party.
- *Finite*—A project by definition has a beginning and a scheduled end. Even when target dates are missed, the project is still time-bound. It will end . . . eventually.

- *Multiple Activities*—Although a project is comprised of a series of tasks, a single activity does not constitute a project. There must be more than one.
- *Specific Goal*—To make it truly a project, the purpose of the activities to be undertaken must be defined. "Going shopping" is not a project, nor is "buying chocolate cake for Johnny's party." The former has no goal. The latter, while it includes a specific objective, is a single activity or a task. Using the example of the birthday party, the project might be defined as "Celebrate Johnny's fifth birthday on October 13 with a party for ten of his friends." It is unique, because Johnny will have only one fifth birthday. It is finite, ending on October 13. Implicit is the fact that arranging the party will involve multiple activities. And it is specific, since the description includes enough information to determine whether the goal has been met.
- *Management*—In the context of this book, management will be defined as "the act or art of directing." Project management is therefore the art of directing a project. It is important to note that while there are similarities between project and general management, what distinguishes project management from general management is the emphasis on a schedule and the temporary nature of both the organization and the work being performed.

Project Constraints

Managing a project is often described as a juggling act with the project manager attempting to keep all aspects of the project in the air at the same time. Another way to illustrate this concept is the use of the project constraint triangle. As shown on Figure 1.1, a project is normally both characterized and constrained by three elements: time, resources, and scope. Time is the schedule; resources are people and budget; scope is the functionality to be delivered.

Project Constraint Triangle

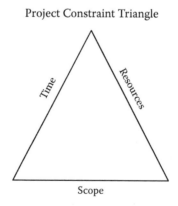

Scope

Figure 1.1   Project constraint triangle.

Out of Balance Project Constraint Triangle

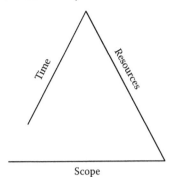

Figure 1.2 Out-of-balance project constraint triangle.

Figure 1.1 shows an equilateral triangle where all three constraints are in balance. While this is normal at the beginning of a project, it is rare to experience no changes during the life of a project. The schedule may be compressed; costs may exceed estimates; customers may request additional functionality. Each of these changes affects the triangle, shortening or lengthening that leg. If any single constraint changes, in order to keep the project in balance, at least one of the others will have to change to compensate. For example, as shown on Figure 1.2, if the time frame is shortened, either scope will have to be reduced or resources will need to be increased so that the legs of the triangle can be joined. This rebalancing or juggling act is the essence of project management.

Types of Project Management

When most people think of project management, they envision a formal process, one that follows a methodology. Although that variety of project management is the subject of this book, it is important to recognize that there are other types.

- *Unplanned*—These are seat-of-the-pants *ad hoc* efforts, where a group of people does its best to accomplish a goal. Under these circumstances, success is unpredictable, and even if it occurs, it cannot be easily replicated because little or nothing has been documented. In a business environment, unplanned projects are undesirable because they lack predictability.
- *Informal*—There are times when an experienced team may decide to run a project without utilizing the complete set of procedures and related documentation that would normally be used. Typically, these are projects of short duration that are very similar to other projects the same group has successfully completed. While success is more likely than in an unplanned project, the informality means that any lessons learned will not be captured for use by

another project team. This is undesirable in a business environment, because the probabilities of success for future projects are increased when team members can learn from others' experiences.

■ *Formal*—This is the most common and most desirable form of project management. An established process is followed; documentation is completed; project results are available as learning tools for future project teams.

Measuring Maturity

Even within companies that employ formal project management techniques, there are variations in the way those techniques are applied. The extent to which techniques are applied is sometimes referred to as maturity. Some professions, including software engineering, define themselves in terms of a maturity path and establish criteria for progression along that path. One of the best known is the SEI CMM. In response to the cost and schedule overruns that frequently plague software development projects, the Software Engineering Institute (SEI) at Carnegie Mellon University created the Capability Maturity Model (CMM). CMM is more than a measurement. It is a methodology designed to improve the development and delivery of software by making the entire process more predictable. The objectives are to prevent runaway projects and to enable an information technology (IT) department to produce every system on time and on budget.

CMM is often referred to as a maturity path with five milestones along the way, its maturity levels. Although CMM is designed specifically for software projects, the levels shown on Table 1.1 can be applied to any type of project and

Table 1.1 SEI CMM Levels

Level	Description	Characteristics
1	Initial	Results are unpredictable, because they are dependent on individuals' skills and efforts.
2	Repeatable	Basic processes have been established on a project level, making it possible to replicate performance on similar projects.
3	Defined	Standard processes have been integrated across the organization and are used consistently on all projects.
4	Managed	Detailed measurements and quantitative controls make it possible to predict results.
5	Optimizing	The organization actively seeks to improve the process through innovation.

can help project managers assess their organization's progress along the path to maturity.

Understanding the Stages of Poor Project Management

Because projects frequently have lengthy durations and are measured in months and years rather than days and weeks, they are often said to have a life cycle with predictable phases. Although its origin is unknown, one cynical version defines the stages of a project as wild enthusiasm, disillusionment, panic, and punishment of the innocent and reward of nonparticipants.

- *Wild Enthusiasm*—These are those heady first days of a project when everyone is excited about the goal and convinced that, no matter how many other similar projects have failed, they will succeed. It is easy to be enthusiastic, because no one has taken a reality check, and no one has worked on those pesky details of schedules and budgets.
- *Disillusionment*—All too soon, reality sets in. The project manager, or whoever is in charge, discovers that the budget is not unlimited and that several of the key people he had counted on for the team are available only part time. Meanwhile, the customer's initial excitement fades when she learns that not all the functions she had been promised will be delivered. The house she envisioned may have four bedrooms and two and a half baths, but on the date she had planned to move in, the project leader tells her there will be only one functioning bathroom, and the kitchen will not be completed until the second phase. Though no longer excited about the project, the team is still convinced that the goal can be achieved. It will simply take more work than they had expected. Lots more.
- *Panic*—This reaction ensues when the team faces the fact that, even if they could work 24/7, the project will not be done on schedule. Fearing that heads will roll, some team members quit, leaving the rest in a deeper state of panic. It is not uncommon at this point for senior management to bring in a consultant to rescue the project. Any remaining esprit de corps evaporates.
- *Punishment of the Innocent and Reward of Nonparticipants*—When the project ends, either by being canceled or delivered with greatly reduced functionality, the witch hunt begins. Team members who did their best in an impossible situation are reassigned to less prestigious projects, their careers are stalled if not destroyed, while the consultants, who may have done nothing more than report the initial team's recommendations, are paid hefty bonuses and publicly feted.

Unfortunately, while these descriptions may seem facetious, this is frequently the course of an unplanned project and is the reason why formal project management is so vital.

Defining the Phases of Formal Project Management

Like the proverbial poor management methodology described above, formal project management can also be divided into four phases: Initiation/Definition, Planning, Execution and Control, and Closeout.

- *Initiation/Definition*—Journalists speak of the Five Ws—who, what, where, when, and why—as the key elements in any article. The Initiation phase of a project seeks to answer those questions. One of the primary objectives of this phase is to temper unrealistic expectations. In other words, it is designed to prevent the natural enthusiasm that greets a new undertaking from spiraling out of control.
- *Planning*—The second phase continues the Definition work begun during the initiation stage, increasing the level of detail. It is during this phase that the team is formed, the schedule is drafted, and detailed specifications of what will—and will not—be included are established. Because expectations were controlled during initiation, it is less likely that this phase will become one of disillusionment.
- *Execution and Control*—Also called Implementation, this is the phase where plans turn into reality. As the name implies, there is a control element to this phase. Designed to monitor progress and resolve problems before they derail the project, the Control function mitigates risks and is key to preventing panic.
- *Closeout*—The final stage of a project is designed to formally end it by releasing the team and celebrating success. Although primarily focused on this particular project, the Closeout phase includes an evaluation of the overall project and documentation of lessons learned—both good and bad. This formal document becomes part of the company's repository and is meant to provide guidance for future project teams.

Table 1.2 provides a reference to the stages of successful and poor project management. Although no one would willingly undertake a project that involves panic

Table 1.2 Project Phases

Successful (Formal) Project Management	Poor (Ad Hoc) Project Management
Initiation/Definition	Wild enthusiasm
Planning	Disillusionment
Execution and Control (Implementation)	Panic
Closeout	Punishment of the innocent and reward of nonparticipants

and punishment of the innocent, without careful planning and attention by the manager, projects can deteriorate. This is why formal rather than *ad hoc* project management is essential. Dramatically different from the proverbial stages of a project, formal project management allows teams to increase their probability of success. Who does not want success?

Chapter 2

Project Management and Change

Project management is difficult. Although it requires all of the skills of general management, the nature of projects increases the complexity and requires skills in addition to those expected of a general manager. One of those additional skills is the ability to manage change. While it is simplistic to say that a general manager does not have to cope with change, the reality is that change is an incidental component of a general manager's life, not the *raison d'être*. A general manager focuses on maintaining status quo, while a project manager changes it. This is a fundamental difference.

In the business world, change is implicit in the definition of a project. After all, there would be no reason to plan, manage, and implement a project if nothing were going to change. Change occurs even in the example of Johnny's birthday party. His parents' finances change as a result of the party expenses. Johnny's collection of toys and other possessions changes after he opens his gifts. Even Johnny's self-esteem changes, because—at least for the length of the party—he is the center of attention.

Change may be positive; it may be negative; but it always has an impact. Because of this, it is important to understand how change affects people, what roles different individuals play during change, how those roles impact their acceptance of change, and how to avoid having poorly managed change derail a whole project.

The Basics of Change

While some people welcome change in their work environment, many others resist it, at least to some degree. The reasons are not hard to find. Change is difficult. There is a learning curve associated with any change, and that means that people who were once regarded as experts may feel as if they are novices. Even if the change is as seemingly simple as moving from one office to another, there are still the initial hurdles of unfamiliarity to overcome.

A classic book that reveals different reactions to change through a parable is Spencer Johnson's *Who Moved My Cheese?** In this parable of two mice's response to change, Johnson presents what he calls "the handwriting on the wall." These are seven statements that range from "change happens" to "enjoy change." While not everyone will enjoy change, if a project is to be successful, the project manager must make the changes associated with it as painless as possible. The first step is to understand how change affects people.

One exercise that is sometimes used in change management classes is to give participants a piece of paper and a pencil and ask them to write their names as if they were signing a check. Although this frequently elicits puzzled looks, it rarely creates a problem. When the facilitator tells the participants to move the pencil to their other hand and repeat the activity, the reaction is different. Nervous laughter and groans can sometimes be heard. The third step is for the participants to discuss the difference between the two experiences. Common responses when describing the second attempt are:

It took longer.
I felt awkward.
It was hard.
I had to think about it; this used to be instinctive.
My signature is illegible.
Why would anyone do this?

The point of the exercise is to understand that change—even as simple a change as writing with the nondominant hand—is difficult, and that when change is first imposed, quality may suffer and schedules may not be met. Furthermore, people may resist change because it takes them out of their comfort zone.

When asked if they think they could master writing with their nondominant hand if given enough time to practice, almost all participants will nod. The challenge in project management is to prepare everyone who will be affected by the change while at the same time ensuring that schedules are met and budgets are not exceeded.

Roles Associated with Change

When dealing with change, it is important to understand the roles individuals may play. Just as people have different roles in the organization and on a project team, so too are there different roles associated with change. In *Managing at the Speed of*

---

* Spencer Johnson, *Who Moved My Cheese?* (New York: G. P. Putnam's Sons, 1998), 76.

*Change,** Daryl Conner identifies four categories of roles: sponsors, agents, targets, and advocates.

■ *Sponsors* are the champions of change, the ones who instigate it. They are the people who identify the problem and seek a solution. It is important to note that Conner's sponsor may not be the same person as the champion that we will discuss in Chapter 5. A sponsor in Conner's terms may be a lower-ranking person within the company who recognizes the need for change and per-suades others of the value of that change rather than the person who becomes its primary defender. In project terms, sponsors are the impetus. They may or may not play an active role once the project is initiated.

■ *Agents* are the activists who make change happen. They are the people who are charged with translating the sponsor's vision into reality. In most projects, the project team members are the primary agents.

■ *Targets* are those who are changed. Normally, these are the ultimate end users or customers, the people whose jobs will be altered, at least to some degree, by the results of the project.

■ *Advocates* support the change. They may be members of the customer depart-ment who are not directly impacted by the change, as well as members of other departments who see the value of the change. While not directly involved in the project, they are vocal about its benefits and may help to sell the solution to the targets.

It should be noted that some people may play more than one role. It is possible for a person whose job will be changed as a result of the project (in other words, a target) to also serve as an agent.

The Impact of Change

The impact of change, of course, varies based on the magnitude of the change and the person's role. Targets are typically the people who feel the greatest effects of change. In her best-selling book *On Death and Dying,*[†] Elisabeth Kübler-Ross defines the stages that people go through as they face their own death or that of a loved one. Further research[‡] revealed that people experience these states not only when faced with mortality; any major life change can trigger them. Being laid off or having responsibilities dramatically changed, both of which can be the result of a project, are among those major life changes.

---

* Daryl R. Conner, *Managing at the Speed of Change* (New York: Villard, 1992), 106–7.
† Elisabeth Kübler-Ross, *On Death and Dying* (New York: Collier Books, 1969).
‡ William A. Borgen, "A Model for Group Employment Counseling," ERIC Digest, 1995, http://www.eric.ed.gov/ERICDOCS/data/ericdocs2sql/content_storage_01/0000019b/80/16/49/db.pdf.

Table 2.1   The SARAH Model

Stage	Characteristic Behaviors
Shock	Surprise and disbelief are the hallmarks of this stage. Irrational behavior is also possible. During Shock, it is impossible to predict what a person will do.
Anger	Productivity suffers as the individual lashes out at either the company as a whole or at specific people. Anger may also be internalized.
Resistance	During this stage, the employee will do the absolute minimum that is required to avoid being fired.
Acceptance	Although productivity may still not be normal, the employee has begun to cooperate.
Hope	In this stage, the employee recognizes that there may be benefits to the change.

Kübler-Ross defines the stages as denial, anger, bargaining, depression, and acceptance. When related to loss of a job or a major change in responsibility, the names of the stages are slightly different. As shown on Table 2.1, they are sometimes referred to as the SARAH model: shock, anger, resistance, acceptance, and hope.

When reviewing the SARAH model and trying to understand people's reactions, it is important to recognize the following:

■ *The speed with which people progress through the stages varies.* Some people will appear to skip stages completely, others to remain mired in one of them.
■ *Relapses occur.* The progression through the stages is not linear. It is possible that a person may have reached acceptance, but an event may trigger anger, and the person will return to that stage.
■ *Not everyone reaches hope.* Although that is the ultimate stage, there are no guarantees that each person will reach it.
■ *Survivor guilt is real.* It is not only the targets who experience these stages. Particularly in the case of layoffs, those who remain may feel many of the same emotions.

Many projects will not invoke the SARAH model, but for those that involve staff changes, relocation, or a major change in responsibility, it is beneficial for the project team to understand how people may react when faced with dramatic change and to be prepared for the various stages of coping with that change. As agents of change, even though they may not have been the instigators, the project team will often be the brunt of targets' anger and resistance.

Components of Successful Change

Change is not always successful. Virtually every company can cite an example of a major change that failed, whether it was the introduction of a product that fizzled or an attempt to implement a new version of a software product that created a rebellion in the customer community. Because of the failures—some of which have been spectacular—people have tried to identify the root causes of the problems.

In *Managing Transitions*,* William Bridges points out that for any change to be successful, it must have the Four Ps: purpose, picture, plan, and part.

■ *Purpose*—If the reason that the change is being implemented is not clear—and clearly communicated—the likelihood of success is diminished. Why would targets support a project whose value they do not understand, particularly when it will cause them more work or might even result in their losing their jobs? There should be no doubt in anyone's mind why a project has been undertaken and what benefits are expected to result.

■ *Picture*—It is not sufficient to understand why a change is occurring. It is equally critical that all persons involved have a clear vision of the end state. What will the company/their department/their individual jobs look like once the change is complete? Trying to implement change without this vision is a bit like trying to assemble a jigsaw puzzle without having seen a picture of the finished product. Although it is possible to assemble the puzzle or implement the change, the process is more frustrating and will take longer.

■ *Plan*—Simply knowing what the end state will be is of little value if the team does not have a plan to reach it. "Plan" is sometimes written "Plan/Process," because processes are needed to implement the plan. As with Purpose and Picture, it is vital that the plan be communicated to everyone who is impacted.

■ *Part*—Lastly, it is important that everyone who is involved in the change understands the role, or part, he (or she) is expected to play and the tasks he is expected to accomplish. Without that understanding, people may be working at cross-purposes or simply not working at all.

Other components of successful change are commitment and sustainability. These will be discussed in Chapters 7 and 23. The key points to remember about change are:

Resistance is normal.
A good plan helps.
Effective, honest communication is essential.

---

* William Bridges, *Managing Transitions* (Cambridge: Perseus, 2003), 60.

Chapter 3

Being Prepared

Though few want to admit it, one of the basic facts of project management is that some projects fail. When that happens, morale plummets and careers are damaged, sometimes irreparably. In many cases, the disaster could have been avoided had the project manager been aware of the warning signs and corrected the problems before they derailed the entire project. Although correction is good, an even more effective approach is to prevent the problems from occurring. An adage states that "A stitch in time saves nine." Managers are more likely to cite the Five Ps when dispensing the same advice, saying, "Prior planning prevents poor performance." No matter how it is phrased, the salient point is that it is far less costly to prevent a problem than to have to correct it.

Because anticipating and avoiding problems is so important, in addition to providing tools and techniques for successful project management, each chapter of this book beginning with Chapter 5 includes a "What Can Go Wrong?" section. Moreover, Chapter 8 is devoted to the issue of risks, providing techniques for identifying them and ways to mitigate them. Chapter 22 has as its sole subject the problems commonly found during the Execution and Control phase of a project. The objective is to prepare project managers by identifying potential problems so that they can be prevented from occurring.

Classic Failures

The annals of project management are rife with tales of spectacular failures. These include:

- Creating a product that few want
- Completing a project so late that the customer has found an alternative
- Delivering a product on schedule but at a cost so high that it is virtually unaffordable

All of these failures relate to the constraints shown on Figure 1.1: resources (which translate into costs), time (schedule), and scope (the customers' requirements). As stated previously, one of a project manager's primary responsibilities is to manage the three constraints so that the end result is a quality product delivered on schedule and at the agreed cost. And that, unfortunately, is not easy. The good news is, there are tools and techniques that increase the manager's probability of success. Some of these are classic project management techniques; others, including a number of tools, are derived from Six Sigma.

Six Sigma and Project Management

What is Six Sigma? Although the term has become synonymous with highly efficient, customer-focused companies that have reduced costs while increasing customer satisfaction, at its most basic level, Six Sigma is a measurement of quality. From its initial focus on measuring and reducing defects, the term is now used to encompass concepts and tools designed to help achieve the goal of nearly perfect processes.

What relevance does this have to project management? Even when a project is creating a one-time product, such as Johnny's birthday party, rather than an ongoing operation like a new assembly line for widgets, project management is a process. As such, it is subject to problems or—in Six Sigma terms—defects. Anything that can eliminate or prevent those defects will increase the probability of delivering a successful end product. Six Sigma techniques can do that.

A little background information may be helpful. The term "Six Sigma" comes from sigma (σ), the eighteenth letter of the Greek alphabet, which is also the symbol for standard deviation. Statisticians determine standard deviation by counting defects and opportunities to have created a defect. They then calculate a ratio of defects found per million opportunities to have created one. By definition, a process or product that is at the Six Sigma level has six standard deviations between its process center and the upper and lower specification limits, or only 3.4 defects per million opportunities. It is not necessary to be a statistician or to understand specification limits to realize that such a result is close to perfection.

To put this in perspective, most companies operate between three and four sigma. As shown on Table 3.1, a four-sigma process has greater than 99 percent accuracy. While that might appear acceptable, consider the third column, which illustrates the difference that increasing the sigma level makes in terms of reducing the number of defects, and the fourth, which translates defects into lost time. These dramatic differences are the reason companies adopted the Six Sigma philosophy and the reason they send their employees to weeks—and, in some cases, months—of training in Six Sigma concepts and tools.

Fortunately for project managers, it is not necessary to attend training or to learn to use all of the Six Sigma tools. It is not even necessary to understand the

Table 3.1 Comparison of Sigma Levels 3 Through 6

Sigma Level	Percent Correct	Number of Defects per Million Opportunities	Lost Time per Century
3	93.3193	66,807	3½ months
4	99.3790	6,210	2½ days
5	99.9767	233	30 minutes
6	99.99966	3.4	6 seconds

underlying philosophy behind Six Sigma. It is only necessary to know that, while many Six Sigma tools are not applicable to project management, others that do not rely on heavy-duty statistics can become valuable components of the project manager's toolbox and can help improve the likelihood of project success.

Six Sigma is built on a foundation that includes the following tenets:

- Prevent defects.
- Reduce variation.
- Focus on the customer.
- Make decisions based on facts.
- Encourage teamwork.

Each of these principles is of value to the project manager.

Defect Prevention

The objective of defect prevention is to anticipate and eliminate problems before they occur. Since it is an axiom of project management that the earlier an error is found, the less it will cost to repair it, prevention is the ultimate way to keep costs under control. By preventing errors from occurring rather than waiting to correct them, fewer resources and less time are expended, increasing the probability of keeping the three project constraints in balance. This is because what a Six Sigma company would call Cost of Poor Quality (COPQ) is reduced. In project management terms, COPQ includes the following components:

- Wasted Resources—The time and other resources the team expended to create something that needs to be modified
- Rework—The effort required to correct the error
- Inspection—The cost of determining that the error occurred
- Reporting—The effort involved in developing and reviewing reports to track errors and their correction

With its focus on detailed analysis, careful planning, and fact-based decision making, Six Sigma helps project managers prevent problems from occurring.

Reduced Variation

Although, as Chapter 1 indicated, by definition each project is unique, there are similarities among them, if only in the processes that are used to initiate and control a project. Use of standard procedures and forms, some of which are adapted from Six Sigma, achieves several desirable results, including reducing the time required to create them and providing a set of easily referenced documentation for subsequent teams.

Customer Focus

One of the causes of project failure is a lack of communication between the project team and the customer. (Customer, for the purpose of this book, is defined as the person or organization that will use the end result of the project.) All too often, customer expectations are not aligned with the project team's understanding of what the project entails, resulting in dissatisfaction when the project is complete. In some cases, whole groups of customers are not included in the process at all. Six Sigma provides techniques for identifying customers, obtaining their requirements, and working with them to prioritize the functionality the project will deliver, thus increasing the probability of success.

Fact-Based Decisions

Six Sigma is characterized by meticulous analysis to ensure that decisions are based on facts rather than intuition. For project teams, this process begins with ensuring that the project being initiated is the right one. This is a corollary to focusing on the customer. A Six Sigma company knows that it is essential to understand what the customer *really* wants, not simply the project team's perception of the customer's needs. Since a defect-free product is of no value if it is not one the customer wanted, this analysis is conducted before beginning any project. It helps restrain the wild enthusiasm that characterizes poorly managed projects and that often leads to disillusionment and panic.

Like customer focus, the reason for insisting on fact-based decisions is simple. By having all the facts before making any change, a Six Sigma company eliminates the rework and waste caused by solving the wrong problem, and a project team avoids the possibility of completing a project only to learn that the functionality delivered is not what the customer wanted or the company needed.

Teamwork

Because project managers rely on teams to accomplish the project goals, many of the Six Sigma concepts of teamwork have direct applicability to project management and can enhance the team's efforts. These include definitions of meeting protocols and team roles as well as tools for the selection of team members.

Although the corporate hierarchy does not disappear in a Six Sigma company, it is of little importance when a team is formed. This is why many meetings begin with the admonition to "check titles at the door." Team members are selected and valued because of their knowledge and expertise, not their position on an organizational chart. The objective is to assemble the right group of people so that decisions are indeed fact based rather than being dependent on incomplete knowledge or assumptions. The same concepts apply to project teams.

Design for Six Sigma

While classic Six Sigma has applicability to project management, Design for Six Sigma (DFSS) tools and techniques are particularly valuable during the first phase of a project: Initiation and Definition. This is because, as its name implies, DFSS focuses on the design of the product or service.

DFSS came into being when companies discovered that classic Six Sigma has limitations. Even when applied rigorously, classic Six Sigma projects rarely exceed a sigma level of 4.5. This represents 1,350 defects per million opportunities, a number that is still too high for most companies. The reason for this shortfall is that traditional Six Sigma focuses on improving existing processes. Although there is no denying the benefit to be derived from reducing variation and eliminating defects in existing processes, this may not be enough.

Classic Six Sigma assumes that the fundamental design of the process being optimized is a good one. It may not be. As Subir Chowdhury states in his book *Design for Six Sigma*, "80 percent of quality problems are unwittingly *designed into* the product."* In that case, because the classic Six Sigma process begins after design is complete, it may be impossible to correct all of the problems and achieve the company's goal of near perfection.

DFSS tackles this problem by starting earlier in the process. Using statistical methodologies and tools, DFSS has as its goal ensuring that the design fully meets the customer's requirements and results in a product that can be produced at the six-sigma level. Because of its focus on the early stages of a product, DFSS has a high level of applicability to project management. "Do it once, and do it right" could be the mantra of DFSS, just as it is the goal of every project manager.

Project managers want their projects to succeed; however, success is not a matter of chance. It is the result of careful planning, attention to detail, and the use of proven methodologies as described in the following chapters.

---

* Subir Chowdhury, *Design for Six Sigma* (Chicago: Dearborn Trade, 2005), 9.

Chapter 4

Introduction to the Case Study

The remainder of this book uses a case study to illustrate many of the principles, tools, and techniques that are discussed. Although the companies in the case study are fictional, the challenges the project team encounters are all real.

The Worldwide Widget Company Headquarters Relocation Project

Based in New Jersey, the Global Widget Company (GWC) is a century-old corporation and the largest manufacturer of widgets in the United States. For years, their metal alloy widgets dominated the market and resulted in GWC's obtaining a 40 percent U.S. market share for large and small widgets; however, recently, because of the changing market and new customer needs, the company expanded its product line to include a medium-sized widget made of rigid polymer.

Despite their name, GWC's customers are primarily located in the continental United States, a fact that has concerned the board of directors. The company's efforts to expand sales to other countries have been unsuccessful, due primarily to competition from Consolidated Asian Widgets (CAW) and a relatively new California-based company, International Widgets (IW).

International Widgets, founded only ten years earlier, is headquartered in southern California. From its inception, IW's senior management realized that they had little chance of overtaking GWC. Instead, they positioned themselves as a complementary rather than a competitive company. Recognizing GWC's market leadership for large and small widgets in the United States, IW specialized in medium-sized widgets designed primarily for the international market. They further distinguished their product by creating flexible widgets, rather than GWC's rigid ones, believing there would be no competition. And there was none, until GWC decided to enter the medium-sized widget market. Then the companies' differences—and their similarities—became important.

Unlike GWC, which has one large manufacturing plant located on the same site as the corporate headquarters, IW has two smaller factories, one each in Mexico and China. The one trait IW has always shared with GWC is that its primary competitor is also CAW, whose good quality and extremely low cost make it a formidable rival to both IW and GWC.

Although the majority of IW's sales are outside the United States, over the past three years IW has begun to erode GWC's market share for medium-sized widgets in the United States. Disturbed by the trend, GWC's senior management team decided the only solution was to crush IW by temporarily lowering their own prices enough to undercut their competitor. This solution might have worked had there not been a global economic downturn. With sales slumping worldwide and profit margins already eroded, the company risked bankruptcy. At the same time, IW's sales plummeted, leaving the company concerned about its ongoing viability. Drastic measures were needed.

The two companies' CEOs met in secret to discuss their alternatives and decided that the scenario most likely to succeed was for their companies to merge. Though reluctant, both boards of directors agreed that they could not continue to watch profits erode. They owed it to their shareholders to preserve what they could of each company, even if it meant creating a new entity. Thus the Worldwide Widget Company (WWC) was formed. Under the terms of the agreement, IW would own 51 percent of the new company, and its CEO, Isabelle Crumpton, would become CEO of the new company, while GWC's current CEO, George Webster, would serve as chairman of the board of WWC.

The shareholders of both companies ratified the plan, fearing their investments would disappear if they did not. Although the Justice Department needed to review the merger to ensure that no antitrust laws were being violated, its approval was expected no later than July 1. The two companies began their plans to merge.

One of the first decisions was to change the location of their corporate headquarters. Both existing buildings—GWC's on its New Jersey manufacturing campus and IW's location in a California high rise—were expensive to maintain. Although there would be layoffs in both corporate staffs, the combined headquarters staff would still exceed the capacity of either existing building. Furthermore, both Isabelle and George recognized the differences in their companies' corporate cultures. GWC was more formal, steeped in a century of tradition, while IW's younger staff members were used to a less-structured environment. Melding the two cultures would be difficult, particularly if the staffs were working at one of the existing locations. George and Isabelle believed that a new building in a different state would send the clear message that this was a new company.

Fortunately for the soon-to-be WWC, the team charged with selecting a new headquarters site had little difficulty in finding one that they believed would be perfect. Located in the Denver suburb of Bluebell, the site would be easily accessible by customers and would provide many of the amenities that both companies' staffs expected, including access to a major metropolitan area with opportunities for both summer and winter recreation as well as cultural and sporting events.

Because of time and cost constraints, the team chose an existing building. Bluebell Industries, which had founded the town, was ceasing operation after more than half a century and sought a buyer for its twenty-year-old building. Preliminary studies revealed that the building was large enough to accommodate the WWC staff and that the town had a pro-business attitude. Best of all, the price was right. Although they knew it would require renovations to modernize the building and incorporate the environmentally friendly features that both George and Isabelle believed were important, the team was confident there would be no problem having everything ready for the staff to move in during the first week in July. Their job was done. They had chosen the site.

Recognizing that there was still much to be done, Isabelle summoned Frank Seely, who had been vice president of Facilities and Services at IW and who would have the same responsibilities at WWC. "This is your lucky day, Frank," she announced when he arrived in her office. "You're in charge of our new headquarters project." Rapidly, she outlined the scope of the project, stating that there were three major components to it:

■ Renovate the interior of the building, constructing individual offices, meeting rooms, etc., and ensuring that wherever possible "green" technology was employed.
■ Redo all landscaping on the campus, incorporating Xeriscaping to minimize ongoing costs.
■ Relocate employees from New Jersey and California to the new campus.

"I know you can do this," Isabelle said. "And *when* you do, there'll be a substantial bonus for you." She continued by explaining that, although every aspect of the project was important, her primary concerns were the design of the lobby and the design and operation of the cafeteria. The first, she said, was important because it was customers' introduction to the company. The second, if well done, would boost employee morale.

Frank's morale was not boosted by Isabelle's announcement that he needed to work with Claudia Canfield, his counterpart at GWC. Though he had met Claudia briefly and knew that she was well respected by the staff, he also knew that she was highly opinionated and that many of those opinions centered on the ability of something called Six Sigma to solve all problems. There were no panaceas. Frank

Table 4.1 Key Players in the WWC Headquarters Relocation Case Study

Name	Title/Role/Background	Former Company
Isabelle Crumpton	Former CEO of IW, she will be CEO of WWC.	IW
George Webster	Former CEO of GWC, he will be chairman of the board of WWC.	GWC
Frank Seely	IW's VP of Facilities and Services; he will have the same position at WWC.	IW
Claudia Canfield	GWC's VP of Facilities and Services; she will leave the company when the merger is complete to establish her own Six Sigma consulting practice.	GWC
Roy Morgan	A fast-track manager within IW's Facilities and Services Department, he becomes the leader of the relocation project.	IW
Jim Wang	An experienced project manager within GWC's Facilities and Services Department and a Six Sigma Black Belt and a Project Management Professional, he serves as the project manager for the overall project.	GWC
Karen Whitson	A member of IW's Communications Department, she serves as the communications representative on the team.	IW
Harry Parr	A member of IW's Customer Service Department, he serves as one of the customer service representatives on the team.	IW
Geraldine Kelly	A member of GWC's Customer Service Department and a Green Belt, she serves as one of the customer service representatives on the team.	GWC
Sarah Alexander	A member of GWC's Finance Department, she serves as the finance representative on the team.	GWC
Michael Dobbs	A member of IW's Human Resources (HR) Department, he serves as the HR representative on the team.	IW

Table 4.1 Key Players in the WWC Headquarters Relocation Case Study (Continued)

Name	Title/Role/Background	Former Company
Emily Lawson	A member of GWC's Information Technology (IT) Department and a Black Belt, she serves as the IT representative on the team.	GWC
Marilyn Engel	A member of IW's Law Department, she serves as the legal representative on the team.	IW
Jonathan Talbot	A member of IW's Procurement Department, he serves as the procurement representative on the team.	IW
Cheryl McNally	A member of GWC's Engineering Department, she serves as the consulting engineer to the project.	GWC
Brad Harding	A member of IW's Health, Safety, and & Environment Department, he serves as the HS&E representative on the team.	IW
Dustin Monroe	A member of GWC's Facilities and Services Department, he becomes the leader of the landscaping project.	GWC
Lori Woods	A member of IW's Facilities and Services Department, she becomes the leader of the interior renovations project.	IW

knew that. Hard work and careful scheduling were what were needed. But he also recognized a command. Like it or not, Claudia Canfield was going to be part of his project, and so was this thing called Six Sigma.

The project had begun.

Table 4.1 provides a list of the various employees involved in the creation of WWC's new corporate headquarters.

THE INITIATION/ DEFINITION PHASE

As the first phase of a project, Initiation or Definition forms the foundation on which that project will be built. Although some project teams have a tendency to compress this phase, believing it to be comprised of unnecessary overhead, it is important that it be solidly constructed, as is true of any foundation. This is truly a case of the Five Ps (prior planning prevents poor performance).

Because a project is only as strong as the people who are executing it, Chapter 5 focuses on selecting the right people. It introduces the concept of project champions, outlines the skills a successful project manager will possess, and discusses reasons why outside advisors and facilitators might benefit a project.

Chapter 6 asks the critical question, "Is this the right project?" and provides the tools to answer it. It explains how to define the problem to be solved, how to identify customers and their requirements, and how to evaluate potential solutions.

In order to avoid both wild enthusiasm and disillusionment on the parts of the project team and customers, Chapter 7 outlines techniques for managing expectations, while Chapter 8 introduces the subject of risk management. This section concludes with the drafting of the business case (Chapter 9).

Chapter 5

Getting Started—Choosing the Right People

It is a simple fact of life that projects do not happen without people. Frank knew that; that is why he planned to make Roy Morgan the project manager for the headquarters relocation project. Roy was a fast-track manager within Frank's department who had successfully delivered a telecommunications upgrade project the previous year. Not only did Roy personally write the Request for Proposal (RFP) for the new phone system, but he also chaired the selection committee and worked nights and weekends to ensure that everything was installed on time. Though Frank had wanted to promote Roy at the conclusion of the telecom project, his recommendation had been denied on the grounds that Roy needed more experience. The new "relo" project would be the perfect opportunity for Roy to prove himself ready for the promotion.

Frank was sure Roy would be the ideal project manager, but—just to be safe—he realized he had better talk to Claudia. After all, Isabelle had insisted that Claudia be involved in all aspects of this project. Neither woman would be pleased if he appointed Roy without at least discussing it with Claudia. "I've got us a great project manager," Frank announced when he entered her office. "His name is Roy Morgan."

Though Claudia did not frown, Frank could see that something was bothering her. "Before we discuss that, let's start at the beginning," she said. "Who's going to be the champion?"

The answer was easy. Frank grinned. "I am."

The Project Champion

Frank knew that every successful project had a champion. Although some companies refer to this person as a sponsor, it is important to distinguish between the person who initiates change, Conner's definition of a sponsor (see Chapter 2), and a true champion. The sponsor initiates change; the champion leads it. The champion is the motivating force throughout the life of the project, the spokesperson, and the destroyer of roadblocks. Although champions need not be involved in the day-to-day activities of the team, they must be accessible to the team.

An effective champion will:

- Believe in the value of the project
- Be fully committed to the project's success, including being willing to invest his or her own time to promote the project
- Have the authority to obtain funding and other resources
- Have enough political clout and persuasive skills to convince others of the project's value

Although it is not mandatory, it is also helpful if the champion has a stake in the outcome, the proverbial "skin in the game." If the champion's budget or personal reputation is at risk, he or she will normally be a more effective advocate of change and will be viewed as having more credibility. It is, after all, easier to advocate change in another person's department than to be willing to implement it within one's own area of responsibility.

Frank Seely met all the criteria.

The Project Manager

When Frank returned the discussion to Roy Morgan's qualifications for project manager, Claudia looked skeptical. "Your job's on the line," she pointed out. "Are you sure Roy's the right person? Is he tough enough?"

Frank had to admit that "tough" was not an adjective he would apply to Roy. The man was a good facilitator. He was highly organized, and no one worked harder. But tough? Not Roy. According to Claudia, that was an essential characteristic of an effective project manager. She cited Neal Whitten, author of *Neal Whitten's No-Nonsense Advice for Successful Projects*, who states, "The No. 1 reason project managers fail is that they are too soft."* Whitten feels so strongly about

---

* Neal Whitten, *Neal Whitten's No-Nonsense Advice for Successful Projects* (Vienna, VA: Management Concepts, 2005), 45.

the need for strong project managers that he entitled the second chapter of his book "Are You a Benevolent Dictator? You Should Be!"* Frank suspected he had lost the argument. No matter what else he was, Roy was not a dictator, benevolent or otherwise.

Although the champion is critical, it can be argued that the project manager is the single most important person on a project. This is because project managers have the ultimate responsibility for the project's success. They lead the rest of the team; they make key decisions; they are involved in the day-to-day activities; they set the tone for the whole project. In other words, they are the linchpins of the project. This is why it is essential that the champion select a project manager who is capable of delivering success.

Characteristics of a Successful Project Manager

In his book *Fundamentals of Project Management*, James P. Lewis uses a pyramid to illustrate the components of a project management system. He places what he calls "human" factors at the bottom, indicating that they serve as the foundation for everything else.† Within the "human" block, Lewis lists six characteristics: motivation, leadership, negotiation, team building, communication, and decision making. While it could be argued that leadership and motivation are components of team building, there is no doubt that each of Lewis's six characteristics is an attribute of a successful project manager.

In one of my earlier books, *Successful Packaged Software Implementation*, I define the critical success factors of a project manager as the following:‡

■ *Project Management Experience*—This is one of the key differentiators between a successful and an unsuccessful project manager. The manager must understand the fundamentals of managing projects, from team dynamics and problem resolution to project schedules. While formal training is important, there is no substitute for experience, and on a large or critical project, only managers with prior experience on *successful* projects should be considered. Note that "successful" was italicized. It is true that project managers may learn valuable lessons working on failed projects and that they can frequently transform those lessons into successes on the next endeavor. However, to minimize risk on mission-critical projects, proven success is desirable.

---

* Whitten, *Neal Whitten's No-Nonsense Advice*, 8.
† James P. Lewis, *Fundamentals of Project Management* (New York: AMACOM, 1997), 10.
‡ Christine B. Tayntor, *Successful Packaged Software Implementation* (Boca Raton: Auerbach, 2006), 23–24.

■ *Ability to Gain Consensus*—More than any other member of the team, it is the leader's responsibility to resolve differences of opinion. This requires an understanding of both general problem-solving techniques and what motivates individual team members. While technical skills may have been responsible for promotions earlier in a person's career, interpersonal skills are essential for successful project managers. (Note: Chapter 22 discusses techniques for conflict resolution.)

■ *Ability to Conduct Meetings*—Since meetings are typically the forum for accomplishing much of the team's work, the leader needs to know how to run effective meetings. This includes establishing and publishing an agenda prior to the meeting, and ensuring that the meeting stays on schedule and that the correct players are invited and attend. While some of the responsibilities may be delegated—for example, a timekeeper may be appointed to ensure adherence to the agenda—the manager has overall accountability and is normally the person who conducts meetings. (Chapter 6 discusses meeting protocols.)

■ *Verbal and Written Communication Skills*—Project managers are normally the day-to-day spokespersons for the project. As such, it is important that they be effective communicators. They may be called upon to present the project to senior management or to workers on the assembly line and should be comfortable in either situation. They must also ensure that all decisions they or the team make are fully documented. Note that during meetings this responsibility may be delegated to a team member, typically called a scribe or recorder, but that the manager is still accountable.

■ *Respect*—It is important that the project manager be well regarded throughout the company. As one of the project's two primary spokespersons (with the champion), the manager must be recognized as an employee whose opinion is valued and whose skills are unquestioned. "Personal influence" is a key characteristic of successful project managers.

Frank had to admit that, based on those criteria, Roy was not the ideal candidate for the project manager role, and so he asked Claudia if she had a recommendation. Her suggestion was Jim Wang, a member of her department. Claudia pointed out that, in addition to running three successful projects, Jim had his Project Management Professional (PMP) certification and was a Six Sigma Black Belt. Though Frank would have preferred someone from IW and hoped that Claudia was not going to spend a lot of time touting the benefits of Six Sigma, he agreed with her suggestion. As she had pointed out, there was too much at stake to have anything less than a fully qualified project manager. They both agreed that Roy would be part of the project team, possibly as the leader of a subproject.

The Initial Project Team

The subject turned to the rest of the team. Both Frank and Claudia knew that the team they were assembling now would be responsible for the Initiation/Definition phase. Although Jim would remain as the manager for the entire project life cycle, it was possible that some of the other team members would leave at the conclusion of the first phase. Most of the team, however, would remain on the project, forming the core of the implementation team that would be organized once the project had been approved.

When Claudia mentioned forming a cross-functional team, Frank agreed. He did not need Six Sigma training to know that, although it might be easier to appoint only members of his department since he could ensure that they had both the motivation and the time required to work on the project, he would have a higher probability of success if he involved all key stakeholders.

Since it was a given that the merger and relocation of the headquarters building would result in many changes to individual employees' daily lives, it was important to have all affected groups' buy-in. Although it is a basic tenet of Six Sigma, Frank had learned from experience that if people were not involved at the early stages and did not believe that they were part of the change process, it was far more difficult to gain their acceptance later. Accordingly, when he began planning the team's composition, he told Claudia that he planned to include representatives from a number of different departments. And since this project involved the merger of two companies, it was essential to include people from both organizations. A team comprised of only IW employees would create an "us vs. them" mentality, something neither Frank nor Claudia wanted.

Frank's creation of a cross-functional team was aligned with the Six Sigma concept of involving people who understand the process and what would be required in the future so that decisions are made based on facts rather than intuition or guesses. Table 5.1 provides a list of support departments that should be considered for team membership. It is important to note that while not all of these functions will be involved in every project, many will participate at some level.

In addition to ensuring that all key functions were involved, Frank knew that it was important to invite the right individuals from each function. Not only did he want people with knowledge of their functional area, but he also wanted employees with a specific set of personal characteristics. Table 5.2 lists the characteristics of effective team members.

Together Frank and Claudia identified a list of potential team members (Table 4.1). Before they could finalize the team's composition, they needed to confer with each candidate's manager to ensure that the employee would be available to participate.

Table 5.1   Support Functions to Be Considered for Team Membership

Function	Reason for Including
Communications	To assist with development of communication plan and package. This is particularly important when the change will impact customers and suppliers.
Customer Service	To provide a "voice of the customer." This is especially helpful if actual customers cannot be involved.
Finance	To aid in developing benefit analyses.
Health, Safety, and Environmental	To identify safety or other environmental issues that should be included in the proposed solution.
Human Resources	To provide assistance with change management, particularly when job functions will be eliminated or substantially altered.
Information Technology	To assist with identification of new technologies that may become part of the solution.
Internal Audit	To identify needed controls and ensure that company procedures are followed.
Legal	To identify any contractual issues that may result from proposed changes. If job functions will be eliminated or substantially altered, HR/legal counsel should be obtained.
Procurement	To identify potential suppliers and the impact of proposed changes on existing suppliers.

Facilitators and outside Advisors

Although the project manager should possess all of the characteristics discussed above, including the ability to conduct meetings and obtain consensus, there are times when a company may want to use a facilitator for these purposes. Facilitators are normally individuals who have received specialized training in group and meeting dynamics. They may be employees of the company or consultants from outside firms.

The advantages that a facilitator brings are twofold: specific skills and objectivity. The skills include high-level expertise in organizing and leading meetings as well as the ability to resolve conflict and obtain consensus. Objectivity is also important. Because facilitators are not full-fledged members of the team, they should have no bias. Their responsibility is to help the team articulate needs and concerns, sort facts from opinions, and make decisions based on those facts. Unlike the champion, they do not have "skin in the game," and this can be an advantage.

Table 5.2   Characteristics of Effective Team Members

Characteristic	Explanation
Commitment	The individual must believe in the project and be willing to do "whatever it takes" to make it successful.
Bias for action	The team member must have a sense of urgency and feel compelled to finish the project successfully.
Flexibility	Since the team's charter is to recommend change, each team member must not only be able to adapt to change but must also embrace it.
Innovation	Successful team members are able not only to embrace change but also to initiate it by finding new ways to accomplish the goal.
Personal influence	Since the team will become agents of change, it is highly desirable for all members to be well respected within their own communities. This is similar to the "personal clout" requirement for project champions and leaders.
Teamwork	No matter how creative and committed individuals may be, unless they can work successfully as part of a team, they should not be part of the core team. Key "individual contributors" who lack cooperative and collaborative skills may be called on to provide expertise at various stages of the project.
Available time	Individuals who are close to burnout because of a too-heavy workload should not be chosen for the team. Not only will they not be effective, but they may also create dissension within the team by missing meetings or failing to deliver on commitments.

In highly charged and emotional situations where two groups appear to be unable to compromise or even to understand each other's position, the facilitator can be viewed as a referee.

Some companies use outside advisors on projects. By definition, advisors are not employees of the company but are from another organization and are selected because of their specific expertise. Typically, they fill gaps in the project team's knowledge. Like facilitators, outside advisors are optional, and the success of the project does not depend on their being used. Indeed, it can be argued that the use of the wrong advisor can have a negative effect on the project. Because of this, it is important to ensure that the right advisor is chosen.

Table 5.3   Outside Advisor Selection Criteria

Question	Reason for Question
How long have you been providing these services?	A company that is new to the business may not have the needed expertise. One exception may be when experienced individuals leave another firm to establish their own company.
Who are your existing and prior clients?	It is important to check references. Depending on the project and the nature of the advice expected, it might be important that at least some of the references were from companies in the same industry. It is also important to note the dates of the reference. If no current or very recent clients are included, the advisor may no longer be well regarded.
Do you have partnerships or affiliations with any other companies?	Depending on the nature of the relationship, the advisor may not be unbiased. If, for example, the project includes the selection and implementation of computer software and the advisor also provides implementation services for one of the software packages being considered, the advisor's objectivity may be questionable.
What is your fee structure?	It is essential to know how the advisor expects to be paid and whether there are any hidden charges. Some consulting firms, for example, bill on an hourly basis but also include an administrative overhead charge that may or may not have been mentioned in advance.

The advantages of advisors are similar to those for facilitators, although instead of providing specific skills, an outside advisor provides access to specific knowledge. In both cases, the company should expect objectivity. This is sometimes more difficult to obtain with advisors. Table 5.3 provides a list of criteria that can help determine whether or not the advisor has the desired background and objectivity. If an advisor is used, it should be made clear that the advisor provides guidance and expertise but is not a voting member of the team. Decisions should be made only by the team members.

Because of her Six Sigma background, Claudia volunteered to serve as the facilitator at the first team meeting. She and Frank agreed that they did not expect to utilize outside advisors. With the core team in place, they were ready to proceed to the next step: defining the project.

What Can Go Wrong?

Though few companies would deny the importance of the project team, there are a number of possible pitfalls in staffing a project. The most common are:

- *No champion*—Unfortunately, some projects are begun without a champion. This may not create major problems on a small, short-term project, but for anything of strategic importance to the company, it is essential that there be high-level sponsorship. Without it, the project's chance of success is diminished. The champion, after all, is the one who breaks down barriers and obtains additional funding, if needed.
- *An ineffective project manager*—Champions should be vigilant when selecting project managers and should ensure that they possess the needed skills. Managers are sometimes chosen for political reasons, to give them experience needed for a promotion, or—worst of all—because they have more free time than anyone else. Although none of those precludes success, those should be only secondary considerations. What is critical is that whoever is chosen has the characteristics of a successful project manager discussed above.
- *The wrong team members*—The project manager may be the head of the team, but the individual members are its arms and legs. Selecting people who lack the needed skills and personal characteristics decreases the probability of success.
- *Absence of the right people*—This is a corollary to the previous point. Although the team might be staffed competently, if key individuals with unique knowledge and skills are not included, the project will suffer.

It bears repeating: projects do not happen without people, and—if the project is to be successful—it is essential that the right people be involved.

Chapter 6

Ensuring It Is the Right Project

Another of the unfortunate facts of project management is that some projects are initiated for the wrong reason. Occasionally it is because a high-ranking employee learns that another company is doing something similar and does not realize that what is being proposed is the proverbial "solution looking for a problem." Other times one department wants to make a change but has not considered the impact of that change on the whole company. In still other cases, the concept is a good one, but the project cannot be cost justified. This is, after all, the stage where wild enthusiasm reigns. As Chapter 1 pointed out, wild enthusiasm leads to disillusionment and panic. To avoid that, an effective project manager ensures that the problem being solved is a valid one and that the proposed solution is both feasible and affordable. In Six Sigma terms, this means making decisions based on facts, not opinions, and not being swayed by wild enthusiasm.

As a Six Sigma company, GWC had a standard procedure for initiating projects. IW followed many of the same steps—they were, Frank insisted, common sense—but there was no mandate to do so. The fundamental difference between the two companies was that all GWC projects used the same methodology, while individual IW project managers decided how best to initiate/define their projects. Using the SEI CMM levels shown on Table 1.1, GWC had achieved Level 3, while IW was between Levels 1 and 2.

Frank agreed that it made sense to follow a proven methodology, especially when his reputation, not to mention a substantial bonus, were on the line, and so he agreed to the steps Claudia proposed.

1. Define the problem.
2. Establish a project charter.
3. Define the scope.
4. Identify customers and other stakeholders.
5. Understand the current state.
6. Identify customer requirements.
7. Prioritize the requirements.
8. Identify potential solutions.
9. Evaluate potential solutions' effect on customer requirements.
10. Define the new state.

Step 1: Define the Problem

A classic cartoon shows an IT manager saying to his staff, "You start coding. I'll figure out what they want." This is analogous to the adage, "If you don't know where you're going, any road will do." No well-managed project should begin without a clear definition of the problem to be solved. The objective of this step is to answer the fundamental question, *Why are we doing this project*? or, in William Bridges' terminology, to establish the purpose for the change.

As Frank and Claudia began to draft their problem statement, they realized that they had three separate projects: the interior renovations, landscaping, and the relocation effort. The remainder of this book focuses primarily on the interior renovations.

Frank's preliminary problem statement was "Because of the creation of a new company, a new corporate headquarters is needed. The objective of this project is to renovate the interior of the former Bluebell Industries building to provide adequate office space, meeting rooms, and a cafeteria for the WWC headquarters staff, while employing 'green' technologies." He and Claudia then measured his statement against the SMART criteria that both GWC and IW used to evaluate problem statements.

SMART is an acronym for:

- *Specific*—The problem must be quantified. Rather than attempting to cure world hunger, which—besides being unlikely to be attainable—is a vague problem, the goal could be defined as "Increase the annual food supply in Country X by 50 percent for each person."
- *Measurable*—The results must be able to be measured. Using the previous example, unless the current per capita food supply has been quantified, it is impossible to measure the increase.
- *Attainable*—The goal must be realistic. It may not be possible to increase the food supply by 50 percent, particularly not within a short time frame.

- *Relevant*—The change being made must satisfy an important customer requirement. In this example, the goal is relevant if the citizens of Country X suffer from malnutrition but not if they have an obesity epidemic.
- *Time-bound*—The expectation must be that the change will be achieved within a specified time frame rather than being open-ended. In an ideal situation, the time frame is measured in months rather than years. To make it time-bound, the world hunger statement could be expanded to read, "Increase the annual food supply in Country X by 10 percent for each person by the end of the current calendar year and by 15 percent for each successive twelve-month period."

Frank realized that his first draft failed to meet four out of five SMART criteria. It was not specific enough, since "adequate office space" could be interpreted in a number of ways. Furthermore, the number of conference rooms was not quantified. Because it was not specific, the results could not be measured. Whether or not the goal was attainable was unclear, largely because of the lack of specificity. Lastly, since the problem statement included no dates, it was not time bound. It was, however, relevant, since there was no question that WWC needed a headquarters building.

Frank revised his problem statement to read, "The objective of this project is to renovate the interior of the former Bluebell Industries building to provide office space for 150 employees, including ten executives, to create five meeting rooms and a cafeteria that will accommodate 100 people, while reducing total building operating costs (defined as water and power) by 25 percent from Bluebell Industries' costs for the prior year. All work must be completed by July 1, 2011." With a SMART problem statement in hand, Frank was ready for the second step.

Step 2: Establish a Project Charter

Although Frank and Claudia had done the preliminary work themselves, it was now time to convene the team for their first meeting. As discussed in Chapter 5, one of the characteristics of a successful project manager is the ability to conduct meetings. Having a defined structure for all meetings ensures consistency and repeatability, which has the result of reducing costs and increasing effectiveness. Cost reduction occurs because meetings are focused and, therefore, shorter; effectiveness is increased because the clear focus and organization keep meetings from wandering and serve to promote decision making.

Claudia suggested that Frank use the meeting structure GWC had established, beginning with GRACE. GRACE was the company's acronym for the components it considered essential to set the tone for a meeting and to keep it focused: goal, roles, agenda, code of conduct, expectations. The first step in each meeting was to review these items.

Table 6.1   Sample Roles and Responsibilities for Meetings

Role	Responsibility
Leader	Has overall responsibility for the success of the meeting; sets purpose and agenda
Timekeeper	Ensures that each agenda item starts and ends on time
Scribe	Is responsible for writing ideas on flipcharts during the meeting
Recorder	Issues minutes of the meeting, including transcribing notes from flipcharts as appropriate
Conduct Monitor	Ensures that all attendees follow the code of conduct
Spokesperson	Serves as the official voice of the team

■ *Goal*—Without a clear objective, a meeting will founder. Although the objective may be implicit, the leader should make the goal explicit by announcing it and providing the team with the opportunity to amend it. In this case, Frank announced that the purpose of the meeting was to kick off the new headquarters building project and begin drafting the project charter. No one objected.

■ *Roles*—Rather than expect the person who chairs the meeting to do everything from leading the discussion to taking notes, a structured meeting delegates some of those responsibilities through the use of a set of clearly defined roles and responsibilities. Table 6.1 provides a list of typical meeting roles. Although not all roles may be needed at all meetings, leader, timekeeper, and recorder are key, since they keep the meeting on track and ensure that the outcome is documented.

For a meeting to be effective, everyone needs to understand who is performing which role. Accordingly, once the meeting's goal has been agreed upon, roles should be established. Under Frank's lead, the team reviewed the list of roles shown in Table 6.1 and decided, as many teams do, to combine scribe and recorder. They also decided that the roles they chose would remain constant throughout the life of this project phase. There are benefits to establishing continuity, but it is not mandatory. Although Jim Wang was the team leader and would chair subsequent meetings, Frank would lead this one. Harry Parr volunteered to be the timekeeper; Sarah Alexander agreed to be the conduct monitor, while Geraldine Kelly accepted the role of scribe/recorder.

■ *Agenda*—To keep them focused, all meetings should have written agendas, including both the topics to be discussed and proposed time frames. Furthermore, those agendas should be sent to all attendees a minimum of

Start and end on time

Have an agenda and stick to it

Come prepared

No side conversations

Check titles at the door

Issue minutes within 48 hours

No speeches

No spectators; everyone participates

There are no bad questions or ideas

Attack ideas, not people

Have fun

Figure 6.1   Sample code of conduct for meetings.

twenty-four hours prior to the meeting. This would allow everyone time to review the agenda and prepare for the meeting. It also allows people to opt out of meetings when they have no interest in the topics being discussed, thus avoiding wasting time. Once the meeting is convened, the team should review the tentative agenda, adjust time frames as needed, and add any new items that they believe are necessary.

■ *Code of Conduct*—Not only should there be designated roles and responsibilities, but all meetings should abide by a code of conduct. As its name implies, a code of conduct establishes rules for behavior and helps ensure that meetings are not derailed by arguments or other divisive actions. A sample code of conduct is shown in Figure 6.1.

The code of conduct should be reviewed at each meeting to ensure that all participants are aware of it. "Checking titles at the door" ensures that everyone on the team has equal authority at the team meetings, regardless of his or her position within the corporate hierarchy. The "no speeches" admonition limits participants to speaking for no more than sixty consecutive seconds, thus both avoiding some people's tendency to monopolize meetings and encouraging full participation.

■ *Expectations*—Since one of the goals of a meeting is to encourage participation by each participant, it is important to have attendees express their expectations for the meeting. This helps calibrate expectations and uncover hidden agendas. Expectations should be listed on flip charts by the designated scribe and reviewed at the end of the meeting to determine whether they have been met.

As their first major task, the team began to develop its project charter. The charter is the first important document in a project, because it serves as a summary of key information about the project. Unlike some documents that remain static once they are created, the charter is updated throughout the life of the project. Although its primary audience is the project team, it may also be distributed to those who are affected by the project.

The charter is designed to help team members clearly understand why the team was formed, what the team members hope to achieve, how long the project will take, and how much time they are expected to spend on it. The benefits of a charter should be self-evident: fewer misunderstandings and greater focus. In short, less variation. Appendix B provides a sample charter with an explanation of what information is expected in each field.

The headquarters relocation team's initial project charter is shown in Figure 6.2. As expected, many of the fields could not be completed during the first meeting. This is normal, since the charter is a living document expected to undergo several revisions before it is finished.

In an ideal situation, the project team would have some input to the target date. Time is, after all, one of the three constraints of a project as shown on Figure 1.1. However, for this project as well as many that are driven by regulatory changes, the completion date was mandated. The only factors the team could change were scope and resources, and even scope had little room for manipulation. The key factor, everyone realized, would be resources.

Though the actual renovation would be done by outside contractors, it was important to understand the involvement of each team member. That is the purpose of the Team Membership section of the charter. It clearly identifies the amount of time each team member is expected to devote to the project. One potential cause of failure for project teams is that—although initial enthusiasm is high—team members' participation wanes as the project progresses, leaving only a few individuals with the majority of the responsibility. The project charter serves as a contract among team members. Although the amount of participation may vary among team members, each person and his or her manager should understand the commitment and agree to it.

Putting time commitments in writing serves several purposes. Not only does it assist the team in developing a realistic project schedule, but it also helps individual team members gain a commitment from their managers that they will be available to participate at the agreed-upon level. This written contract increases the probability of success by ensuring that people, always a key resource, will be available when needed.

The project charter as currently drafted reflects responsibility only for the Initiation/Definition phase. The Implementation team, as noted previously, will be substantially larger. At the point that it is established, similar commitments will be required from all new team members and their managers.

Summary			
Project Name	New Headquarters Building Interior Renovation	Total Financial Impact	
Team Leader	Jim Wang	Champion	Frank Seely
Start Date	November 1, 2010	Target Completion Date	July 1, 2011
Project Description	Provide office space for 150 employees, including ten executives; create five meeting rooms and a cafeteria that will accommodate 100 people; reduce total building operating costs (defined as water and power) by 25% from Bluebell Industries' costs for the prior year.		
Departments Impacted	All employees being relocated to Bluebell		
Processes Impacted	Ongoing building maintenance; cafeteria operation; landscaping and maintenance of grounds		

Benefits					
	Units	Current	Goal	Actual Achieved	Projected Date
Cost Reduction	$(000)	100	75		
Increased Sales					
Customer Sat					
Other Benefits					

Team Membership			
Name	Role	Department	% Time
Jim Wang	Leader	Facilities and Services	100
Karen Whitson	Team Member	Communications	15
Harry Parr	Team Member	Customer Service	50
Geraldine Kelly	Team Member	Customer Service	50
Sarah Alexander	Team Member	Finance	25
Michael Dobbs	Team Member	Human Resources	10

Figure 6.2   Initial project charter.

Emily Lawson	Team Member	Information Technology	75
Marilyn Engel	Team Member	Law	30
Jonathan Talbot	Team Member	Procurement	50
Cheryl McNally	Team Member	Engineering	25
Brad Harding	Team Member	Health, Safety and Environmental	10
Dustin Monroe	Team Member	Facilities and Services	100
Lori Woods	Team Member	Facilities and Services	100

	Support Required		
Training Required	None		
Other Support Required	Team requires dedicated meeting room. Once construction has begun, team will require project trailer at the new site.		

		Schedule			
Milestone/ Deliverable	Target Date	Owner	Estimated Cost		Comments
Feasibility study	11/30/10	Jim Wang			

	Critical Success Factors and Risks
Critical Success Factors	Outside contractors must be available when needed.
Risks	Environmental and other regulatory concerns may delay the project beyond July 1.

Figure 6.2   (Continued)

Approvals		
Role/ Title	Name	Date
Revision History		
Revision Number	*Authors*	Date
0	*Jim Wang*	November 1, 2010

Figure 6.2   (Continued)

Step 3: Define the Scope

Although the initial problem statement attempts to define the scope of a project, it is only a first draft and needs to be refined. This is particularly true in a case like the headquarters relocation project where the time frame is fixed. It is essential to establish a scope that can be accomplished within the mandated time frame. In most cases, this involves reducing the problem statement to focus on one or two objectives. Teams typically have initial scopes that are too broad, but by narrowing the scope to a more manageable scale, the project has a greater likelihood of success.

Although the team recognized that they would not be able to define the scope during this first meeting, they began the process by brainstorming, asking questions that would help them determine what would be inside the project boundaries. Table 6.2 shows some of the questions they developed. In many cases, Frank indicated that he could obtain the answers by speaking with Isabelle and George. Other answers, however, required more detailed analysis and consultation with customers of the project. Realizing that their definition of the scope was still incomplete, the team moved to the next step, identifying customers and other stakeholders.

Table 6.2 Result of Scope Brainstorming Session

Question	Responsibility	Answer
Will there be an open or a closed floor plan?	Frank Seely	
Will executives have offices with their departments or on a separate "executive row"?	Frank Seely	
Will meeting rooms be centrally located or on each floor?	Frank Seely	
What are the telecommunications/ networking needs?		
Does the project's responsibility include furnishing the offices and conference rooms?	Frank Seely	
Will furniture be moved from existing buildings?	Frank Seely	
Where will copier/printer/supply rooms be located?		
How much seating is required in the lobby?		
What amenities should be included in the lobby (phones, wireless Internet, coffee)?		
What décor is expected for the lobby (fresh flowers, plants, fish tank)?		
Will there be an executive lunchroom in addition to the cafeteria?	Frank Seely	
How extensive should the menu be?		
Will the cafeteria utilize a traditional one-line design or will there be individual stations (salads, sandwiches, hot food, desserts, etc.)?		
What size tables are required?		
Will dishes be disposable or permanent?		
Will customers eat in the cafeteria?	Frank Seely	

Step 4: Identify Customers and Other Stakeholders

Although many companies use the traditional definition of customer, namely someone who *purchases* a product or service, Six Sigma companies use a broader definition and consider customers anyone who *uses* a product or service, even employees of the company. They make a distinction between internal and external customers and divide each of those categories into subcategories.

- *External Customers.* These are normally easily identified. In the case of GWC and IW, these were the companies who purchased their widgets. They were not, however, always the ultimate customers.
  - *Ultimate Customers.* These external customers can also be classified as end users or consumers. If Great Auto, one of GWC's external customers, incorporates GWC's widgets on the cars it manufactures, the person who buys one of Great Auto's cars is GWC's ultimate customer.
- *Internal Customers.* These are the company's departments and individual employees who use a product or service. In the relocation project, they are primary customers, since the majority of the work that is being done is for their benefit. Internal customers come in two varieties: immediate and intermediate.
  - *Immediate Internal Customers.* These are the departments that are directly impacted by the project. For the relocation project, that includes all employees. If the project addressed the manufacturing process, with the end product being a finished widget, the immediate internal customer would be the Packaging Department, since it is the first department to use the widget.
  - *Intermediate Internal Customers.* Intermediate customers stand between an immediate internal customer and an external customer. For the relocation project, there are no intermediate internal customers. However, using the example of the widget manufacturing process, the Shipping Department would be an intermediate customer. Shipping receives a product or service (a widget) from the immediate customer (Packaging).

The primary reason for categorizing customers is to help the team think beyond the traditional or external customer and to consider everyone who uses the products or services that are part of the project. Since one of the objectives of any project should be to make decisions based on what will have the greatest positive effect on customers, it is vital to be able to identify all customers.

Although customers are critical to the project's success, they are not the only groups that impact a project. Suppliers, influencers, and other stakeholders are also important. Unfortunately, all too often, their views are not considered until the project is underway and key decisions have been made. This may result in unnecessary rework when their requirements are revealed.

■ *Suppliers.* As the name implies, suppliers provide input to a process. For the headquarters relocation project, suppliers include the outside contractors who would do the actual construction work; the companies that would provide furniture, carpeting, and office equipment; the local utilities (power, water, sanitation); and, for the ongoing operation of the cafeteria, the purveyors of food, spices, and other ingredients needed to prepare the meals.

■ *Influencers.* These are outside agencies, normally governmental, that regulate one or more aspects of a project. For the headquarters relocation project, influencers include the local departments of health and building permits as well as the fire department. Other influencers might be the Environmental Protection Agency and state agencies that regulate the use of land. Failing to address influencers' requirements at the earliest stage of a project can result in delays as well as additional expense.

■ *Other Stakeholders.* Although they are not directly impacted by the corporate relocation, the interests of the shareholders of the new company must be considered. Those include minimizing costs to help maintain the stock price.

With key customers, suppliers, and influencers identified, the team was ready for the next step.

Step 5: Understand the Current State

Very few projects involve the creation of something completely new. For the rest, it is important to understand the current or what is sometimes called the "as is" state, since this will provide the foundation for the development of the ultimate or "to be" state. When a complex process is involved, it is helpful to create a diagram, often called a functional process map, to illustrate the steps. Creating a process map for both the current and the projected states provides a visual representation of the changes that will occur and can aid in the selling of a project. Appendix C details the creation of a functional process map.

Because the relocation project was relatively simple, the team decided to describe the current state using a tabular form. Table 6.3 displays the results of the team's initial survey. Although the team had realized there were cultural differences between GWC and IW, they were surprised at how pervasive they were. This exercise pointed out the value of describing the current state, since it helped them understand some of the challenges they would face as part of their project.

Table 6.3 Current State

Item	GWC	IW
Executive offices	Located in separate wing	Colocated with department
	Special furniture (chosen by each executive)	Same furniture as rest of staff
Employee work space	Cubicles for grades 1–6; offices for higher grades	Cubicles for all (executives have offices)
Meeting rooms	1 per floor	All located in core area near elevators
Cafeteria	2 lines (hot and cold)	1 line (all food)
	2 checkout lines (hot and cold)	Single checkout line
Customer/executive dining	Catered; served in executive conference room	Catered; served in one of the meeting rooms

Step 6: Identify Customer Requirements

If a project is to be successful, it is essential to understand what the customers want and need. A Six Sigma company would call this the "voice of the customer"; everyone should call it common sense. The first steps in this chapter were devoted to understanding why the project was being initiated. This one continues by asking the key question: what is the project expected to accomplish?

The previous paragraph states that it is essential to understand what customers *want* and *need*. The use of both italicized words was deliberate. As noted before, this is the project stage that, if not properly managed, can become characterized by wild enthusiasm. This is the time when customers believe that their new project will do everything they have ever wanted and perhaps cure world hunger at the same time. Customer needs may be far simpler than their wants, but at this stage, both tend to run rampant. Understanding and managing customer expectations is critical to the success of the project and will be described in more detail in Chapters 7 and 12.

Clearly understanding requirements before making any changes is a critical component of fact-based decision making. As discussed in Chapter 2, it is essential to understand why a change is needed and what impact it will have before making any modifications.

Customer requirements can be determined in a number of different ways. The most common techniques are shown in Table 6.4 along with the advantages and

Table 6.4   Tools for Determining Customer Requirements

Tool	Advantages	Disadvantages
Surveys	Relatively inexpensive to administer; require minimal effort from team	Unless carefully constructed, may not elicit important information
Focus groups	Provide opportunity to digress from agenda and discover underlying problem; group setting may encourage participation and "building on" another's response	Require more time to conduct than surveys; group setting may intimidate some participants
Individual interviews	Excellent way to discuss sensitive topics and to obtain specialized information that might be boring to others in a group setting; ideal for people who are uncomfortable in groups	Most time-intensive method
Site visits	Excellent way to see the effect of problems and to meet customers who would otherwise be inaccessible	Can be expensive; customers may be unwilling to host site visits
Customer complaints	Lowest cost	Provides only one perspective; does not address problems that other customers have not expressed; unbalanced, since it does not include positive comments

disadvantages of each. The team decided to conduct focus groups with representative groups of employees as their primary method of identifying customer requirements. Recognizing that the executive staff had different requirements and would not be amenable to a focus group meeting, the team agreed that Jim Wang, as the team leader, would conduct one-on-one interviews with key executives.

In preparation for the interviews and focus group meetings, the team's final task during their initial meeting was to draft a customer requirements matrix. The purpose of this document was to identify what the team believed customers expected and what would delight them. This "straw man" document, which is shown in Table 6.5, would be validated during the focus groups. It should be noted that, although the ranking scale is from 1 to 10, the team uses only four values: 1, 4, 7, and 10. This simplifies ranking and provides greater differentiation in the results.

Table 6.5   Preliminary Customer Requirements Matrix (Cafeteria)

Customer: Employees		
Requirement	*Importance to Customer**	*Current Satisfaction***
Menu must include both hot and cold entrees and hot and cold sandwiches		
Main entrees must be different each day of the week		
Menu must accommodate special diets (low-fat, low-calorie, diabetic, gluten-free, etc.)		
Cost of full meal (entree, vegetable, starch, dessert and beverage) must not exceed $10		
Time in line (from picking up tray to exiting the checkout line) must not exceed 5 minutes		
Customer: Senior Management		
Requirement	*Importance to Customer**	*Current Satisfaction***
Initial cost must not exceed $200,000		
Ongoing net operating costs must not exceed $5,000/month		

* Importance Ranking Scale:

1 = not very important

4 = moderately important

7 = very important

10 = extremely important

** Satisfaction Ranking Scale:

1 = not very satisfied

4 = moderately satisfied

7 = very satisfied

10 = completely satisfied

Although it is possible to begin requirements-gathering sessions with a blank piece of paper and to simply ask customers to list their requirements, the team believed that it would be helpful to have a starting place for the discussions. Even if the requirements they drafted were inaccurate, this "priming the pump" would serve as both an icebreaker and the basis for establishing accurate requirements. The team would also be able to work with the customers to apply SMART criteria to the draft requirements, making them more specific.

Step 7: Prioritize the Requirements

When the team convened their second meeting, the first item on the agenda was a review of the focus group meetings and executive interviews. Both revealed surprising information. Although the team had believed that menu variety would be the most important employee requirement, they learned that low cost and fast service were of greater importance. And, although it was expected that minimizing costs would be the highest priority for the executive staff, Jim explained that his discussions with the executive staff revealed a new requirement: safety. The executives were concerned about the number of accidents that occurred from people cutting around others in the cafeteria line, spilling food, and slipping on the wet floor. This, the CEO decreed, must stop. Table 6.6 shows the results of the meetings.

The team's next objective was to prioritize the requirements. Although it would have been simple to place primary focus on the items with an importance ranking of 10, Jim pointed out that current satisfaction needed to enter into the equation. He suggested using a streamlined version of a Design for Six Sigma tool, the Quality Function Deployment (QFD) matrix. QFD is not new to DFSS or even to classic Six Sigma. Like many of the quality tools, it was developed in Japan and became part of the American business lexicon during the quality movements of the 1980s. The objective of a QFD is to provide a tool that translates customer needs ("what") into product features ("how"), ensuring that the project is focused on the right things—namely, those that will provide the greatest customer satisfaction. In its full form, QFD is anything but simple, but the basic concept of using weighting factors and standard calculations can help simplify the process of prioritizing requirements.

Figure 6.3 illustrates a mini-QFD. The first three columns are the same ones shown on the customer requirements matrix (Table 6.6). The other columns are completed as follows:

■ *Satisfaction Goal for New Solution*—The team made an assessment of how satisfied they wanted customers to be. It is important to note that they did not expect total satisfaction (a 10) for each requirement. In determining the satisfaction goal, the team considered the importance and current satisfaction rankings the customers had provided. For the first three items, where customers rated their satisfaction equal to or higher than importance, the team decided that the customers were not seeking any improvement.

Table 6.6 Customer Requirements Matrix (Cafeteria) after Focus Group Meetings and Executive Interviews

Customer: Employees		
Requirement	Importance to Customer*	Current Satisfaction**
Menu must include both hot and cold entrees and hot and cold sandwiches	4	7
Main entrees must be different each day of the week	1	7
Menu must accommodate special diets (low-fat, low-calorie, diabetic, gluten-free, etc.)	7	7
Cost of full meal (entree, vegetable, starch, dessert and beverage) must not exceed $10	7	1
Time in line (from picking up tray to exiting the checkout line) must not exceed 5 minutes	10	1
Customer: Senior Management		
Requirement	Importance to Customer*	Current Satisfaction**
Initial cost must not exceed $200,000	7	N/A
Ongoing net operating costs must not exceed $5,000/ month	10	4
Design must minimize accidents (current average is 1 per month)	10	1

* Importance Ranking Scale:

1 = not very important

4 = moderately important

7 = very important

10 = extremely important

** Satisfaction Ranking Scale:

1 = not very satisfied

4 = moderately satisfied

7 = very satisfied

10 = completely satisfied

Requirements		Importance	Satisfaction with Current Solution	Satisfaction Goal for New Solution	Improvement Required (Negative Values are Converted to 0)	Development Priority
1	Menu: hot and cold entrees and sandwiches	4	7	7	0	0.0
2	Menu: different entrees each day	1	7	7	0	0.0
3	Menu: special diets	7	7	7	0	0.0
4	Cost: full meal < $10	7	1	10	9	63.0
5	Time: start to checkout < 5 minutes	10	1	10	9	90.0
6	Cost: initial (setup) cost < $200K	7	0	10	10	70.0
7	Cost: monthly net operating cost < $5K	10	4	10	6	60.0
8	Design: minimize accidents (<1/qtr)	10	1	10	9	90.0
9						
10						

Figure 6.3   Priorities requirements (Mini-QFD).

Therefore, the satisfaction goal was the same as current satisfaction. The other items, however, indicated a substantial disparity between importance and satisfaction. In all cases, satisfaction was rated as 4 or less, whereas importance was 7 or 10. These, the team realized, were important requirements. The satisfaction goal for them should be total, a 10.

■ *Improvement Required*—This is a simple calculation, subtracting current satisfaction from the satisfaction goal. It indicates how much improvement is required. Once again, it would have been simple to stop here and declare that the items that deserved the greatest focus were those with the greatest discrepancy between current and desired satisfaction. Based on the Improvement Required column, it appeared that the menu did not need to be changed and that the highest priority should be ensuring that the initial cost did not exceed $200,000. Jim indicated that this column presents only part of the picture. The customer's importance ranking also needs to be considered. That happens in the final column.

■ *Development Priority*—This is a calculation, multiplying the Improvement Required by the Importance. Because it incorporates the importance ranking as well as the needed improvement in satisfaction, it provides a more accurate reflection of requirements priorities than simply considering any of the previous four columns by itself. Based on this column, the employees' requirement that a meal cost less than $10, which had an importance ranking of 7, is a higher priority than the executives' requirement that monthly net operating costs be less than $5,000, even though that one had an importance ranking of 10. And, although the cost of a meal and the time requirement had the same improvement required score, their development priorities varied because of the difference in their importance rankings.

Based on this analysis, the team realized that their highest priorities were to minimize accidents and time in line.

Step 8: Identify Potential Solutions

The team recognized that their two top priorities were related and that the design of the cafeteria was critical to satisfying those requirements. Their next task was to identify potential solutions. Although there are a number of different ways to do this, they used brainstorming, basing their suggestions on their experience with cafeterias. The team determined that they would consider three basic designs:

- Single line, the approach that both companies employed in their current cafeterias (GWC had two single line operations)
- Stations, with separate lines for hot and cold entrees, salads, desserts, and beverages
- Hybrid, with a single line for trays, utensils, and beverages, followed by stations for other food items.

Step 9: Evaluate Potential Solutions' Effect on Customer Requirements

There are a number of techniques that can be used to evaluate multiple choices, including developing a matrix of solutions and requirements and assigning weighting factors to each intersection. This is often referred to as a Cause and Effects or C&E matrix. Although the C&E matrix is a highly effective method, the team decided to use a standard Six Sigma tool, the Pugh Concept Selection matrix.

The primary difference between the Pugh matrix and the evaluations the team had already conducted was that, instead of ranking each alternative using the 1-4-7-10 scale, Pugh uses a simpler scale to indicate whether each solution is better, worse, or the same as the baseline. Typically the scale is plus, minus, and zero, although some companies replace the zero with an "S" for "same." Others use color coding, with red being worse, green better, and white neutral.

The headquarters relocation team used the standard plus, minus, zero scale. They then tallied the number of pluses, minuses, and zeros for each solution. This simplicity translated into an approach that was easy to complete and understand. While it lacks the precision of the 1-4-7-10 rankings in a standard C&E, at this point the team did not need precision. Their goal was to quickly identify strengths and weaknesses of potential solutions. Pugh is ideal for that.

Figure 6.4 shows the use of a Pugh concept selection matrix to evaluate the team's proposed solutions. Although the stations and hybrid approaches had similar

Requirements		Satisfaction With Current Solution	Possible Solutions*			
			Single Line	Stations	Hybrid	
1	Menu: hot and cold entrees and sandwiches	7	0	0	0	
2	Menu: different entrees each day	7	0	0	0	
3	Menu: special diets	7	0	+	+	
4	Cost: full meal < $10	1	0	0	0	
5	Time: start to checkout < 5 minutes	1	–	+	+	
6	Cost: initial (setup) cost < $200K	0	+	–	0	
7	Cost: monthly net operating cost < $5K	4	–	+	0	
8	Design: minimize accidents (<1/qtr)	1	–	+	+	
9						
10						
	Totals	**Plus**	1	4	3	
		Minus	3	1	0	
		Neutral	4	3	5	

Figure 6.4   Pugh concept selection matrix.

results, the team believed that the stations approach was the best one. Not only did it have one more plus than the hybrid solution, but that plus was a critical one, since it was for ongoing operating costs. The team believed that this outweighed the higher initial cost. Before proceeding with this assumption, though, the team asked Frank to present their findings to the executive committee. He agreed that he would do that, once they had completed the final step.

Step 10: Define the New State

As was true for the definition of the current state, if a process was being changed, the team would use a process map to create a pictorial representation of the proposed or "to be" state. However, since this project was relatively straightforward, the team decided to use a verbal explanation. Their description of the "to be" state for the cafeteria was: "The cafeteria will feature individual stations for hot entrees and sandwiches, cold entrees and sandwiches, salads, soups, desserts, beverages, and special diets. There will be six checkout lines, and customers will pick up utensils at checkout, eliminating the cost of washing excess utensils. The design will ensure that there is sufficient space between stations to eliminate bumping and other accidents."

After conducting similar analyses for the other aspects of the new headquarters building, the team members presented their findings and recommendations to their champion, Frank, confident that what they had defined was worthwhile and feasible. When Frank asked whether they believed it was the right project, the answer was a resounding "yes."

What Can Go Wrong?

Although there are a number of potential pitfalls to this step, the most common are:

- *Incomplete or inaccurate definition of the problem*—Since this is the stage of wild enthusiasm, it is not surprising that some project teams jump into a project without completely understanding what is involved. This is, however, a critical mistake and one that invariably increases overall costs. It is essential to have the facts before proceeding.
- *Lack of involvement by key groups*—Although it is unlikely that a project team would neglect to include primary customers, all too often the ancillary groups—what this chapter refers to as influencers and stakeholders—are forgotten. This provides another possibility for cost overruns later in the project when the team discovers that there are legal or regulatory implications to the work they are doing.
- *Incomplete requirements definition*—Admittedly, the requirements that are gathered during this stage are preliminary and will be refined as the project

proceeds; however, it is important to identify key categories. In the case of the relocation project, if the team had not identified safety as a major concern, they might have chosen a different solution, with the result that the final cafeteria design would have been unsatisfactory.

■ *Solution selection without complete analysis*—Once again, under the influence of wild enthusiasm, it is tempting to choose the first solution that appears to meet the requirements. While this may prove to be an effective solution, it is also possible that it will not.

Chapter 7

Managing Expectations

"When we move to the new building, we'll have individual offices, and all of them will have windows."

"Did you hear about the cafeteria? It's going to be completely subsidized. Who said there's no such thing as a free lunch?"

When Jim Wang overheard two colleagues' conversation, he realized that his project was already behind schedule in at least one critical area: managing expectations. Rumors, some of them with no basis in reality, had begun to spread. "Team, we've got a problem," he announced at the next meeting. "If we're not careful, we're going to wind up with some mighty disappointed customers."

Jim knew that if the unrealistic expectations—what Table 1.2 calls wild enthusiasm—were not curtailed, they would turn to disillusionment. His responsibility, and that of the team, was to control the enthusiasm and channel it into the project. To do that, they needed to manage expectations.

When Jim explained what he had overheard, Harry Parr nodded. "I heard that, too. I also heard all of us on the team would receive 10 percent bonuses when the project's done and that we're guaranteed no overtime."

Jim frowned. The problem was bigger than he had feared. He had been so focused on ensuring that the project was doable that he had neglected to ensure that everyone had realistic expectations of both the "to be" state and their roles in creating that state.

"It's never too late," he assured Frank when they met later that day. "Here's what we're going to do." Jim outlined the four steps he planned:

1. Develop a list of what would *not* be included in the project scope.
2. Develop measurements of success for the proposed solution.
3. Gain customer buy-in.
4. Calibrate team expectations.

Step 1: Develop a List of What Will *Not* Be Included in the Project Scope

At this point in the project, the team had concentrated on what the project would entail. They had been working to clarify the scope, eliminating items to make the overall goal achievable. While this was important, Jim knew it was also important to document what would not be included and the reasons for the omissions.

Although the project team had never contemplated individual offices, with or without windows, for all employees, and the commitment from senior management was that the cafeteria would continue the existing 8 percent subsidy that both GWC and IW currently had, the initial requirements-gathering had revealed some expectations that could not be met. This is typical of a project. Not all requirements can be satisfied, but none should be ignored or allowed to fall into the proverbial black hole. Every project needs a repository of documentation, and that documentation should include all decisions.

In the case of the relocation project, three requests were denied. Customer interviews revealed that many employees wanted to be able to eat outdoors. The team realized this would not be feasible, at least for the initial stage of the project, since the additional costs for outdoor tables and chairs would exceed the start-up budget. Furthermore, the potential for lost and broken dishes and utensils might jeopardize the ongoing operating budget. Employees also wanted the cafeteria to be open from 10:00 until 3:00, but traffic patterns from the existing cafeterias revealed that only a few people used it before 11:00 and after 1:00. The cost of keeping it open the extra hours could not be justified.

Similarly, the request from a member of senior management that the windows have solar coating to reduce energy costs was not feasible for the first phase. In this case, although the cost was within the budget, the timing was not. The contractors were unable to begin work on the windows until October.

In addition to documenting the reasons for not including these features in the project, it is essential that the entire project team and the customers who requested the features understand what will not be included and why. Not only is informing the requestors common courtesy, but it is also a way of avoiding unrealistic expectations. Even if an idea was presented during a brainstorming session rather than being formally requested, it is important that everyone involved in the brainstorming session understand that the idea will not become part of the project. Otherwise, rumors may spread, creating false hopes.

Notifying the team is important, because team members are often the source of informal information about the project. If they do not understand the scope and the reasons why specific items were eliminated, they cannot provide accurate responses when asked.

Step 2: Develop Measurements of Success for the Proposed Solution

One part of managing expectations is to ensure that everyone—whether team member or customer—understands how success is being defined. Customers have a right to expect that the promised functionality will be delivered and that it will have an acceptable level of quality; however, it is important for both them and the team members who will deliver that functionality to have a common understanding of what constitutes "completion" and how "well done" will be determined. One way to do this is to ensure that all requirements are SMART.

One of the most frequently cited employee requirements was "Time in line (from picking up tray to exiting the checkout line) must not exceed five minutes." Evaluating this requirement using the SMART criteria reveals the following:

- *Specific*—Yes. There is adequate specificity to determine whether or not the requirement is met.
- *Measurable*—Yes. It is possible to measure time in line.
- *Achievable*—Perhaps. The goal may or may not be achievable. A person waiting for a grilled cheese sandwich to be cooked and then debating over a choice of salads might require more than five minutes to exit the checkout line.
- *Relevant*—Yes. There is little doubt that the requirement is important to employees.
- *Time bound*—Yes. The requirement specifies a time. Furthermore, it implies that each and every transaction will be subject to the same criteria.

As noted above, the problem with this requirement is that it may not be achievable for every person who uses the cafeteria's services. One way to mitigate the problem is to use averages; however, average time in line may not satisfy the employees' requirements. If half the people exit in one minute and the other half in nine, the requirement would be technically fulfilled. It is unlikely, though, that employee satisfaction would be high.

An alternate version of the requirement is "Ninety-eight percent of all customers will spend no more than five minutes in line (measured from picking up their trays until they have exited the checkout line). The remaining 2 percent will spend no more than seven minutes in line. Calculations will be done on a calendar month basis, with reports provided no later than the fifth working day of the following month." This definition, which is similar to a service-level agreement, provides a high level of specificity and leaves no doubt about what is expected or how success will be defined.

Each requirement should be subjected to similar scrutiny to ensure that everyone understands how the project will be measured. Like everything else on the project, these definitions should be written, added to the project repository, and distributed to key personnel. Key personnel include the person or department that specified the requirement and the team members who will be responsible for turning the requirements into reality. It is also important to note that the definition of success should not be created by either the project team or the customers alone. The two groups should work together to ensure that the definition meets the customers' needs and that it can be accomplished by the team.

Step 3: Gain Customer Buy-in

Also called commitment, buy-in is a key component of successful change as discussed in Chapter 2. If a change is to be successful, everyone involved, whether customers or team members, must be fully committed to turning the vision into reality. Mere acceptance is not enough.

One aspect of gaining commitment is ensuring that everyone who is involved understand their part. They need to know what roles they will play on the project and what is expected of them. That is only the beginning. The project's champion and the entire team need to ensure that the stakeholders "buy into" the project and work to achieve its success. The key to this commitment is effective communication. In their book *Project Management That Works*, Rick Morris and Brette Sember state, "A PM's [project manager's] role is 90 percent about communication."*

Projects by definition create change. Change is often difficult, and some people will resist it. Those are facts; nothing will alter them. However, effective communication can help ease the negative aspects of change and reduce resistance. When seeking successful change, it is not enough to develop the Four Ps or to establish a direction as discussed in Chapter 2. Unless these elements are communicated effectively, the likelihood of obtaining commitment is low, and there will be no change to sustain. In short, the change will not be successful.

Realtors stress the importance of three things: location, location, location. The project management equivalent is communication, communication, communication. Realtors really mean good location, and project teams need *effective* communication. Simply preparing a PowerPoint slide show or hosting a town meeting is not enough. To be effective, communication must be clear, consistent, targeted, and ongoing.

■ *Clear*—Whether it is a PowerPoint presentation, a newsletter, or an oral briefing, it is important that there be no ambiguity. The KISS (Keep it Simple, Stupid) principle applies to all communication but is particularly relevant when explaining major changes.

---

* Rick A. Morris and Brette McWhorter Sember, *Project Management That Works* (New York: AMACOM, 2008), 97.

- *Consistent*—It is important that everyone who has a role in communicating information about the project delivers the same message. This point is so critical that some companies provide scripts for anyone who will be providing oral briefings. They may also channel all written communications through a single person to ensure consistency. Mixed messages not only create confusion, they can also hinder the development of commitment.

- *Targeted*—All projects have a variety of audiences. Just as business cases often contain an executive summary designed for senior management, as well as more detailed descriptions of costs and benefits for the Finance Department, so too is it important to consider the needs of everyone who will be affected by the project. Although everyone has a need to know the overall schedule and progress in meeting it, the detailed information provided to the project team will differ from that provided to the customers. Even within the customer community, depending on the project, there may be different communications to managers and to workers. The format as well as the content may vary based on the target audience. While a poster hung on the break-room door may serve the production line workers' needs, managers may require additional detail in the form of a memo or newsletter.

- *Ongoing*—Simply delivering the message once is not enough. People have short attention spans and competing priorities. They need to be reminded of what is happening, why, and when. Not only is it important to reiterate the reasons for the project and the overall schedule, but it is also critical to provide regular updates on progress. While some people may believe that no news is good news, many equate an absence of news with an absence of progress.

Communication is so critical to the success of a project that Chapter 18 is dedicated to the development of a formal communication plan. The WWC team decided that at this stage of the project, they would:

1. Develop a website to contain all customer-related information.
2. Create posters with photos of the Bluebell Industries building and distribute them to all departments. The photos would also be available on the website.
3. Create an FAQ (frequently asked questions) document with weekly updates. This would be distributed to all employees via e-mail and would be posted on the website. Its goal was to address questions like the cafeteria subsidy and individual offices and prevent the spread of wild enthusiasm.

Step 4: Calibrate Team Expectations

It is not only customers whose expectations may run wild. So, too, as Jim discovered, may the team's. It is important that all team members understand exactly what is expected of them and what they can expect from the project manager.

When Harry raised his question during their expectation-setting meeting, Jim had the unwelcome task of telling his team that bonuses were unlikely and that substantial overtime might be required. As he had expected, his announcement was met with groans mingled with quiet resignation. The team was aware that bonuses were rare and overtime was, after all, an occupational hazard on many projects.

Jim knew that although the team as a whole had certain expectations, individual team members had others. That is why although he held group meetings, he also met with each member of the team individually. During the one-on-one sessions, he confirmed his own expectations, including the percentage of time he expected the team member to devote to the project, and sought to learn what the individual wanted to accomplish as well as what concerns he or she had about being part of the new headquarters building project. Jim's goal was to begin establishing a relationship based on mutual respect and trust. Chapter 11 discusses other aspects of team development.

What Can Go Wrong?

The potential pitfall of this stage is the failure to complete each of the steps shown above. This chapter has focused on two elements of a successful project: what and who. It is essential that everyone understands what is to be accomplished and—just as importantly—what will not be part of the project scope. It is also important that success be clearly defined and that that definition be understood and agreed upon by key shareholders. Unless this happens, unrealistic expectations may continue to flourish, only to be followed by the predictable next stage: disillusionment and disappointment.

On the "who" side, it is vital that both customers and the entire team be committed to the project's success. Customers are the reason for the project, and team members are the arms and legs, not to mention the brains, that will make the project a success. They must be included and kept aware of progress and problems. In a classic adage, if they are not part of the solution, they may become part of the problem.

The single most common cause of failure when establishing and managing expectations is a lack of communication. Project managers, as Morris and Sember state, must communicate—constantly.

Chapter 8

Identifying and Avoiding Risks
The Initial Risk Assessment

Jim was a realist. He knew that every project entails risk. Like most managers, he dreaded the thought of a risk becoming reality and turning his project into a disaster. Although not as risk averse as some managers, Jim was surprised when he read Tom DeMarco and Timothy Lister's book, *Waltzing with Bears: Managing Risk on Software Projects*, and discovered that they have a different attitude. Far from decrying risk as a bad thing, DeMarco and Lister claim, "Projects with no real risks are losers. They're almost always devoid of benefit; that's why they weren't done years ago."* Jim was chuckling as he headed to the team's next meeting. Since the primary purpose of the meeting was to identify and then mitigate the impact of risks, he would begin by sharing the DeMarco and Lister quote with the team. If there was a direct correlation between risk and benefits, the GWC–IW merger and the relocation to Bluebell was certain to have many benefits, because it certainly had enough risks.

In *Project Management Recipes for Success*, Guy DeFuria divides risks into two categories: threats and opportunities.† Threats pose a potentially negative impact on the project, while opportunities can have a positive effect. This categorization may result from the SWOT analysis that Kathy Schwalbe discusses in *Information*

---

* Tom DeMarco and Timothy Lister, *Waltzing with Bears: Managing Risk on Software Projects* (New York: Dorset House Publishing, 2003), 9.
† Guy L. DeFuria, *Project Management Recipes for Success* (Boca Raton: Auerbach, 2009), 129.

Technology Project Management* in which teams identify their project's strengths, weaknesses, opportunities, and threats as part of a strategic plan. While there is no doubt that it is important to identify opportunities, this book will use the classic definition, what DeFuria calls a threat, when discussing risk. It should be noted, however, that many of the techniques discussed for assessing and mitigating risks can be used to assess and implement opportunities, thus providing a project with additional benefits or reduced costs.

Risk management should be repeated at various stages of the project. Although the scope under consideration will vary with each iteration, the process remains constant. The four basic steps are:

1. Identify the risk.
2. Evaluate the potential effects and severity of the risk.
3. Prioritize the risks.
4. Develop a mitigation plan.

The Failure Modes and Effects Analysis (FMEA), a tool commonly used by Six Sigma companies to assess process risks, can also be used to provide a standard way of documenting project risks. The objectives of an FMEA, which originated in NASA, are to:

■ Identify ways in which a process—or, in this case, a project—might fail to meet customer requirements (the failure mode).
■ Determine which potential failures would have the greatest effect on the customer.
■ Evaluate current controls that are designed to prevent the failure. In the case of a project, there are no current controls. Instead, this section can be used to document the initial plan for dealing with the risk.
■ Develop a corrective action or formal mitigation plan to prevent the most critical failures. In a process environment, the FMEA is also used to document the results of the corrective action.

Appendix D provides detailed instructions for the development of an FMEA. It should be noted that this FMEA has been modified from the standard process-related one used as part of a Six Sigma process-improvement project to be more applicable to any type of project.

---

* Kathy Schwalbe, *Information Technology Project Management* (Cambridge, MA: Course Technology, 2000), 77.

Step 1: Identify the Risk

The first step in risk management is to understand what problems or risks may occur. There are a number of possible techniques for identifying risks. Several of these are shown on Table 6.4, Tools for Determining Customer Requirements. Specifically, surveys, focus groups, and individual interviews can be used to identify potential problems. Brainstorming, in which participants offer ideas and a scribe records them, is a commonly used technique and one that the relocation team employed for its own risk identification.

DeFuria suggests two other methods: records analysis and nominal group technique.* Records analysis involves reviewing documentation from previous projects to determine what risks they encountered. In nominal group, unlike brainstorming (which is verbal and voluntary), each participant is asked to make a written list of potential threats. At the end of a designated time period, the facilitator asks each participant to share one threat, then proceeds to the next participant, going around the room as many times as needed to list all the risks the team identified. The advantage of this approach over brainstorming is that there is more reflection, greater participation by the whole group, and reduced possibility of manipulation by a small group of participants.

Once the raw list of potential risks has been created, it is important to categorize them. DeMarco and Lister[†] postulate that there are five core risks to a software project:

■ A schedule flaw
■ Scope creep
■ Employee turnover
■ Specification breakdown (ambiguity in requirements)
■ Poor productivity

Although their book focuses on software projects, the categories have relevance for many other types of projects. Other risk categories might include contractors and technology.

The relocation team had identified environmental and regulatory concerns as possible risks when they drafted the project charter. Knowing that there were more potential problems, they held a brainstorming session. Jim, serving as the facilitator, began the session by asking, "What is the worst thing that could happen?" When the team members had exhausted their answers, he asked, "What is the next worst thing?" and continued with "What else could go wrong?" Only when the team was exhausted and flip charts of possible problems papered the walls was this stage of the process complete.

---

* DeFuria, *Project Management Recipes*, 133–37.
[†] DeMarco and Lister, *Waltzing with Bears*, 102.

Although many more risks were identified, five will be used to illustrate the risk assessment process.

1. The new building is destroyed by a tornado.
2. Critical contractors fail to meet their schedules.
3. Local building regulations and inspections delay the schedule.
4. "Green" materials (VOC-free paint and low-emissions carpet) are not available when needed.
5. Plates and utensils with the new corporate logo are not available on July 1.

These risks were entered into the "potential failure mode" column of the FMEA spreadsheet (Figure 8.1). When choosing the "project phase," although the building's destruction would be a risk at any phase of the project, the team believed that it was most critical during Execution and Control, which is why they showed that as the stage when the risk was highest.

Step 2: Evaluate the Potential Effects and Severity of the Risk

All risks are not created equal. Some, although potentially catastrophic, are unlikely to occur. Others whose probability of occurrence is higher may have lesser impact on the final outcome of the project. It is important to make distinctions and to quantify the effects.

Under Jim's guidance, the team began to answer the next question, "What would be the consequences if this risk materialized, and how severe would those consequences be?" The answers to the first part of the question are recorded in the "potential failure effects" column, while the estimated severity ranking is placed in the "severity" column. As they had when ranking requirements, the team used a 1-4-7-10 ranking scale. The results of their evaluation are shown on Figure 8.1.

It should be noted that the team ranked the use of a nongreen material as a lower severity than missing the target date. In determining severity, they believed that the project schedule was of primary importance, with budget secondary, and specific scope items, including the use of green materials, tertiary. In terms of the project constraints triangle (Figure 1.1), they believed that the time leg was fixed, that resources (including costs) had some flexibility, and that the greatest level of flexibility was in scope. When they reviewed their work with Frank Seely, the project champion, he disagreed. Both Isabelle Crumpton and George Webster had insisted that schedule could slip, if needed, but the building had to be as green as possible. The team revised the severity rankings on their FMEA and continued with the process of assessing risk. Figure 8.2 shows the final results of the team's assessment.

Project Name:	New Headquarters Building Interior Renovation		Date Prepared:November 2, 2010	Revision Number:
Prepared By:	Jonathan Talbot		Revised By:	Revision Date:

	What Could Happen?				Why and How Often?			What Will We Do?	Action Plan			
	Project Phase	Potential Failure Mode	Potential Failure Effects	S E V	Potential Causes	O C C	R P N	Proposed Action (Avoidance, Containment, Mitigation, Evasion)	Actions Recommended	Resp.	Target Date	Date Completed/ Comments
	Execution and Control	The new building is destroyed by a tornado	The company's relocation is delayed until the building can be rebuilt or a new one chosen.	10								
			The project budget is exceeded.	7								
	Execution and Control	Key contractors fail to meet their schedules	The project or portions of it are delayed, possibly delaying the relocation date.	7								

Figure 8.1   Initial risk assessment (FMEA).

What Could Happen?				Why and How Often?			What Will We Do?	Action Plan			
Project Phase	Potential Failure Mode	Potential Failure Effects	S E V	Potential Causes	O C C	R P N	Proposed Action (Avoidance, Containment, Mitigation, Evasion)	Actions Recommended	Resp.	Target Date	Date Completed/ Comments
Execution and Control	Local building regulations and inspections delay the schedule	The project or portions of it are delayed, possibly delaying the relocation date.	7								
		The project budget is exceeded.	7								
Execution and Control	"Green" materials (VOC-free pain and low-emissions carpet) are not available when needed	Alternate materials with a higher environmental impact would need to be utilized.	4								
Execution and Control	Plates and utensils with the new corporate logo are not available July 1	The cafeteria would need a temporary source of plates and utensils.	1								

Figure 8.1 (Continued)

Project Name:	New Headquarters Building Interior Renovation	Date Prepared: November 2, 2010	Revision Number: 1.0
Prepared By:	Jonathan Talbot	Revised By: Jonathan Talbot	Revision Date: November 3, 2010

What Could Happen?			Why and How Often?				What Will We Do?	Action Plan			
Project Phase	Potential Failure Mode	Potential Failure Effects	S E V	Potential Causes	O C C	R P N	Proposed Action (Avoidance, Containment, Mitigation, Evasion)	Actions Recommended	Resp.	Target Date	Date Completed/ Comments
Execution and Control	The new building is destroyed by a tornado	The company's relocation is delayed until the building can be rebuilt or a new one chosen.	10	Act of God	1	10	Evasion				
		The project budget is exceeded.	4	Act of God	1	4	Evasion				
Execution and Control	Key contractors fail to meet their schedules	The project or portions of it are delayed, possibly delaying the relocation date.	7	Initial schedule is too aggressive	4	28	Containment				

Figure 8.2 Final risk assessment (FMEA).

	What Could Happen?			Why and How Often?				What Will We Do?		Action Plan		
Project Phase	Potential Failure Mode	Potential Failure Effects	S E V	Potential Causes	O C C	R P N		Proposed Action (Avoidance, Containment, Mitigation, Evasion)	Actions Recommended	Resp.	Target Date	Date Completed/ Comments
			7	Sub-contractors are not available when needed	7	49		Containment				
Execution and Control	Local building regulations and inspections delay the schedule	The project or portions of it are delayed, possibly delaying the relocation date.	7	Incomplete understanding of local regs	4	28		Mitigation	Obtain copies of all local regs; meet with officials to determine scheduling constraints	Cheryl McNally	12/1/10	
		The project budget is exceeded.	4	Schedule does not include "wait" time	4	16		Mitigation				
Execution and Control	"Green" materials (VOC-free pain and low-emissions carpet) are not available when needed	Alternate materials with a higher environmental impact would need to be utilized.	10	Manufacturer has insufficient inventory	4	40		Mitigation	Contact manufacturer to advise them of future order and the plan to feature the green building in the company's annual report.	Frank Seely	1/15/11	

Figure 8.2 (Continued)

Project Name:	New Headquarters Building Interior Renovation	Date Prepared: November 2, 2010	Revision Number: 1.0
Prepared By:	Jonathan Talbot	Revised By: Jonathan Talbot	Revision Date: November 3, 2010

What Could Happen?				Why and How Often?			What Will We Do?		Action Plan		
Project Phase	Potential Failure Mode	Potential Failure Effects	S E V	Potential Causes	O C C	R P N	Proposed Action (Avoidance, Containment, Mitigation, Evasion)	Actions Recommended	Resp.	Target Date	Date Completed/ Comments
Execution and Control	The new building is destroyed by a tornado	The company's relocation is delayed until the building can be rebuilt or a new one chosen.	10	Act of God	1	10	Evasion				
		The project budget is exceeded.	4	Act of God	1	4	Evasion				
Execution and Control	Key contractors fail to meet their schedules	The project or portions of it are delayed, possibly delaying the relocation date.	7	Initial schedule is too aggressive	4	28	Containment				

Figure 8.2   Final risk assessment (FMEA).

What Could Happen?			Why and How Often?				What Will We Do?		Action Plan		
Project Phase	Potential Failure Mode	Potential Failure Effects	S E V	Potential Causes	O C C	R P N	Proposed Action (Avoidance, Containment, Mitigation, Evasion)	Actions Recommended	Resp.	Target Date	Date Completed/ Comments
Execution and Control	Local building regulations and inspections delay the schedule	The project or portions of it are delayed, possibly delaying the relocation date.	7	Sub-contractors are not available when needed	7	49	Containment				
			7	Incomplete understanding of local regs	4	28	Mitigation	Obtain copies of all local regs; meet with officials to determine scheduling constraints	Cheryl McNally	12/1/10	
		The project budget is exceeded.	4	Schedule does not include "wait" time	4	16	Mitigation				
Execution and Control	"Green" materials (VOC-free pain and low-emissions carpet) are not available when needed	Alternate materials with a higher environmental impact would need to be utilized.	10	Manufacturer has insufficient inventory	4	40	Mitigation	Contact manufacturer to advise them of future order and the plan to feature the green building in the company's annual report.	Frank Seely	1/15/11	

Figure 8.2 (Continued)

Phase	Risk	Consequence	Likelihood	Cause	Likelihood	Impact	Score	Strategy	Mitigation	Owner	Date
Execution and Control	Plates and utensils with the new corporate logo are not available July 1	The cafeteria would need a temporary source of plates and utensils.	10	Contractor fails to order with sufficient lead time	7	70		Mitigation	Ensure that contract includes detailed schedule and. penalties if schedule is not met	Marilyn Engel	1/15/11
			1	Logo design is delayed	7	7		Containment			
			1	Supplier cannot meet schedule	4	4		Containment			

Figure 8.2 (Continued)

The next two questions Jim asked the team to consider were "What is the cause of the potential problem?" and "How likely is it to occur?" The answers to these questions are recorded in the "potential causes" and "occurrence" columns.

Step 3: Prioritize the Risks

It is essential to know which risks are most likely to occur and which would have the greatest negative effect. As Harold Kerzner states in *Project Management: A Systems Approach to Planning, Scheduling and Controlling*, risk is a function of likelihood and impact or, to express the concept as an equation, risk = f (likelihood, impact).* On the FMEA, this is referred to as the Risk Priority Number, or RPN. It is calculated by multiplying Severity by Likelihood of Occurrence. As shown on Figure 8.2, the failure mode/cause with the highest RPN is that contractors would fail to order green materials with sufficient lead time, resulting in the unavailability of the environmentally sound paint and carpet when needed. The risk with the second-highest RPN is the potential unavailability of subcontractors, leading to a delay in the overall project schedule.

Step 4: Develop a Mitigation Plan

Once the team has identified and prioritized risks, the remaining step is to determine what, if any, actions should be taken to minimize the likelihood of the risk becoming reality. DeMarco and Lister propose four different approaches to any risk: avoidance, containment, mitigation, and evasion.†

- *Avoidance*—Elimination of the portion of the project that poses the risk
- *Containment*—Establishment of contingencies (schedule and budget) to deal with the risk if it occurs
- *Mitigation*—Actions taken to prevent the risk from occurring
- *Evasion*—The risk does not materialize, although the team has taken no action; this can also be described as luck.

The team decided that avoidance was not appropriate for the project, since all portions of the project were critical; however, they believed that evasion was the correct action for the first risk, destruction of the building by a tornado. There was simply no way to mitigate or contain that risk. They could only hope that it would not occur.

---

* Harold Kerzner, *Project Management: A Systems Approach to Planning, Scheduling and Controlling*, 9th ed. (Hoboken: John Wiley & Sons, Inc., 2006), 709.
† DeMarco and Lister, *Waltzing with Bears*, 63.

As shown on Figure 8.2, the team decided to mitigate the risks associated with unavailability of the green paint and carpet and the possibility of delays due to regulatory agencies. The mitigation plans, person responsible, and target date are all shown on the "Action Plan" section of the FMEA.

With their initial risk assessment complete, the team was ready to begin development of the business case.

What Can Go Wrong?

The four primary risks associated with risk assessment are:

- *Failure to identify key risks*—It is impossible to mitigate an unknown risk. That is why it is essential that every project include formal risk management. This is one of the areas where companies with Project Management Offices (PMOs) and extensive project documentation excel, because they can use both of those resources to identify the source of possible risks.
- *Underestimation of potential severity*—At the beginning of a project, optimism reigns. It is important to look beyond the early enthusiasm and clearly assess the possibility of failure. Only by being realistic about the project's potential pitfalls can the team be prepared to deal with them.
- *Incorrect response to a risk*—Although evasion is the least costly method of dealing with a potential risk, it is rarely the correct one. The team needs to evaluate each risk and choose the response category that will increase the probability of success.
- *Failure to update the risk assessment*—Risks change as the project progresses. New ones develop; others become of lesser importance. In order to minimize serious problems, the risk assessment/FMEA must be a living document, updated periodically throughout the life of the project.

Chapter 9

Drafting the Preliminary Business Case

The team was nearing the end of the Initiation/Definition phase with only two major tasks remaining: drafting the business case and obtaining approval to proceed with the project. These steps marked the culmination of the work they had done thus far. Presentation of the business case is a critical point in all projects, for it is the first "go/no-go" decision. While the funding and approval process varies by company and size of project, in most cases the team will have only one chance to obtain funding. It is therefore important to create a bulletproof business case. The Five Ps (prior planning prevents poor performance) definitely apply to this process. Since many companies require a formal business-case document that will be read in detail by the Finance Department as well as a summary presentation for senior management, the remainder of this chapter addresses the preparation of those two items.

What Is Involved?

Although the champion is normally the person who presents the business case and seeks funding, the preparation of the materials for that presentation is typically done by the project team. Such was the case for the WWC headquarters project. Jim and his team developed the business case. A few team members would accompany Frank to the meeting where it would be presented and discussed, but their role at the meeting was as spectators. Unless one of the decision makers posed a question that Frank could not answer, Jim and the others would not be active participants. That made it all the more critical that the business case was complete and able to stand on its own.

When developing the business case and the related presentation, it is important that the team understands the perspective of the audiences. While the Finance Department will want to ensure that every calculation is correct and that all benefits assumptions are valid, senior management will focus primarily on two questions:

- Why is this project important?
- How much will it cost?

These questions help senior management balance competing priorities and choose the projects that will provide the greatest benefit, relative to their cost.

The business case itself is normally a text document. Since business cases can become lengthy, many of the details are relegated to appendices, which can be read as needed. In addition, while the base document is primarily text, some of the appendices may be graphical, providing readers with a visual representation of the facts. The adage of a picture being worth a thousand words applies particularly when explaining concepts like cost/benefit ratios and break-even analysis.

Also, because the business case may be a longer document than some of the decision makers choose to read, it is customary to include an executive overview in addition to the full business case. The executive overview, which is placed first in the packet of information, should not exceed three pages and typically has the following sections:

- *Introduction*—This provides a summary of the problem and the proposed solution. Although costs are not included in the introduction, this section provides a condensed version of the whole executive overview, answering the question, "What is involved?"
- *Background*—In addition to a description of the problem that is being addressed, the background section should include a very brief summary of the events that led to the recommendation. This answers the question, "Why is this project important?"
- *Recommendation*—The proposed solution is described here, including the names of any outside firms that will be employed to assist with its implementation.
- *Cost/Benefit*—A summary of the Return on Investment (ROI) calculation, including the payback period is the primary content of this section. Its purpose is to answer the second critical question, "How much will the project cost?"

Contents of Business Case

The table of contents of a typical business case is shown on Figure 9.1. Although not all sections are required for each project, each is discussed below. As a key component of the approval process, the objective of a business case is to answer the Five Ws: who, what, where, when, and why.

1.0 Project Background

    1.1 Problem or Mission Statement

    1.2 Scope of Project

    1.3 Project Objectives

    1.4 Actions-to-Date

2.0 Drivers for Change

    2.1 Deficiencies of Current Solution

    2.2 Need for New Functionality

    2.3 Other

3.0 Overview of Proposed Solution

    3.1 Description of Proposed Solution

    3.2 Mapping of Recommendations to Objectives

4.0 Alternate Solutions

    4.1 Identification of Alternate Solutions and Reasons Not Selected

5.0 Benchmarking

    5.1 List of Companies Contacted

    5.2 Results of Benchmarking

    5.3 Independent Advisors' Recommendations

6.0 High Level Project Plan

7.0 Project Organization and Staffing

8.0 Project Performance Criteria

9.0 Critical Success Factors and Constraints

10.0 Assumptions

11.0 Risks and Recommended Mitigating Actions

12.0 Overview of Costs

13.0 Benefits

    13.1 Cost Reduction

    13.2 Cost Avoidance

    13.3 Improved Quality

    13.4 Increased Functionality

    13.5 Other Benefits

14.0 Cost/Benefit Analysis

Figure 9.1 Business case table of contents.

Project Background

This section provides a brief description of why the project was undertaken and what has occurred to this point. As Figure 9.1 shows, there are four components: problem or mission statement, scope, objectives, and actions-to-date.

The Problem or Mission Statement uses as its foundation the one that was created as Step 1 in Chapter 6. For the business case, the WWC team included an introductory sentence, explaining that the two companies were merging, that neither existing headquarters building would meet the needs of the new corporation, and that the maintenance costs of both existing buildings were deemed excessive. This was followed by the mission statement Frank and Claudia had drafted.

Although few would question that the Project Scope Definition should include those items that will be included, it is also important to list those that will not. This helps calibrate expectations and avoid the problems of wild enthusiasm. In addition to a verbal description, it is also beneficial to include a diagram showing inclusions and exclusions. Figure 9.2 provides an example of the WWC relocation project's scope diagram. The different shading in the boxes and the word "excluded" make it clear which elements are out of scope for this project.

Scope Diagram

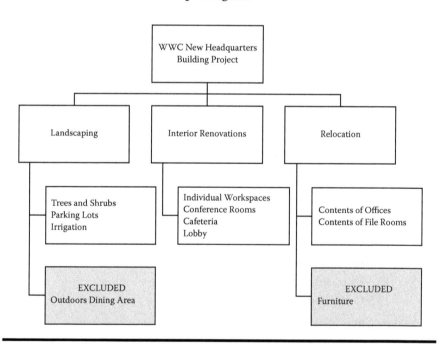

Figure 9.2 Scope diagram.

The Project Objectives section should expound on the goals outlined in the mission statement, clearly explaining what the project is expected to accomplish, while Actions-to-Date lists the primary tasks the team has undertaken thus far.

Drivers for Change

This section answers the question of *why* the project is necessary. Although problems are alluded to in the problem or mission statement, they should be detailed here. Since projects are often undertaken to provide new functionality as well as resolve existing problems, there is a separate section for listing those requirements. And, if there are other reasons for initiating the project that do not fit into either of the first two categories, they can be shown in the "other" section.

When the WWC team drafted their Drivers for Change section, they stressed the need for additional space and lower operating costs as deficiencies of the current solution. New functionality included the ability to track time in line at the cafeteria.

Overview of Proposed Solution

If the previous section answered the question *why*, this one describes *what* will be done. In addition to an explanation of the proposed solution, it is also helpful to include a chart illustrating how specific recommendations and/or portions of the proposed solution will meet the desired objectives. Table 9.1 shows a portion of the team's recommendation-objective mapping.

Alternate Solutions

The question this section is designed to answer is "Why not?" In it, the team should describe the other solutions they considered and the reasons why those solutions were not selected. If a Pugh Concept Selection matrix (Figure 6.4) was used, it may be included here.

Table 9.1 Mapping of Recommendations to Objectives

Objective	Recommendation
Reduce ongoing operational costs	All landscaping will be xeric.
	All shrubs and trees will have drip irrigation.
	All interior lights will have motion-sensitive switches and will turn off automatically if the room is empty.

Benchmarking

Although the WWC team did not conduct any benchmarking, depending on the project, the team might have contacted other companies to understand their experiences. Typically, benchmarking is done with companies that are considered leaders in the specific area under consideration. In this case, if the team had done benchmarking, it might have been with companies noted for their use of green technology and Xeriscaping.

As shown on the table of contents, the Benchmarking section provides the opportunity to list the companies whose practices were reviewed as well as the results of those reviews. If independent advisors were consulted, their recommendations are also included in this section.

High-Level Project Plan

This section of the business plan explains *when* the project will be complete. Although at this point the team has only a preliminary and high-level plan, it is important that it be included. Normally, this will be a Gantt chart, a simple bar chart that shows major tasks and milestones. Gantt and other project-charting methods are discussed in more detail in Chapter 13. Figure 9.3 shows the WWC team's high-level schedule in Gantt format.

Project Organization and Staffing

Who will be doing the work? That is the question the project staffing section of the business case answers. Although some members of senior management may skim these pages, it is important to indicate the main players as well as the percentage of time each is expected to devote to the project. This part of the business case can be seen as an expanded version of the Team Membership section of the project charter (Figure 6.2).

In addition to listing company staff who will be involved, the business case should also indicate any outside advisers or contract staff who may be involved. While individual names may not be known at this point, the extent of reliance on outside staff should be clearly explained. It is also wise to include an organization chart so that there is no misunderstanding about reporting relationships on the project.

Project Performance Criteria

This portion of the business case addresses the question of how project success will be determined. Once again, it is important to manage expectations by clearly explaining the success criteria. The measurements identified in Step 2 of Chapter 7 form the basis for this section of the business case.

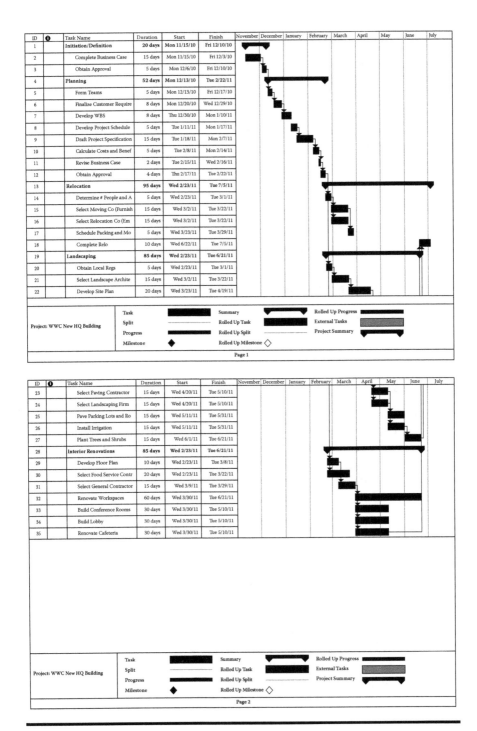

Figure 9.3   Gantt chart for WWC headquarters building project.

Critical Success Factors and Constraints

This section of the business case is an expansion of the Critical Success Factor (CSF) section of the project charter. It seeks to answer the question, "What must occur or be present if the project is to be successful?" Although not always considered a CSF, DeFuria recommends including unusual resource requirements. By this, he means "people with specialized training or experience, plus materials or equipment not available in the organization."* As he points out, obtaining these resources may require a different procurement process, turning them into a project constraint.

Assumptions

All projects are based on assumptions. To avoid misunderstandings and potentially dissatisfied customers, it is important to list all assumptions.

Risks and Recommended Mitigating Actions

What can go wrong? How do we plan to deal with the risk? Those are the questions this portion of the business case seeks to answer. The FMEA/risk assessment that the team created as Figure 8.2 forms the basis for this section.

Overview of Costs

As noted above, one of the most critical questions senior management will ask during the decision-making process is how much the project will cost. This section should include all known costs and any contingency that the team believes is appropriate. Costs are typically divided into two categories: one-time and ongoing. Although it should be understood, it is important to specify that all costs shown are preliminary and will be updated during the Planning phase.

Benefits

This is the opposite side of the cost equation and is even more important than costs. After all, benefits are the reason the project was initiated. Although some initial projection of benefits may have been outlined on the project charter (Figure 6.2), in order to create a complete business case, all potential benefits need to be identified and quantified. At the conclusion of this step, the project charter should be updated with the revised numbers.

Benefits are typically grouped into four categories: cost reduction, cost avoidance, quality improvement, and increased functionality.

---

* Guy L. DeFuria, *Project Management Recipes for Success* (Boca Raton: Auerbach, 2009), 14.

■ *Cost Reduction*—For many projects, this category of benefits is the most important because reduced costs can be used to justify the expenditures involved in the new project. That was the expectation on the WWC project, since the new headquarters building was projected to be less costly to maintain than either of the existing headquarters locations. In some cases, the proposed solution will result in a reduction in staff. In this case, it is important to use fully burdened salaries, which include fringe benefits, and to add an annual inflation rate for salaries. When including manpower savings, the team should distinguish between time that is freed up for other work, which does not translate into a reduction of the bottom line, and the ability to eliminate one or more positions.

■ *Cost Avoidance*—Even though it is less concrete than cost reduction, cost avoidance is also a key benefit area. The costs that are avoided are often additions to staff, whether temporary or permanent. Streamlined processes that require less effort may not only reduce costs but also help avoid incurring additional costs. If, for example, the company anticipates a dramatic growth in sales but does not want to increase its staff of order takers, a new computer system that allows the current staff to take more orders in the same time or that encourages customers to enter their orders online may avoid staff increases. When calculating the costs that were avoided, the team should include not only the fully burdened salaries but also hiring costs (employment agency fees, managers' time to interview candidates, pre-employment physicals, etc.) and the costs of acquiring workstations or other equipment for the new hires.

■ *Quality Improvement*—Although it is more difficult to assign a dollar value to this category and the following one, the team should try to quantify all benefits. Almost no one doubts that improved quality is important. The challenge is to quantify its value. If outside advisors have been used during the Initiation/Definition phase, they may be able to assist in this process. If the quality impacts external customers, there may be research that demonstrates either increased sales due to improved quality or less erosion of the customer base. This same research may help to quantify the extent of those changes. Increased quality is often difficult to quantify, with the result that it is rarely the deciding factor in a cost/benefit analysis.

■ *Increased Functionality*—Like quality improvement, this can be a difficult category to quantify. Sometimes increased functionality is instrumental in identifying new products and new markets. This can be translated into increased sales. In that case, those projected revenue increases should be shown as a benefit. Similarly, new functionality may reduce the time to get a product from the conceptual stage to market. The revenue that would be generated during the time between the streamlined introduction date and the one that would have been the result of the old process can be quantified as a benefit of increased functionality. If, on the other hand, the new functionality is needed to meet governmental regulations, the benefits can be categorized as cost avoidance, since failure to meet those regulations would result in penalties.

■ *Other Benefits*—Benefits that do not fit into any of the previous four categories should be listed here. In the case of the WWC project, an additional benefit is the increased safety in the cafeteria. Although there is a cost avoidance component to improved safety, since there will be fewer workers' comp claims and less lost work time, the morale boost of a safer environment cannot be reduced to dollars and cents but should still be listed as a benefit.

Even when cost reduction alone is sufficient to justify the project, it is helpful to include all categories of benefits to present a complete picture of the project and its benefits.

Cost/Benefit Analysis

Later in the project, as discussed in Chapter 15, a full Return on Investment (ROI) calculation will be performed. At this point, since complete costs are not yet available, a simpler cost/benefit analysis that compares the known costs with the quantifiable benefits is sufficient.

Appendices

If the explanation of any one of the preceding elements exceeds two or three pages, it is helpful to provide a summary in the body of the business case and to include the full detail in an appendix. This allows reviewers to understand the basic business case and to refer to an appendix if more detailed information is required.

The Approval Process

The formal presentation delivered to senior management is typically accompanied by slides that summarize the key points that are detailed in the business case. The sections of a presentation are similar to those of the executive overview; however, there is no summary at the beginning. Instead, the presentation builds the business case, explaining why a change is needed, what steps the team members took to reach their recommendation, what those recommendations are, and the cost and benefits to be derived.

Although not mandatory, when there are a number of competing priorities for funding or when the project is politically sensitive, some companies increase their likelihood of gaining approval for a project by preselling the solution to influential members of the decision-making group. This preselling consists of one-on-one meetings, normally between the project champion and the decision maker, to outline the project and obtain commitment. If preselling is effective, the next step becomes almost a formality.

The final step is to deliver the presentation and obtain funding approval. This is the culmination of the work that has been done and represents a major milestone for the project. Depending on corporate culture, the champion may present the business case alone or may be accompanied by key team members. In addition to the presentation itself, the champion will typically provide copies of the full business case to all members of the decision-making group. Depending on corporate culture, the business case may be distributed in advance of the meeting to allow participants to study it before the official presentation.

The WWC team had no difficulty receiving approval for their project. Both Isabelle Crumpton and George Webster applauded the efforts to date and agreed to fund the project. The team had successfully completed the first project phase, Initiation/Definition, and was ready to proceed to the next phase, Planning.

What Can Go Wrong?

Although there are two common problems in the development and approval of a business case, only the first is under the team's control.

- *An incomplete or unconvincing business case*—As stated at the beginning of this chapter, the team typically has only one chance to gain approval for the project. It is essential that the business case be a compelling one, that each benefit be clearly outlined, and that no attempt be made to understate risks. The team should also consider the corporate culture and ensure that the presentation is one that will appeal to each of the decision makers. Prior planning does indeed prevent poor performance.
- *A shift in corporate priorities*—Unfortunately, priorities change. Sometimes the changes are the result of economic forces. In other cases, the champion or other staff who supported the project initially may leave the company or take positions with a different area of responsibility. In either case, the result is the same: a project with a compelling business case is not approved. There is nothing the team members can do other than return to their normal jobs and hope that the project will be revived at some future date.

THE PLANNING PHASE, PART 1: WHO IS INVOLVED?

While the Initiation/Definition phase of the project established the foundation, the Planning phase builds on that foundation, translating the initial objectives into concrete deliverables and a detailed schedule. In terms of the journalistic Five Ws, the first phase answered the question "why?" and gave preliminary responses to the other questions. The purpose of planning is to provide detailed answers to the remaining questions: who, what, when, and where.

Because planning is such a critical—and often short-changed—part of a project, two sections of this book have been devoted to it. The three chapters of Section III concentrate on the "who" component of a project. Chapter 10 discusses the question of leadership, distinguishing between management and leadership, and outlining characteristics of a successful leader. It also introduces the concept of the Project Management Office.

Since no project would be possible without a team, Chapter 11 focuses on the team. It includes a discussion of team size and roles, presents the advantages of various sourcing options, and discusses team dynamics.

The last critical part of the "who" equation is the customer. Since this is the project phase where wild enthusiasm can turn into disillusionment, Chapter 12 discusses methods for establishing good customer relations.

Chapter 10

The Critical Question
Who Is Leading the Project?

With the project approved and funding secured, the team had reached the beginning of the second project phase: Planning. A plan, according to Merriam-Webster, is "an orderly arrangement of parts of an overall design or object."* The first step in creating that orderly arrangement of parts is determining who will be involved, starting with the individual leading the project. For the WWC project, the answer was easy: Jim Wang would continue as project manager. It should be noted that although the project manager who led the Initiation phase typically remains in charge of the project throughout its life, it is possible that a new manager will be appointed at this point. This may occur because the champion believes a different set of skills is needed for planning and execution than for initiation or because the person who led the initiation phase has been reassigned. In general, however, it is desirable to maintain continuity and to have the same leaders—both champion and project manager—for the project's duration.

As this chapter's title indicates, the critical question is "Who is in charge?" That is, who is ultimately responsible? It might appear that the answer to that question is the champion. After all, champions have committed their power and influence to the project. That is undeniably important; however, the day-to-day responsibility for the project rests on the project manager. It is project managers whose careers will be enhanced or hindered by the outcome of the project. Yes, the champion will suffer if the project fails, but the reality is that project managers have the most to lose. While they may share the glory of a

---

* *Merriam-Webster's Collegiate Dictionary*, 10th ed. (Springfield: Merriam-Webster, Incorporated, 1993), s.v. "plan."

successful project with the champion, project managers are the ones who bear responsibility—and blame—for failure. Project managers set the tone for the project and determine whether the team members function as a true team or as a loosely connected group of individual contributors. Managers are the pivots around which projects turn.

It is possible that the project will be divided into multiple projects and that each of those will require a manager. Such was the case with the WWC relocation project. While it could have been managed as a single project, both the time constraints and the fact that the work affected three different functions led Jim to tell Frank and Claudia that he planned to divide it into three separate projects as shown on Figure 9.2. It is important, however, to note that those project managers all report to Jim and that he is the manager for the overall relocation project, maintaining a single point of contact for Frank and the primary customers, and establishing clear accountability for the full project.

An Important Distinction

Before discussing the responsibilities and characteristics of a successful project manager, it is important to distinguish among three terms: supervision, management, and leadership. Supervision, according to Merriam-Webster, is "a critical watching and direction (as of activities or a course of action)."* In contrast, in their classic book *Management of Organizational Behavior*, John Hersey and Kenneth Blanchard explain that management is "the process of working with and through individuals and groups and other resources to accomplish organizational goals," while "leadership occurs any time one attempts to influence the behavior of an individual or group, regardless of the reason."†

The differences are significant. As Figure 10.1 shows, the amount of control exerted over an individual is greatest at the lowest level of the pyramid, supervision. Conversely, it is those individuals at the top of the pyramid, the leaders, who wield the greatest influence. Note that Hersey and Blanchard use the word "influence" as a key descriptor of leadership but do not mention it when describing a manager.

A supervisor focuses on specific tasks, instructing individuals how to do a job. A manager focuses on the attainment of goals, and a leader is instrumental in establishing those goals. In *Project Management Demystified*, Sid Kemp points out that leaders define what needs to be done, provide the initial inspiration, and develop commitment.‡ Although this book is titled "project management," using the definitions presented above, project managers are expected to lead as well as manage.

---

* *Merriam-Webster's Collegiate Dictionary*, s.v. "supervision."
† Paul Hersey and Kenneth H. Blanchard, *Management of Organizational Behavior* (Englewood Cliffs: Prentice Hall, 1988), 5.
‡ Sid Kemp, *Project Management Demystified* (New York: McGraw-Hill, 2004), 13.

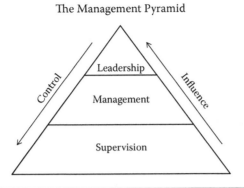

Figure 10.1 Management pyramid.

Characteristics of Successful Leaders

It can be argued that there are many characteristics of successful leaders; however, three are particularly pertinent to managers of projects. Successful leaders:

- Use power prudently
- Enable others to succeed
- Accept ultimate responsibility for the project

Use of Power

Schwalbe identifies five types of power: coercive, reward, legitimate, expert, and referent.* Coercive power, as its name implies, involves forcing others to comply, normally by threatening punishment or penalties. Reward is the opposite side of coercive, in that it promises something positive if the individual complies. Legitimate power is based on the authority managers have through their position within the organization, while expert power resides in the manager's personal experience or expertise. Referent power, which Schwalbe points out is rare, is the result of a person's charisma.

A successful leader must understand the types of power and the effects of each in order to use them wisely. There are times when a project manager needs to use each of these powers. Coercive power may be required when all else fails. Although rewards are normally more effective in motivating employees than threats, positive reaction to the promise of rewards varies by individual. Project managers use legitimate power on a daily basis, since most team members respond to their direction simply because the project managers have been appointed as leaders. Knowing that expert power can help to win over distrusting team members, most companies

---

* Kathy Schwalbe, *Information Technology Project Management* (Cambridge, MA: Course Technology, 2000), 215.

choose project managers with technical expertise as well as project management experience. The key to success is for managers to know their staff well enough to recognize which type of inducement is most effective for each team member.

Enabling Others

No matter how talented they are, no matter how many hours they work each day, managers cannot accomplish everything alone. They need the rest of the team. How they deal with those team members determines the culture of a project, whether employees work eagerly or under threat of punishment, whether they are committed to the project's success or simply consider it part of their job. Managers set the standards and the tone. This is where the differences between supervision, management, and leadership are visible.

Managers can supervise the team, providing explicit instructions on how to accomplish each task. The work will probably be completed; however, if there is a simpler or more effective way to do it, it is unlikely that anyone will volunteer the suggestion. Why should they, when they are only cogs in a wheel?

Alternatively, managers can manage the project. In that case, they explain what needs to be done but leave the "how" up to the individuals actually doing the work. This increases the probability that team members will seek ways to improve productivity or quality. In the best projects, managers lead as well as manage. They create an environment where team members are eager to contribute, because they know that their efforts will be acknowledged and appreciated.

Managers' influence increases when team members realize that they stand to gain if the project is successful. Once again, it is critical that managers understand what motivates each member of the team. In this case, it is important to know team members' goals and to identify ways to help them achieve those goals. That was one of the reasons Jim scheduled one-on-one meetings with each member of the team. He wanted to know them as individuals, not simply names on an org chart.

Hersey and Blanchard developed a concept they call situational leadership and have identified four leadership styles associated with it: telling, selling, participating, and delegating.* As the name "situational leadership" implies, the style a manager chooses will vary based on the situation. An effective project manager understands both the situation and the individuals involved and chooses the correct style to manage or lead the team. The use of situational leadership is discussed in more detail in the next chapter.

Accepting Responsibility

Harry Truman is famous for stating that the buck stopped with him, indicating that he had ultimate responsibility. The same statement is true of project managers.

---

* Hersey and Blanchard, *Management of Organizational Behavior*, 171.

They bear the ultimate responsibility for the project. Unfortunately, not all project managers accept that fact, and some are quick to assign blame when something goes wrong.

A truly effective team is built on a foundation of trust. Team members know that they can trust each other to accomplish their assigned tasks. Even more importantly, trust is established when they are confident there will be no scapegoats. That is not to say that performance problems will be tolerated. One of the project manager's responsibilities is to address poor performance by correcting the underlying problem. But there is a major difference between dealing with a problem and blaming an individual for everything that has gone wrong. The successful project manager understands the difference and is careful to publicly acknowledge good performance and privately seek to improve less than stellar work.

What does all this mean? There are numerous theories of management, most of which agree that it is critical to involve employees, to recognize their goals and help them achieve them, all the while ensuring that the overriding corporate goals are met. Whitten calls this benevolent dictatorship and says, "A benevolent dictator leads by actively soliciting information and opinions from project members and others—listens, then demonstrates the leadership, courage and boldness to personally make the right decision and stand accountable for that decision."* While the term *dictator* may appear to be politically incorrect, the concepts are valid and are the ones Jim planned to employ with his team.

The Role of Mentors

While project managers normally focus on their teams when answering the question of who will be involved, they should also consider mentors. The concept of mentors has been around at least as long as Greek mythology. Initially mentors were teachers, deriving their name from the man who provided Odysseus' son, Telemachus, with his education. Now mentors are recognized as counselors or coaches rather than teachers. Although not all corporate cultures encourage them, mentors can be invaluable, particularly to a new project manager.

Mentors do not form part of the official project team; instead, they serve as advisors or coaches to the project manager. Like the outside advisors described in Chapter 5, they provide specialized expertise, in this case, experience managing projects and dealing with employees and customers. Mentors frequently act as sounding boards for the project manager, helping to defuse tension and providing advice. It is important to note that mentors typically come from within the organization rather than an outside firm, since knowledge of the company is a critical

---

* Neal Whitten, *Neal Whitten's No-Nonsense Advice for Successful Projects* (Vienna, VA: Management Concepts, 2005), 8.

element of the project manager's success. For mentorship to be effective, a project manager should not report to the mentor, and there should be no connection between the mentoring sessions and the manager's performance appraisals.

The Project Management Office

Recognizing the importance of learning from experience, some companies have established a separate organizational structure called the Project Management Office (PMO) or Project Office. What is a PMO or what Schwalbe also calls a Center of Excellence (COE)?* In *The PMBOK Guide*, the Project Management Institute defines the PMO as "an organizational unit to centralize and coordinate the management of projects under its domain."† Although this might sound as if the PMO actually managed projects, that is not the case in most organizations. Jack Meredith and Samuel Mantel's *Project Management: A Managerial Approach* claims that the purpose of the PMO is to establish consistent project management standards and methodologies. They point out that the PMO is an enabler or facilitator of projects, not the doer.‡ In *Project Management Survival*, Richard Jones confirms this by stating that the project office is responsible for the quality of the information it maintains but has no formal authority.§

In summary, the PMO can be viewed as a type of mentor, an organization designed to provide guidance as well as standards for future projects. It is a repository and a resource. A well-run PMO is also a valuable tool in increasing the company's project-management maturity level. But, like a good mentor, while it provides many benefits to a project manager, it does not do the actual work of managing the project. The distinction is an important one.

What Can Go Wrong?

Not surprisingly, the most common problem when determining who is in charge is the selection of the wrong project manager. Although there are variations on this theme, two are noteworthy when they occur on a critical project.

- *An inexperienced project manager*—Although every project is a learning experience, choosing an individual without a proven track record can be a serious mistake, since problems and errors are magnified when the project

---

* Schwalbe, *Information Technology Project Management*, 70.
† Project Management Institute, Inc., *A Guide to the Project Management Body of Knowledge (PMBOK® Guide)*, 3rd ed. (Newtown Square: PMI, 2004), 17.
‡ Jack R. Meredith and Samuel J. Mantel Jr., *Project Management: A Managerial Approach*, 6th ed. (Hoboken: John Wiley & Sons, 2006), 207.
§ Richard Jones, *Project Management Survival* (London: Kogan Page, 2007), 141.

is critical. A project manager in this situation needs a strong mentor, either in the form of a PMO or an individual—or both. The ideal situation is for the less-experienced employee to serve in the number-two role on this project, gaining expertise that would enable him or her to succeed on the next project.

■ *An experienced project manager who is new to the company*—Occasionally a company faced with an important project will hire someone who has had experience with similar projects at a different company to manage this one. While this may sound like a wise decision, the potential problem is the new manager's unfamiliarity with the corporate culture. Depending on the company and the project, this may create friction within the team and with the customer base. A better solution would be to have this individual serve as an advisor for the project.

As stated previously, the project manager is the linchpin of the project. Selection of a qualified manager is essential to the project's success.

Chapter 11

Forming the Team

Although the project manager is critical to its success, when planning a project, the answer to the question of "who" involves more than the leader. The second component is the team, specifically, those individuals selected as team members. Chapter 5 addressed some of the issues involved in team selection when it described the formation of the team for the Initiation/Definition phase. While most of these still apply, there are additional considerations for the working team, the one charged with implementation of the project. Not only are there more people involved during execution, but they have different responsibilities, and that raises new concerns.

Number of Teams

Before individual team members are chosen, it is important to determine the overall project organization. Some project managers enjoy the Cecil B. DeMille effect. Named for the legendary film director whose credits included a number of epic movies, a Cecil B. DeMille project has a cast of thousands, all reporting directly to a single project manager. That is power, this type of project manager believes. The reality is closer to chaos. DeMille may have had casts of thousands in his epics, but the vast majority of them were walk-ons who required virtually no direction. A project is different. Team members are expected to do more than simply show up and put on a costume; they are expected to be active participants, each contributing to the project's success.

Where project team size is concerned, less is more. Jones advocates keeping the core team as small as possible* and points out that if more than six people are working on the same task, when estimating the time required to complete that task, it is necessary

---

* Richard Jones, *Project Management Survival* (London: Kogan Page, 2007), 46.

WWC Project Organization

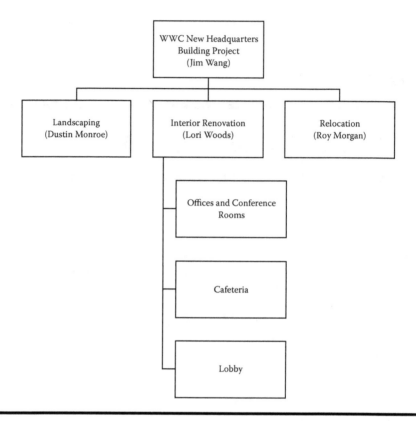

Figure 11.1 WWC project organization.

to add an extra 10 percent for each person above six because of the increased complexity and extra communication required when sharing tasks.* At this point in the project, the issue is not task sharing, but the principle remains valid. A simpler, smaller organization is a more effective one. It is easier to communicate within a lean team, and accountability is more easily established when the team size is relatively small.

Some projects by their very nature are large. The WWC headquarters building project was one of those. Jim Wang knew that he would have over two hundred people involved at the peak of the Implementation phase. He also knew that that large a group would be unwieldy and that if he attempted to manage all of them personally, his chance of success was low. He needed smaller teams.

Dividing a project into pieces can be accomplished by a variety of methods, two of which are creating multiple projects and establishing subprojects. The goal in either case is to develop a team of manageable size. As shown on Figure 11.1,

---

* Jones, *Project Management Survival*, 122.

Jim decided that his project required both multiple projects and subprojects. Landscaping, interior renovation, and relocation are separate projects, while offices and conference rooms, cafeteria, and lobby are subprojects of interior renovation.

The difference is in reporting and, typically but not always, leadership. Multiple projects have unique project managers and schedules, and their status and other reporting is not combined with any other team's. Though team members on the relocation project are familiar with the schedule and status of their project, they do not normally see details of landscaping or interior renovation. In contrast, the three subprojects (offices and conference rooms, cafeteria, and lobby) are considered an integral part of the interior renovation project. Although each has its own schedule, the three are combined for reporting purposes. While each team operates individually on a day-to-day basis, members are aware of the progress the other two teams have made and the problems they face. Furthermore, although the three teams meet individually, there are also group meetings, confirming the fact that they are all part of the same project. For the WWC project, all three of these subproject groups report directly to Lori Woods. In other cases, separate project leads may be established for each of the subprojects, but there will be a project manager assigned to the main project, in this instance, the interior renovations.

Selecting Team Members

Once the project manager has established the overall organization and knows what skills will be needed and in what quantity, the next step is to identify the individuals who will become team members. Table 5.2 identified characteristics of effective team members for the Initiation/Definition phase. Many of these characteristics apply to the team being assembled during this phase; however, the focus is somewhat different. For the first phase, the champion and project manager sought people who could serve as change agents, identifying and promoting change. The ability to persuade others and sell the solution was an important characteristic of that team's members. For the remaining phases of the project, the emphasis is on performing, doing the actual work rather than convincing others of its merit.

When selecting team members, the first priority should be what DeFuria calls capability.* This means that the individuals have the skills, the experience, and the training to accomplish the tasks they will be assigned. Other important characteristics, as shown on Table 5.2, are available time, commitment, teamwork, and bias for action. Although desirable, flexibility, innovation, and personal influence are of lesser importance once the Initiation/Definition phase is complete.

---

* Guy L. DeFuria, *Project Management Recipes for Success* (Boca Raton: Auerbach, 2009), 113.

Team Sourcing

Although in many cases all project tasks are completed by the company's staff, there are times when the company lacks either the needed expertise or the number of employees required for a specific project. In that case, the manager may choose to use staff augmentation or outsourcing to fill the gaps. Before deciding which is more appropriate for the project, the manager needs to have a clear understanding of the distinctions between the two. Table 11.1 outlines key differences, the most critical of which is day-to-day management of the staff.

In staff augmentation, whether they are called contractors or consultants, the people who are hired function as an extension of the company. Except for the facts that their salaries and benefits are paid by a different company and that their services are temporary, they are virtually identical to permanent staff. This is the reason that co-employment concerns can arise. Co-employment is the legal argument that two companies share the management of an individual. It is of concern to most companies that hire contractors since, if co-employment is proven, the company may be responsible for providing benefits to the contractors. This is why many companies limit the

Table 11.1 Differences between Staff Augmentation and Outsourcing

Characteristic	Staff Augmentation	Outsourcing
Company contracts for	Individual contractor's work	Predefined service or product
Selection of staff to perform work	Company's (company staff interviews prospective contractors)	Outsourcer
Day-to-day direction of staff provided by	Company	Outsourcer
Pricing	Time and materials; hourly rate or per diem	Fixed price, typically payable monthly or on completion of specific deliverables
Location of staff	Company site	Either company or outsourcer's site
Co-employment concerns	Possible, if lengthy assignment	None
Measure of success	Individual tasks	Deliverables
Key to success	Individual contractor	Outsourcer

length of time any one contractor can perform work for them. Staff augmentation should be viewed as a temporary solution to a lack of staff or specific expertise.

Outsourcing is different. In outsourcing, the company contracts for a service or deliverable, not for an individual. Responsibility for a specific body of work is given to the outsourcing firm, making it their responsibility to decide who will perform specific tasks and to ensure that deadlines and quality standards are met. There are no co-employment considerations with outsourcing. This is one reason companies consider outsourcing a long-term solution. As part of the new headquarters building project, WWC decided that it would outsource maintenance of the grounds. Although that work had been performed by GWC's internal staff, IW had always outsourced the services and found it to be a cost-effective method of maintaining their landscaping.

Although sourcing from outside the company may be the best solution for the project, it is not without potential problems, one of which is decreased employee morale. If the company chooses to outsource or augment staff, it is essential to explain to in-house staff the reasons for the decision. This is particularly critical when there are employees capable of performing the tasks that are being outsourced, since staff may fear that their jobs will be eliminated. This occurred at WWC when the decision to outsource grounds maintenance was announced. Claudia had expected the GWC Facilities and Services staff whose jobs were being eliminated to be upset, but she had not anticipated the ripple effect that occurred. Staff responsible for interior maintenance, none of whose positions were scheduled for elimination, were convinced that she had told them only half the story and that they too would be laid off. When repeated assurances did not assuage the employees' fears, Claudia provided each of them with a memo, stating the facts.

Although outsourcing is often the more contentious decision, staff augmentation is not devoid of potential problems. In addition to notifying its employees, if the company decides to use contractors for staff augmentation, it needs to be certain that in-house staff is available to manage the contractors' day-to-day work and that potential co-employment issues are reviewed with both the Human Resources and Legal departments.

Team Dynamics

Simply choosing staff and assigning them to a team does not mean that the project manager has a true team. What exists at that point is a group of individuals whose names are on the project organization chart. Whether or not they become a team is determined by the project manager's actions. Teams are built; they do not come into existence merely because of a piece of paper.

An ideal method for beginning the team-building process is to hold an off-site meeting where everyone has a chance to meet others in an informal setting. Although typically billed as a project kickoff, the primary purpose of the meeting is to begin establishing personal rapport among the various team members. The goal is to have everyone on the team relate to each other as human beings, not simply names on an organizational ("org") chart. This is one occasion where it is often helpful to have an outside facilitator who is skilled in team dynamics and can lead activities designed to help build the team.

When Jim developed the preliminary project budget, he included expenses for a kickoff meeting in Bluebell. Although the location required everyone to travel, he believed it was important for all team members to see the new location. Furthermore, because everyone would be staying in a hotel rather than some returning home at the end of each day, there would be no distinctions among team members.

The exercises the facilitator planned included a walk-through of the building followed by a brainstorming sessions to answer the question, "What could we do to make this a building that would delight both employees and customers?" Although few of the suggestions were feasible, the idea of using widget casings on one lobby wall piqued enough interest that it led Jim to include it in his recommendations.

While a kickoff meeting is helpful, it does not in itself create a team. Instead, it is only the first step in the team-building process. It is normal for teams to go through various stages. One model, identified by Bruce Tuckman in 1965, calls the stages forming, storming, norming, and performing. What is important is to recognize that the stages exist and that, as Lewis points out, to be effective the project manager needs to apply different managerial styles at each stage.* The styles Lewis proposes correspond to the situational leadership styles Hersey and Blanchard developed (telling, selling, participating, delegating), which were introduced in Chapter 10.

During forming, the newly appointed team members are unsure of their roles and need a high level of direction, or in Hersey and Blanchard's term, telling. Although the manager may not be a true dictator, there is little involvement of the team in decision making, in large part because the team is still coalescing. When they reach the storming phase, individual team members have begun to question the team's overall goals and to vie for position within the team. A manager's selling skills will explain why the project is important and what roles each person has, thus helping to resolve the problems.

Once the team enters the norming phase, working processes have been established and agreed to. In other words, the group is close to becoming a functional team, not simply a collection of individuals. At this point, the most effective managerial style is participating, since the team is now ready to take on more responsibility and make more decisions. The performing phase, as its name implies, is the one where the team is fully formed and productive. The preferred managerial style at this point is delegating. The team has resolved its problems and no longer needs close supervision.

Just as individuals move through the various phases of the SARAH model at different speeds, teams progress through these four stages at different paces. The project

---

* James P. Lewis, *Fundamentals of Project Management* (New York: AMACOM, 1997), 103–5.

manager's responsibility is to accelerate the movement toward performing, since only then will the team be fully productive and the project on track for success. This can be accomplished most effectively by understanding the various stages of team dynamics and using the managerial style that is most appropriate for each stage.

What Can Go Wrong?

In forming a team, there are two classic failure modes: the wrong team size and the wrong team members.

Wrong Team Size

As discussed above, it is important to keep teams at an optimum size. One that is too large will encourage chaos, while one that is too small can be easily dominated by a single individual. Although sizes vary based on the project and corporate culture, smaller is normally better.

Wrong Team Members

When project managers realize that they have made a poor selection, it is normally because of one of three reasons.

- *Correct skills but insufficient time*—In this case, although employees have the ability to accomplish the work, they are overscheduled and cannot devote the time necessary for success. It is vital to ensure that team members are available when needed, ideally assigned to the project team on a full-time basis.
- *Available time but lacking skills*—As was discussed in Chapter 5, critical projects are not the ideal training ground. Staff should not be selected simply because they have nothing else to do.
- *Poor attitude*—Everyone has met them, the employees whose presence has a negative effect on a team. In *The Everything Project Management Book*, Rich Mintzer outlines four personality types that can create problems on a team: tigers, prima donnas, passive-aggressives, and people-pleasers.* Tigers, as their name implies, are overly aggressive and not suited to a team, and neither are prima donnas, with their need to be constantly in the limelight. Passive-aggressive individuals, who are often obstructionists, are as ill suited to a team as people-pleasers, whose need to be accepted prevents them from taking initiative and identifying problems.

Choosing the right team is not easy, but it is essential for project success.

---

* Rich Mintzer, *The Everything Project Management Book* (Avon: Adams Media, 2002), 185.

Chapter 12

Dealing with Customers and Stakeholders

Customers and other stakeholders are the last part of the answer to, "Who is involved in the project?" Although they may not have daily involvement in the project's execution, they are critical to the overall success. Customers, as Chapter 6 explained, are those individuals who will use the product or service that is the end result of the project. Stakeholders include everyone who will be impacted by the project, either positively or negatively. Using this definition, customers are a subset of stakeholders.

In *Advanced Project Management*, Alan D. Orr claims, "If stakeholder management is undertaken successfully, the project will run more smoothly."* He is, of course, correct. The problem is that managing customers is only one part of the project manager's job. Meredith and Mantel point out that a project manager has responsibilities to three constituencies: customers (who represent the project), the project team, and the corporation as a whole.[†]

As shown on Figure 12.1, these can be competing responsibilities that may, and frequently do, pull the manager in different directions. Customers expect the project to satisfy all their requirements and requests, some of which may not be cost justifiable, at the same time that the corporation expects a suitable return on investment. Clearly, it will be difficult to satisfy both groups. Meanwhile, the members of the project team seek challenging work that includes the possibility for career

---

* Alan D. Orr, *Advanced Project Management* (London: Kogan Page, 2004), 8.
[†] Jack R. Meredith and Samuel J. Mantel Jr., *Project Management: A Managerial Approach*, 6th ed. (Hoboken: John Wiley & Sons, 2006), 122.

Competing Responsibilities

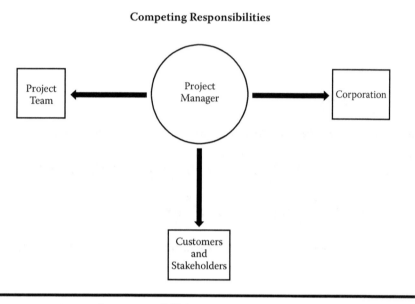

Figure 12.1 Competing responsibilities.

advancement while allowing them to maintain a reasonable work–life balance, whereas the project may require substantial overtime but not involve anything new and exciting. This creates another one of the project manager's juggling acts: trying to keep all three groups' needs and expectations in balance.

Classifying Customers and Stakeholders

The first step in a successful relationship with customers and stakeholders is to identify them. Chapter 6 outlined methods for identifying groups of customers and other influencers. It is important to note, however, that at that point, the team was focused on identifying groups with a vested interest in the project's success. DeFuria correctly states, "Some stakeholders will want to see the project fail."[*] Although it is unpleasant to contemplate, the team needs to recognize that there are stakeholders who may have a negative effect on the project. Just like the potential problems identified on the Failure Modes and Effects Analysis (FMEA) (Figure 8.2), negative stakeholders pose a risk to the project's success. Whether they are simply naysayers who seek to undermine the project with their negative comments or individuals

---

[*] Guy L. DeFuria, *Project Management Recipes for Success* (Boca Raton: Auerbach, 2009), 18.

who attempt active sabotage, they need to be classified as risks and treated like any other project risk.

Roy Morgan, the head of the relocation project, was worried about the file rooms. He had heard stories of key files going missing during IW's last reorganization. At that point, a few people were laid off, and it was thought that one of those employees was responsible for the missing files. Since layoffs would be more extensive as a result of the two companies' merger, Roy feared a repetition of the sabotage. Although he had never used an FMEA prior to this project, he remembered how useful it had been in identifying risks and developing action plans to mitigate them. That was why he decided to use the tool to address his concerns. As shown on Figure 12.2, Roy determined that the risk of losing files must be mitigated and that two mitigating actions would be taken: installing a combination lock on the file-room door and instituting a sign-out policy for all files.

Establishing Expectations

As Table 1.2 shows, unless properly managed, this second phase of a project can become one of disillusionment. Normally, disillusionment is a result of a mismatch between expectations and reality. On the surface, there should have been no problem. Initial customer expectations were developed as part of the requirements-gathering process and documented on Table 6.6. The team had even followed the advice given in Chapter 7 and had communicated what would *and would not* be included in the project scope. They knew that was critical, because one way to avoid disillusionment with the project is to ensure that everyone affected by it is operating with the same set of expectations. Customers need to know what they will receive when the project is complete. The team must understand what they are expected to do to accomplish the customer's goals, and the corporation must be clear about what benefits will result.

Despite the team's initial efforts, there was still the possibility of mismatched expectations. This is due in part to the fact that customers often believe expectations are unidirectional. That is, customers establish requirements, and the team delivers. The reality is, the team has expectations of the customer. Customers play roles on the project beyond simply defining what is to be done. At a minimum, they should be responsible for reviewing and approving the results of the project. Ideally, customers should be active participants at various stages of the project.

Keeping customers involved has many benefits. Because they are the ones with the greatest stake in the project and the ones who best understand what needs to be accomplished, their input to the design and testing of the product is invaluable. Additionally, having them involved throughout the project's life keeps them engaged (the all-important customer buy-in discussed in Chapter 7) and helps prevent disillusionment. Unfortunately, unless the project team explains the roles

Project Name:	WWC Headquarters Relocation					Date Prepared: 11/15/2010	Revision Number:				
Prepared By:	Roy Morgan					Revised By:	Revision Date:				

	What Could Happen?			Why and How Often?			What Will We Do?	Action Plan			
Project Phase	Potential Failure Mode	Potential Failure Effects	S E V	Potential Causes	O C C	R P N	Proposed Action (Avoidance, Containment, Mitigation, Evasion)	Actions Recommended	Resp.	Target Date	Date Completed/ Comments
Execution and Control	Key files are lost or stolen	Trade secrets are lost.	10	Sabotage	7	70	Mitigation	Install lock on file doors	Sally Harmon	11/20/10	
		New product launch is delayed because of missing formulas and blueprints	10	Sabotage	7	70		Establish policy that all files must be signed out by Administrative Assistant	Roy Morgan	11/20/10	

Figure 12.2 Negative stakeholder FMEA.

and responsibilities it envisions for customers, they have no way of knowing what is expected of them. Communication is key.

To clarify overall responsibilities, many project teams develop RACI charts or matrices. RACI is an acronym for responsible, accountable, consult, inform. A RACI chart lists either individuals or groups on one axis, project components on another, and the associated role in each intersection. Figure 12.3 shows a RACI chart developed by the WWC landscaping project.

	Project Team	Landscape Architect	Bluebell Township Dept. of Land Use	WWC Trademarks Dept.	WWC Facilities & Services	Paving Unlimited	Shrubs 'R Us	WWC Executive Committee
Overall site plan		R	C					A
Parking lot design	A	I			R	I		
Shrub and tree selection	A	I					R	
Front gate signage	R			C				A
Site security	R				A			
Irrigation	A		C				R	
Weekly status reports	R/A							I
Legend								
R = Responsible								
A = Accountable/ Approve								
C = Consult								
I = Inform								

Figure 12.3 Landscaping project RACI chart.

Since there may be some confusion about the difference between responsible and accountable, some organizations substitute "approve" for "accountable." In either case, the responsible group is the one actually performing the work, while the entity designated as accountable/approve is the one that must approve the work. Although multiple groups may consult or be informed, typically there is only one responsible and one accountable group.

Using slightly different terminology, Schwalbe suggests creating a matrix with five possible roles. She proposes the acronym PARIS (participant, accountable, review required, input required, sign-off required).* Whichever approach the team chooses, once the chart has been developed, it should be reviewed with and approved by all stakeholders.

Gaining Trust

As discussed in Chapter 10, an effective team is built on a foundation of trust. The same statement can be made of good relationships with customers and other stakeholders. Although there are a number of methods of establishing trust, there are three fundamental elements: respect, involvement, and communication.

Respect

Mutual respect is one of the hallmarks of a successful relationship. To gain respect in a business environment, it is important that the two groups understand each other's roles and responsibilities. One way of developing this understanding is to have members of the two groups work closely together. Depending on the nature of the project, the project team may benefit from having someone serve a "tour of duty" in the customer's department. By functioning as a member of the department for a few weeks, the "tourist" will learn how the customers work and—just as importantly—why they do things the way they do. This can be invaluable, particularly when the project involves reengineering the customer's procedures.

Although it is less common for customers to serve a tour of duty, they can benefit from a briefing on the team's organization and the tasks that are involved in completing the project. Without that, they have no way of understanding the complexities of the typical project and may become frustrated with the length of time required to complete what they believe to be a simple task.

Involvement

Customers need to be actively involved in the project. They cannot simply submit a request for a new project and disappear. At a minimum, they should prioritize their

---

* Kathy Schwalbe, *Information Technology Project Management* (Cambridge, MA: Course Technology, 2000), 223.

requirements, develop completion criteria, and, where appropriate, identify methods for testing. Customers should also be responsible for final or acceptance testing.

The primary impetus for involvement rests on the project team. Ideally, customer input should be solicited and considered throughout the project, and customers should attend key meetings, but not as simple observers. This does not always happen, in part because project teams do not necessarily encourage customer involvement. They should. Recognizing, as a Six Sigma company does, that the customer is the driving force behind a project, the team should expect—and require—frequent involvement. That is one of the reasons for developing a RACI or PARIS matrix: to clarify the roles each group will play. It is the project team's responsibility to develop, communicate, and enforce those roles.

Customers, however, are not absolved of all responsibility for involvement. They should recognize that it is important for the project team to be aware of changes in their department and should, wherever possible, invite a representative from the project team to attend all critical departmental meetings.

Communication

All too often customers regard a project as a black hole, the place where project requests disappear. They submit a request and wait months—or, in some cases, years—to see any results. During that time, their needs may change, with the result that the project deliverables no longer meet their requirements. That creates the classic lose–lose situation. To avoid these problems, there must be frequent bidirectional communication. The team should keep customers fully informed of their progress and any problems they have encountered. For their part, customers must notify the project team when priorities or requirements change.

For all three components, the key is honesty. Delivering only good news or deliberately excluding one group from critical meetings will foster an environment of hostility. Only when both groups recognize that they are part of the same team, working toward a common goal, will there be true trust.

Recognizing the importance of establishing and maintaining a positive working relationship with its customers, the WWC team instituted weekly meetings with representatives from each of the two companies' departments. Although these were designed as briefings, with a primary objective to inform everyone of the project's progress and any challenges the team faced, they allowed a substantial amount of time for Q&A and featured guest speakers from customer departments on alternate weeks. The guest speakers' presentations focused on the actions their departments were taking in preparation for the move and the problems they encountered.

Because of the logistics problems associated with the two companies being located on opposite sides of the country and three time zones apart, the meetings were held by teleconference, alternating between GWC and IW's current headquarters buildings. Initial cost considerations dictated that an IW team member lead the meetings held in the IW building, while the GWC staff chaired the others. After only a few weeks, it was apparent that while this approach saved money, it perpetuated the us-vs.-them mentality that George and Isabelle expressly wanted to eliminate. To resolve the problem, two team members—one from each company—attended each meeting, with the IW employee leading meetings at GWC's headquarters and vice versa.

As a result of this experience, the team added a new item to their code of conduct: we are all green. GWC's corporate logo had been blue, IW's yellow. Isabelle and George had decided that the new WWC needed both a new logo and a new color. They chose green. Not only was it the combination of blue and yellow, but it also reflected WWC's commitment to the environment.

What Can Go Wrong?

The two most common problems when dealing with customers and stakeholders are ignoring potential troublemakers and allowing a breakdown in communication. Although identification of naysayers and others who may have a negative impact on the project may appear to be a one-time effort, it is not. Team dynamics change as the project progresses, and new problems may arise. The project manager needs to be aware of potential problems and address them as soon as they are apparent rather than allow them to fester.

The project manager is also responsible for ensuring frequent, complete, and accurate communication both within the project team and with customers and other stakeholders. As the project enters the Execution and Control phase, time constraints typically become more stringent, and it may be tempting to delay communication, believing it to be unnecessary overhead. As Chapter 18 will explain in more detail, communication is essential.

Customers form the foundation of the project, and other stakeholders can have a substantial influence on the project's success. Project managers ignore them at their peril.

THE PLANNING PHASE, PART 2: WHAT, WHERE, AND WHEN

Planning—or, more precisely, accurate, complete planning—is an essential component of a successful project. It is during this phase that the manager develops the detailed road map that will keep the project from deteriorating into disillusionment and answers three more of the journalistic Five W questions. Section II answered why; Section III dealt with who; now Section IV addresses the remaining questions: what, when, and, to a lesser extent, where.

For some people, a project is synonymous with a schedule. This is because the work is finite, and that leads managers to focus on a schedule. That focus is one of the characteristics distinguishing project management from general management. Chapter 13 has as its primary subject the schedule. It outlines the steps involved in creating a road map for the project, explaining how to develop Work Breakdown Structures and to translate them into network diagrams and a project schedule, thus answering the fundamental question "When will the project be complete?"

Until this point, what the project will accomplish has been described in general terms. The subject of Chapter 14 is project specifications, the documents that translate generalities into a detailed description of exactly what needs to be done and how each output or deliverable will be measured.

Chapter 15 describes the final steps in the Planning phase. It is at this phase that one of senior management's primary questions is answered: namely, "How much will all this cost?" This chapter describes methods for estimating costs and explains how to calculate Return on Investment (ROI).

Chapter 13

Establishing the Road Map

Every journey needs a map, or at least it does if the goal is to reach a specific destination, not simply wander. This chapter, which is a continuation of the planning phase of a project, outlines the steps required to develop a road map.

For a project, the road map is not a literal map but a detailed schedule, showing who will do which tasks when. Like a more traditional map, the schedule shows the start and end points, the sequence of destinations along the way, and the distance/time between them. Creating such a schedule requires time and attention to detail. It is at this point that many project teams, eager to begin what they perceive as "real" work, have a tendency to take shortcuts. Although understandable, those shortcuts can be the cause of the project entering a stage of disillusionment (Table 1.2) when the team realizes how much work is involved. A successful project needs to be properly planned. No shortcuts allowed.

Planning is important, yet according to Larry Richman, author of *Project Management Step-by-Step*, "The average organization spends only 5 percent of the total project effort on planning." He adds, "A good rule of thumb is to spend at least 25 percent of the project effort in concept and development and 75 percent in implementation and termination."*

Why is it important to spend so much time in planning? The answer is simple. Planning prevents future problems from occurring. And, if it cannot completely eliminate problems, good planning minimizes their effect, because it leads to early identification of missing requirements, incorrect assumptions, and

---

* Larry Richman, *Project Management Step-by-Step* (New York: AMACOM, 2002), 50.

unrealistic scheduling. This is critical to a project's success, because the earlier a problem is found, the lower the time and cost involved in fixing it. Kemp quantifies the differences, using factors of 1:10:100. According to him, a change costs ten times as much if it is made during construction rather than during the planning phase and a hundred times more if it is not implemented until after the project is complete.* It clearly behooves the project team to minimize changes after the planning phase.

That is the philosophy behind Design for Six Sigma (DFSS). The goal of DFSS is to do everything right the first time, eliminating the rework and redesign loops that occur far too often in projects. A pictorial representation of the reason for doing effective planning at the beginning of the project, ensuring that all requirements are captured and understood before the execution phase begins, is shown in a figure from one of my earlier books, *Six Sigma Software Development*. Figure 13.1 introduces the concept of the DFSS lever.† This is another case of the Five Ps: prior planning prevents poor performance.

The team is now entering the second part of the Planning phase, where the questions of "what" and "when"—and, to a lesser extent, "where"—will be answered. While it is important that this planning be done and that it be complete and accurate, there is one other consideration that some teams forget—namely, involving the right people. As Lewis instructs, "The people who must implement a plan should participate in developing it."‡ While this may seem like common sense, since the workers are the ones who best understand all that is involved in a task and can provide the most accurate estimates, all too often planning is done by managers without input from the rest of the team. This can be a fundamental mistake.

Lori Woods made that mistake. A veteran IW employee, she had participated in the building of the current IW headquarters and applied her experiences with that project to develop the plan for the office and conference room renovations. Confident that she could complete the plan more quickly if she worked alone, Lori did not involve the rest of her team. It was only when Jim expressed surprise at the lower-than-expected cost that she realized she had forgotten a key task: upgrading the electrical system.

Work Breakdown Structure

The first step in creating a complete road map is to develop a Work Breakdown Structure (WBS). A WBS is a hierarchal list of all work that will be required to complete a project. The use of a hierarchy is important because it provides a logical grouping of work activities. As shown on Figure 13.2, a WBS may have multiple

---

* Sid Kemp, *Project Management Demystified* (New York: McGraw-Hill, 2004), 23.
† Christine B. Tayntor, *Six Sigma Software Development*, 2nd ed. (Boca Raton, FL: Auerbach, 2007), 133.
‡ James P. Lewis, *Fundamentals of Project Management* (New York: AMACOM, 1997), 22.

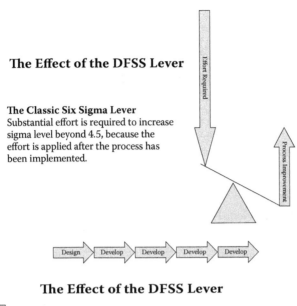

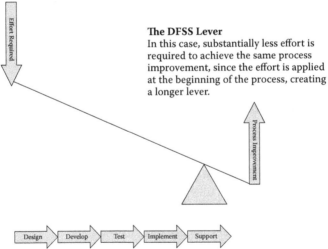

Figure 13.1   Effect of the DFSS lever.

levels, and the number of levels under each major (*x*.0) level need not be consistent. In all cases, however, the lowest level is the task or activity. The higher levels serve as summaries of the tasks.

There are three rules commonly used when developing a WBS. Each applies to the task level.

1.0 Project Management
    1.1 Project Plan
        1.1.1 Develop Project WBS
        1.1.2 Develop Network Diagram
        1.1.3 Develop Project Schedule
        1.1.4 Obtain Sign-Offs
        1.1.5 Conduct Team/Stakeholder Briefings
    1.2 Monitor Project
    1.3 Conduct Closeout

2.0 Floor Plan
    2.1 Develop Floor Plan Sketch
    2.2 Obtain Approval
    2.3 Create Blueprint

3.0 Food Service
    3.1 Draft RFP
    3.2 Identify Potential Suppliers
    3.3 Issue RFP
    3.4 Review Responses and Select Supplier Short List
    3.5 Conduct Detailed Evaluation
    3.6 Select Supplier
    3.7 Negotiate Contract

4.0 Furnishings
    4.1 Wall Coverings
        4.1.1 Determine Requirements
        4.1.2 Identify and Evaluate Potential Products and Suppliers
        4.1.3 Place Order
        4.1.4 Install Wall Coverings
    4.2 Floor Coverings
        4.2.1 Determine Requirements
        4.2.2 Identify and Evaluate Potential Products and Suppliers
        4.2.3 Place Order
        4.2.4 Install Floor Coverings
    4.3 Food Preparation Equipment
        4.3.1 Determine Requirements

Figure 13.2　Work Breakdown Structure (cafeteria project).

4.3.2 Identify and Evaluate Potential Products and Suppliers

4.3.3 Place Order

4.3.4 Install Food Preparation Equipment

4.4 Food Serving Equipment

4.4.1 Determine Requirements

4.4.2 Identify and Evaluate Potential Products and Suppliers

4.4.3 Place Order

4.4.4 Install Food Serving Equipment

4.5 Dishes and Utensils

4.5.1 Determine Requirements

4.5.2 Identify and Evaluate Potential Products and Suppliers

4.5.3 Place Order

4.5.4 Install Dishes and Utensils

4.6 Seating

4.6.1 Determine Requirements

4.6.2 Identify and Evaluate Potential Products and Suppliers

4.6.3 Place Order

4.6.4 Install Seating

Figure 13.2   (Continued)

1. A task should require no more than eighty hours to complete. Ideally, it should be able to be accomplished in forty hours or less. The reason for this stipulation is that tasks with shorter durations are easier to track and, just as importantly, if they fall behind schedule, they can be mitigated before they create a major ripple effect. Early detection results in less damage to the overall schedule than if the problem were not identified for months. Remember Kemp's 1:10:100 factor.
2. A task must produce a deliverable. The reason for this is simple. If there is no deliverable, there is no way to determine whether the task has been completed.
3. A task should be described using a noun and a verb. The reason for this convention is to stress the fact that it is an activity. It should be noted that higher levels are typically described as noun phrases. On Figure 13.2, the summary level 1.1 is Project Plan, a noun, while each of the tasks below it is a noun/verb combination; e.g., 1.1.1 Develop Project WBS. In this example, the noun, Project WBS, is the deliverable, making it easy to understand what will be accomplished during this activity.

When developing a WBS, it is not necessary to indicate logical sequence or dependencies. The objective is to identify the work to be done without worrying about the order in which specific activities must occur. Sequence and dependencies will be addressed in the next step, the network diagram.

There are a number of ways of organizing a WBS. DeFuria provides detailed examples and templates for three different organizational methods: deliverable, department providing the work, and time phase.* A deliverable-based WBS focuses on what will be done without regard to the organization doing the work, while a department-based WBS is organized by the provider of goods or services rather than the work being done. A time-phased WBS divides activities into logical chronological groupings. If the cafeteria project WBS had been organized by time phases, major groupings might have been Before Construction, During Construction, and After Construction.

The WWC team chose to organize its WBS for the cafeteria project by deliverables, as shown on Figure 13.2. It should be noted that this WBS is incomplete, because it does not include all the detail that would normally be shown. For example, items 1.2 (Monitor Project) and 1.3 (Conduct Closeout) would typically be renamed Project Monitoring and Closeout and divided into lower-level tasks.

The reason for including a task breakdown is to ensure that no activities are forgotten. Lewis points out, "One frequent reason projects fail is that a significant part of the work is forgotten."†

Network Diagrams

Once the team has identified the detail of the work that must be done, the next two questions to answer are: *how long will it take,* and *what dependencies exist?* Network diagrams are used to document the responses to those questions.

Duration

Few would dispute that the duration of a task depends on the amount of work involved. What may not be as obvious is that there are two other factors: the proficiency of the person (or persons) assigned and the availability of those individuals. The reality is that a junior employee doing an activity for the first time will require longer to accomplish the task than someone who has done it many times before. And even the most productive employees will take longer to complete an activity if they have competing priorities. All these factors make estimating the duration of a task a challenge.

If a Project Management Office (PMO) exists, it may have historical records that can be used for estimates. Similarly, the cost-estimating methodologies outlined

---

* Guy L. DeFuria, *Project Management Recipes for Success* (Boca Raton, FL: Auerbach, 2009), 44–47.
† Lewis, *Fundamentals of Project Management,* 37.

in Chapter 15 (Table 15.1) can be applied to estimating duration. An alternative approach is PERT, a technique developed by the Navy. PERT, which stands for Program Evaluation and Review Technique, uses three different estimates and creates a weighted average. Before PERT can be used, the team must develop three separate estimates for each activity: the best-case scenario (the optimistic estimate), the worst-case (pessimistic), and the most likely. These are entered into the following equation:

PERT duration = [optimistic + 4(most likely) + pessimistic]/6

If the optimistic estimate is six weeks, the pessimistic fourteen and the most likely seven, the equation becomes

PERT = [6 + 4(7) + 14]/6

The numerator is 48, with the resulting duration being 8.

Dependencies

Once duration has been estimated, the next step is to identify the relationships among the tasks. Relationships, often called dependencies or precedences, reflect the reality that not all tasks can begin at the same time. Some cannot begin until a preceding one has finished. This is the most common type of dependency, namely finish-to-start (FS). In the WWC example, installation of wall coverings (activity 4.1.4) cannot occur until the order has been placed (activity 4.1.3). This is a finish-to-start relationship.

In a finish-to-finish (FF) dependency, two tasks must finish at the same time. Since the WWC team wanted all major construction in the cafeteria to end on the same day, it assigned the installation of food preparation equipment (activity 4.3.4) and the installation of food serving equipment (activity 4.4.4) finish-to-finish dependencies.

Start-to-start relationships (SS) indicate that two tasks may begin on the same day. For the cafeteria project, development of the floor plan (major task 2.0) can begin at the same time as selection of the food service supplier (major task 3.0).

Figure 13.3 shows a high-level dependency chart, also called a network diagram, for the WWC cafeteria project. As shown on the chart, tasks 2.0 and 3.0 have an FS relationship with task 1.0. They cannot start until the project plan (1.0) is completed. (For simplicity's sake, only the high-level task groupings have been shown on Figure 13.3. The reality is, tasks 2.0 and 3.0 cannot begin until task 1.1.5 is complete. Subsequent task groupings are not dependent on tasks 1.2 and 1.3, which are shown on Figure 13.2.) Task 4.0 (furnishings) has an FS dependency on task 2.0. There are no dependencies between tasks 2.0 and 3.0, meaning that, as indicated above, they could be considered to have a SS relationship.

One benefit of a network diagram is that it identifies what schedulers call paths, groupings of tasks that can be performed independently of each other. Figure 13.3

High-Level Network Diagram

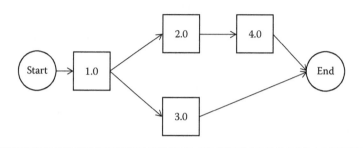

Figure 13.3 High-level network diagram.

illustrates the fact that the WWC project has two paths: the upper one, which includes tasks 1.0, 2.0, and 4.0, and the lower one, which consists of tasks 1.0 and 3.0.

Critical Path

With relationships among the tasks determined and the paths established, the team was ready to add the task durations it had estimated in the previous step to the dependency chart. This would allow them to establish the project's critical path. Critical path is an important term in project scheduling, because it identifies the shortest time in which a project can be completed. Any delays in tasks on the critical path result in delays to the entire project.

Critical path is determined by calculating the length or duration of each path on the network diagram. As shown on Figure 13.4, the shortest path, the one which

Network Diagram Showing Critical Path

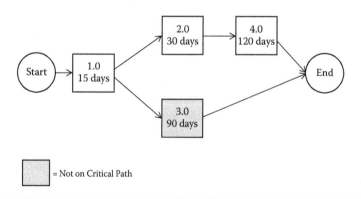

Figure 13.4 Network diagram showing critical path.

includes task 3.0, is 105 days (task 1.0 plus 3.0), whereas the other path's duration is 165 days (task 1.0 plus 2.0 plus 4.0). No matter how quickly the bottom path tasks can be accomplished, the project cannot finish until the top path is completed. The critical path, therefore, is the path with the longest duration. In this case, the project's minimum duration is 165 days, and any changes to the duration of tasks 1.0, 2.0, and 4.0 will affect the overall end date.

When calculating critical path and project duration, it is important to understand three duration-related terms: lag, lead, and float. The first two are determined by the project team; the third is created by the schedule itself and is a result of the varying path lengths.

Lag

There may be times when the team wants to delay an activity, even though the dependency chart would indicate that it could start as soon as the preceding activity was completed. This is called "lag" and is indicated on the duration chart by placing a plus sign along with the number of days lag on the arrow connecting the two activities, thus extending the duration. For the cafeteria project, although obtaining sign-offs (task 1.1.4) requires two days, it could not occur until a regularly scheduled executive committee meeting. A lag of 33 days was added to the schedule to reflect that delay. This is shown in the predecessors column of task 6 on the Gantt chart (Figure 13.6).

Lead

Lead is the opposite of lag and allows a task that has a finish-start dependency to begin before the predecessor task is complete. Lead is indicated by placing a minus sign and the number of lead days on the arrow connecting the two activities, thus accelerating the start of the second activity and effectively shortening the overall duration. There were no tasks where lead time was needed on the cafeteria project.

Float

Float, which is also referred to as slack, is the time by which an activity may be delayed without impacting either a dependent task or the entire project. To determine float, it is necessary to first calculate early and late start and finishes. Figure 13.5 expands the network diagram developed in Figures 13.3 and 13.4 by adding the start and finish days.

As shown on Figure 13.5, early start (ES) and early finish (EF) are indicated at the top of the task box, while late start (LS) and late finish (LF) are shown at the bottom. In each case, the notation reflects the number of days, not a specific date. Actual dates can be determined once the overall start date has been identified.

Network Diagram Showing Critical Path

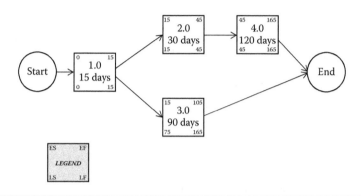

Figure 13.5 Network diagram showing early and late start and finish.

Early start and finish begin with the "start" box and proceed along the path to the right. They are calculated as follows:

ES = EF of preceding task, adjusted for either lag or lead, if present. For the first task, ES is always equal to zero.
EF = ES plus the duration of this task.

The calculations for late start and finish begin with the "end" box and proceed along the path to the left. They are calculated as follows:

LF = LS of successor task, adjust for either lag or lead, if present. For the last task, the one closest to the end-of-project circle, LF is always equal to the LF of the entire project.
LS = LF minus the duration of this task.

Float is calculated by subtracting the late finish from the early finish for each task. As shown on Figure 13.5, there is no float for items on the critical path; however, activity 3.0 has 60 days' float.

Project Schedule

A schedule is a critical component of every project. As Scott Berkun points out in *The Art of Project Management*,* a schedule serves three purposes. It:

---

* Scott Berkun, *The Art of Project Management* (Sebastopol, CA: O'Reilly Media, 2005), 22–23.

- Makes commitments
- Lets participants see their roles in meeting those commitments
- Allows for tracking of the project

While it may seem like an oversimplification, without a schedule, there is no project. This is because a project by definition is finite, and whether or not the schedule is formal, there is always an expected end. A well-managed project has a formal schedule.

Although they may be considered a type of schedule, the network diagrams shown in the previous examples are at best only preliminary. Their objective is to identify dependencies and the critical path. While a network diagram achieves those goals, it has several deficiencies. Not only does it not have dates associated with durations, but it is has not addressed resource loading questions. Durations for each task were based on a single person doing the work for the activity. The final schedule reflects the actual number of people assigned to each activity as well as their availability, including vacations, holidays, and other assignments.

Although it is possible to create the schedule manually, computer software simplifies the work, which is why most project managers use a software package designed to track projects. Figure 13.6, which illustrates a Gantt chart for the cafeteria project, was created using Microsoft Project. It shows activities in a hierarchical

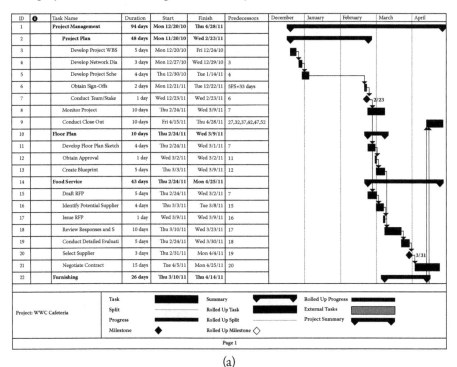

(a)

Figure 13.6 Gantt chart for cafeteria project.

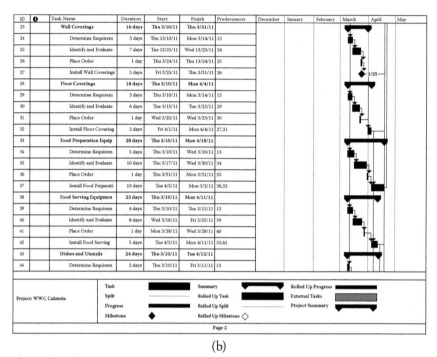

ID	❶	Task Name	Duration	Start	Finish	Predecessors	December	January	February	March	April	May
23		**Wall Coverings**	**16 days**	Thu 3/10/11	Thu 3/31/11							
24		Determine Requirem	3 days	Thu 13/10/11	Mon 3/14/11	13						
25		Identify and Evaluate	7 days	Tue 13/25/11	Wed 13/23/11	24						
26		Place Order	1 day	Thu 3/24/11	Thu 13/24/11	25						
27		Install Wall Coverings	5 days	Fri 3/25/11	Thu 3/31/11	26					3/25	
28		**Floor Coverings**	**18 days**	Thu 3/10/11	Mon 4/4/11							
29		Determine Requirem	3 days	Thu 3/10/11	Mon 3/14/11	13						
30		Identify and Evaluate	6 days	Tue 3/15/11	Tue 3/22/11	29						
31		Place Order	1 day	Wed 3/23/11	Wed 3/23/11	30						
32		Install Floor Covering	2 days	Fri 4/1/11	Mon 4/4/11	27,31						
33		**Food Preparation Equip**	**28 days**	Thu 3/10/11	Mon 4/18/11							
34		Determine Requirem	5 days	Thu 3/10/11	Wed 3/16/11	13						
35		Identify and Evaluate	10 days	Thu 3/17/11	Wed 3/30/11	34						
36		Place Order	1 day	Thu 3/31/11	Mon 3/31/11	35						
37		Install Food Preparati	10 days	Tue 4/5/11	Mon 3/2/11	36,32						
38		**Food Serving Equipmen**	**23 days**	Thu 3/10/11	Mon 4/11/11							
39		Determine Requirem	4 days	Thu 3/10/11	Tue 3/15/11	13						
40		Identify and Evaluate	8 days	Wed 3/16/11	Fri 3/25/11	39						
41		Place Order	1 day	Mon 3/28/11	Wed 3/28/11	40						
42		Install Food Serving	5 days	Tue 4/5/11	Mon 4/11/11	32,41						
43		**Dishes and Utensils**	**24 days**	Thu 3/10/11	Tue 4/12/11							
44		Determine Requirem	2 days	Thu 3/10/11	Fri 3/11/11	13						

Project: WWC Cafeteria	Task	▬▬▬	Summary	▼▬▼	Rolled Up Progress	▬▬▬
	Split	....	Rolled Up Task	▬▬▬	External Tasks	▬▬▬
	Progress	▬▬▬	Rolled Up Split	....	Project Summary	▼▬▼
	Milestone	◆	Rolled Up Milestone	◇		

Page 2

(b)

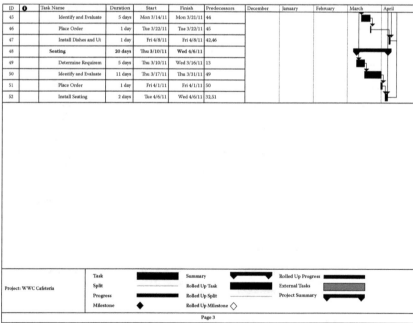

ID	❶	Task Name	Duration	Start	Finish	Predecessors	December	January	February	March	April
45		Identify and Evaluate	5 days	Mon 3/14/11	Mon 3/21/11	44					
46		Place Order	1 day	Tue 3/22/11	Tue 3/22/11	45					
47		Install Dishes and Ut	1 day	Fri 4/8/11	Fri 4/8/11	42,46					
48		**Seating**	**20 days**	Thu 3/10/11	Wed 4/6/11						
49		Determine Requirem	5 days	Thu 3/10/11	Wed 3/16/11	13					
50		Identify and Evaluate	11 days	Thu 3/17/11	Thu 3/31/11	49					
51		Place Order	1 day	Fri 4/1/11	Fri 4/1/11	50					
52		Install Seating	2 days	Tue 4/6/11	Wed 4/6/11	32,51					

Project: WWC Cafeteria	Task	▬▬▬	Summary	▼▬▼	Rolled Up Progress	▬▬▬
	Split	....	Rolled Up Task	▬▬▬	External Tasks	▬▬▬
	Progress	▬▬▬	Rolled Up Split	....	Project Summary	▼▬▼
	Milestone	◆	Rolled Up Milestone	◇		

Page 3

(c)

Figure 13.6 (Continued)

form similar to the WBS and includes the dependencies that were determined in previous steps. Dependencies are listed in the "predecessors" column. Other views of the project schedule display the resources assigned to each task and indicate when a resource has been overloaded.

Although computer software can perform many aspects of project scheduling, it relies on human input for its accuracy. There are also some things it cannot do, one of which is determining milestones. Milestones are important. As their name implies, these are critical steps along the way. Jones describes them as "specific outcomes rather than a set of activities."* Although they are frequently on the critical path, they may not always be. This is one of the reasons why milestones are not determined by a software product but are, instead, chosen by the project team. The WWC team determined that the milestones for the cafeteria project were the team/stakeholder briefings (activity 1.1.5), the selection of the food service supplier (activity 3.6), and the installation of wall coverings (activity 4.1.4). These were marked as milestones in Microsoft Project and are shown as diamonds on the Gantt chart.

When the team generated the schedule, they were surprised that it indicated they would have no trouble meeting the July 1, 2011 target date and that they would, in fact, have four months' slack time. They knew something was wrong. A closer look at the schedule indicated a major flaw with the furnishings tasks. Although they had included tasks for placing the orders for wall coverings and the other components, and although they had allowed time for installation of those items, they had not factored in the time required for the supplier to obtain the materials. In the case of the floor coverings, this could be up to six weeks. They revised the plan, including lag times for each of the "install" tasks. Their new schedule was substantially longer but reflected reality.

What Can Go Wrong?

There are three common problems associated with the development of the road map.

■ *Not All Work Included*—Although the project team is normally past the stage of wild enthusiasm, they may neglect key portions of the work when creating the WBS. This is one reason why companies have established PMOs, since the PMO's repository of documentation about previous projects can be invaluable in identifying forgotten tasks. Some PMOs have created WBS templates for different classes of projects, providing further guidance to the project team. Historical records and templates are valuable, but they do not eliminate the need for personal expertise. Even if a PMO exists, it is important to involve those individuals who will be performing the work in the development of the WBS, since they have firsthand knowledge of what is needed.

---

* Richard Jones, *Project Management Survival* (London: Kogan Page, 2007), 70.

■ *Unrealistic Estimates*—Even when all tasks are included in the WBS, it is not uncommon for estimates of the amount of time required to accomplish those estimates to be too low. One way to address this issue is to use PERT. Although PERT requires additional work to create the three different estimates, the advantage is a schedule with a higher probability of accuracy.

■ *Failure to Account for Nonproductive Time*—Realistic time estimates are only one component of a successful schedule. A second, and equally important one, is the admission that employees are not productive forty hours a week. In addition to accounting for holidays and vacation, it is important to apply a nonproductive factor to the schedule to account for administrative tasks, illness, and other nonworking activities.

Creating the road map is a major step on the path to project success. Although it may require more time than some project managers prefer, it should not be short-changed. After all, without a good road map, how will the project team know where they are headed and when they will arrive at their destination?

Chapter 14

Project Specifications and Statements of Work

The Work Breakdown Structure created in Chapter 13 listed all tasks required to complete the project. The next step is to define each of them in sufficient detail that the staff assigned knows exactly what is to be done, what deliverables will be produced, and how they will be evaluated. The documents that contain these definitions are often referred to as Project Specifications or Statements of Work (SOWs). Although the terms can be used interchangeably, some companies—including the newly created WWC—make a distinction, referring to Project Specifications as descriptions of work that will be done by company staff, whereas tasks performed by outside contractors are detailed in SOWs.

Project Specifications

The detailed content of specifications will vary based on the type of project. Building the space shuttle is, after all, substantially different from renovating Bluebell Industries' cafeteria to accommodate WWC's needs. The objective, however, remains constant: to explain what is to be done.

Table 14.1 shows the components of one specification document, including instructions on how to complete each section. The WWC cafeteria team used that template to draft their specification document for activity 3.5, the detailed evaluation of food service suppliers. Table 14.2 is the result.

It should be noted that, although the format of specification documents will vary from company to company, it is important to establish a consistent format.

Table 14.1   Contents of Specification Document

Component Name	Instructions for Completing
Activity Name and Number	Enter the name of the activity and the number assigned during the development of the WBS.
Description	Include a brief description of the work to be done.
Scheduled Start	This field shows the scheduled start date, taken from the project schedule. If the task is not on the critical path, both early and late start dates may be included.
Scheduled End	This field shows the scheduled end date, taken from the project schedule. If the task is not on the critical path, both early and late end dates may be included.
Estimated Work Effort	This field is used to indicate the total amount of work effort required, regardless of the number of people assigned. It may be reported in either days or hours, but in either case, the unit of measure should be indicated. Normally, this field is used to indicate work effort that the company controls either through use of its own staff or through staff augmentation.
Other Costs	The cost of materials and outsourced labor should be included in this section. Note that outsourced work is not included in the work effort section, since the company does not control the number of hours involved and pays for deliverables rather than hours worked.
Total Costs	The sum of all costs. Estimated work effort should be converted to a dollar amount and added to the Other Costs estimate.
Inputs	For engineering-related projects, this section describes classic inputs to the process. For other projects, it should include a description of the outputs of previous tasks that are required to begin work on this activity.
Work to Be Done	This is normally the longest section of the specification, since it includes a detailed listing of all the work that is to be done. In engineering terms, this is the process to be performed.
Deliverables	Whether they are called outputs or deliverables, these are the items produced by the activity. This section should include a detailed description of them.

Table 14.1   Contents of Specification Document (Continued)

Component Name	Instructions for Completing
Test Plan	Although test plans are most often associated with engineering-related projects, the reality is that all work needs to be verified for accuracy, adherence to specifications, and quality. How that verification will be done is the subject of this section. The testing/verification process that will be used should be detailed. For engineering- or process-related projects, a formal test plan should be developed, including test cases.
Acceptance Criteria	This is the corollary to the test plan. It describes the conditions that must be met for the work to be approved. In the case of an engineering- or process-related project, this section would indicate the expected results from each test case.
Approvals Required	Enter the name and title of each person whose approval is required before the work can be considered complete.
Risks	A risk assessment should be performed for each activity. If a substantial number of risks are identified or if they are deemed likely to occur, a formal risk assessment using the modified FMEA shown in Appendix D should be completed.

In Six Sigma terms, this reduces variation, with the result that less time is spent in developing each specification, since the author does not have to decide which elements to include. Furthermore, life is easier for the staff assigned to do the work, since each specification they receive has the same format, and they know where to look for which pieces of information.

As Table 14.1 indicates, the work accomplished under a Project Specification needs to be approved. Depending on the nature of the project and the specific activity, the approval of the final deliverables may be performed by a number of different functional organizations within the company. At a minimum, there should be a review by the team and one conducted by the customers. Quality Assurance may also be involved, as may the Finance or Law department, depending on the deliverable.

In addition to this review, there is another approval process that occurs before any work begins. This review is of the document itself and involves two groups, working independently. The first review, which is normally conducted by peers, has as its objective to ensure that everything necessary is included in the document and that the contents appear reasonable. Peers may or may not understand the intricacies of the work being done, but they can provide an assessment of reasonableness. The second review is performed by customers and focuses on the work to

Table 14.2   Specification Document for WBS Task 3.5

Component Name	Contents
Activity Name and Number	3.5—Conduct detailed evaluation of food service vendors
Description	Following the review of the responses to the RFP and the selection of the short list of vendors, evaluate the qualifications of each of the short-list vendors. The final output of this activity will be the recommendation of the supplier to provide food service to the WWC cafeteria.
Scheduled Start	March 24, 2011
Scheduled End	March 30, 2011
Estimated Work Effort	20 person-days (It is anticipated that a team of four will be assigned to this activity.)
Other Costs	$1500 in travel expenses to visit short-list suppliers' customers and conduct reference checking
Total Costs	$13,500
Inputs	Short-list suppliers' responses to the RFP
Work to Be Done	1. Develop the evaluation matrix, showing each factor that will be used in the evaluation and the weighting to be assigned to it.
	2. Develop the questionnaire to be used for phone reference checking.
	3. Develop the checklist to be used at customer sites.
	4. Conduct reference checks (phone interviews of at least three customers per supplier).
	5. Update evaluation matrix based on results of reference checks.
	6. Determine which customers to visit for on-site reference checking (one per supplier).
	7. Conduct on-site reference checking, including eating in the customer's cafeteria.
	8. Update evaluation matrix based on results of reference checks and complete evaluation.
	9. Develop recommendation.

Table 14.2   Specification Document for WBS Task 3.5 (Continued)

Component Name	Contents
Deliverables	1. Completed evaluation matrix. This will include all factors that were rated, a weighting factor for each factor, and the score developed as a result of the reference checking.
	2. Formal presentation of recommendation to project champion and executive staff.
Test Plan	1. Peers will review the evaluation matrix and questionnaires prior to their use to determine that all critical items are included and that the weighting factors reflect customer requirements.
	2. A secondary review of the evaluation matrix will occur prior to making the final recommendation.
Acceptance Criteria	1. The evaluation matrix must be complete and must include explanations of any items rated 1 or 0.
	2. The presentation must include a review of the recommended supplier's financial stability, the proposed pricing for meals and the expected profit margin.
Approvals Required	Jim Wang, Project Manager
	Frank Seely, VP of Facilities and Services
Risks	The primary risk is that customers may not be available for on-site visits during the scheduled timeframe. Since supplier selection is not on the critical path, this risk will not be mitigated.

be accomplished, the deliverables, the test plan, and the acceptance criteria. The objective, as has been true throughout the Planning phase, is to ensure that the work is complete and accurate, thus preventing future problems.

Statements of Work

As noted above, a statement of work is similar to a Project Specification in that its objective is to clearly outline the work to be done. The differences are that an SOW is typically developed for use by an outside contractor rather than the company's employees and that, as such, it forms a legal contract between the company and the contractor. As a result, even greater specificity is required, since changes may be costly. It is essential to minimize the need for interpretation.

An SOW should include the following:

- *Detailed Description of Work to Be Done*—The more information the company can give the contractor, the more likely the deliverables are to meet the company's expectations. Although this is not an activity well suited to outsourcing, if the detailed evaluation of suppliers shown on Table 14.2 were being conducted by an outside contractor, the Work to Be Done section would include details of the categories of factors that the company expects to be included in the evaluation matrix and in the reference checks. In this case, there would be additional deliverables, since the company would want to review the evaluation matrix and questionnaire developed in Steps 1 and 2 before they were used.
- *Format of Deliverables*—If the company wants documentation provided in a specific format or expects training to be delivered in a particular manner, the SOW should indicate that, including references to standards and formats. Using the example of the food service supplier evaluation, the Deliverables section would include the desired format for both the evaluation matrix and the presentation.
- *Schedule for Delivery*—A detailed schedule, showing the date on which the *final* version of each deliverable will be given to the company, is needed. The word *final* was italicized, because some companies have experienced problems when contractors who were having difficulty meeting deadlines and fearing imposition of a late delivery penalty delivered poor-quality products, claiming that they had satisfied the contract even though this was only an interim deliverable. As noted above, the SOW, like any legal document, should be written so there is no ambiguity. If the company wants to review interim versions of the deliverable, those may be added to the schedule; however, it should be noted that penalties for late delivery normally apply only to the final version of a deliverable.
- *Schedule for Review*—The date on which the company will complete its review of each deliverable should be included in the SOW. This is an item that is often omitted, but in fairness to the contractor it should be specified. Since payment is often contingent on review and acceptance of deliverables, the contractor has a right to know when that review will be completed.
- *Acceptance Criteria*—Each deliverable should be accompanied by a clear indication of the criteria that will be used to determine whether or not the company will accept it. As is true of other sections of the SOW, there should be no room for interpretation of acceptance criteria.
- *Fees*—Payment of fees is one thing that distinguishes an SOW from a Project Specification. Although companies may have internal chargeback systems where one department charges another for the work performed, there is typically less emphasis on chargebacks than there is on payments to an outside contractor. From a contractor's view, it can be argued that fees and the

dates on which they are payable form the most important part of the SOW. Contractors are anxious to be paid; companies are normally less eager to write a check. Recognizing this, it is to the company's advantage to tie payments to acceptance rather than delivery of deliverables, since there is no guarantee that the contractor will provide a quality product the first time. It is also helpful to establish a warranty period and to make final payment contingent on resolving all problems identified during the warranty period.

- *Terms and Conditions*—If the company has done business with the contractor in the past and has a Master Services Agreement (MSA) with the contractor, the terms and conditions (Ts and Cs) will have already been established. If not, Ts and Cs that specify the terms under which the two companies will do business should be drafted. Although some project teams may dismiss them as legalese, terms and conditions are important. They can be viewed as a form of risk mitigation, since they provide legal protection should problems arise. Ts and Cs include contractual clauses related to confidentiality and breach of contract as well as ownership of deliverables, limitations of liability, and insurance requirements.

The most critical components of an SOW are the description of the expected deliverables and the acceptance criteria. In both cases, they must be SMART. Since WWC does not have an architect on staff, activity 2.1, Develop the floor plan sketch for the cafeteria, will be outsourced to an architectural firm. If the project team gave the architect no direction other than to create the sketch, there would be no way of evaluating the deliverable. The architect could give them almost anything, claiming it was what they had requested. A better, SMARTer description of the work to be done is "Using the existing space in the Bluebell, Inc. cafeteria, develop a sketch for a new cafeteria that will provide seating for 100, using tables for two, four, and eight individuals. The design must include a food preparation area, four food service stations (hot entrees and sandwiches, cold entrees and sandwiches, salad bar, desserts and beverages) and six checkout lines, all adequate to service 100 persons each half hour. The design must minimize cross-traffic and potential collisions among patrons, must incorporate low-energy-use lighting and appliances, and may not exceed $200,000 for construction and furnishings." This detailed description of work can be readily translated into specific and measurable deliverables and acceptance criteria. Although no reference is made to a time frame in this example, the "time-bound" element of SMART is addressed in the Schedule section of the SOW.

As was true of Project Specifications, there are two levels of approval needed for a SOW. When conducting the first review, the one of the document itself, unless the company already has an MSA with the contractor, there should be a legal review, ensuring that the Ts and Cs are complete and protect the company. This is in addition to the peer review. Although it is important that the customer review of Project Specifications be complete, special attention should be given to the description of deliverables and acceptance criteria in an SOW, since changes will result in additional costs.

What Can Go Wrong?

The greatest risk in developing either a Project Specification or an SOW is a lack of specificity. Although it is important when developing specifications for work by in-house staff, it is essential that SOWs contain no ambiguity. Defining the work to be accomplished is a critical part of the planning process, and the time spent on careful planning will be paid back during execution when there are fewer disputes over definitions and less rework. In addition to meticulous attention to detail, the team should apply the SMART criteria as a technique for determining whether or not the needed level of specificity has been achieved.

Complete and accurate specifications and SOWs form the foundation for the actual work to be done and are fundamental elements in the overall success of a project.

Chapter 15

Completing the Plan

The team had reached the final steps of the planning process. They now had enough information to update the business case and present the final version for approval. This would be the second of what are sometimes called tollgates or major decision points in the project. The first was the go/no-go decision at the end of the Initiation/Definition phase when the initial business case was presented. Like tollgates on a highway, project gates require the team to stop, at least briefly, while a transaction occurs. On a highway, the transaction is payment of a toll; on a project, it is a review of the progress to date.

As Kerzner points out,* there are four possible decisions each time a tollgate is reached:

- Continue as planned
- Revise objectives and then continue
- Wait for more information before making a decision
- Cancel the project

The team was, of course, hoping for approval to proceed as planned. To gain that approval, they needed to incorporate the results of their planning into the business case.

Figure 9.1 provides a sample table of contents for a business case, and Chapter 9 explains how to develop one. At the point that the initial business case was created, everyone involved understood that some information was preliminary. What was provided at that point was enough to gain approval to conduct the Planning phase,

---

* Harold Kerzner, *Project Management: A Systems Approach to Planning, Scheduling, and Controlling*, 9th ed. (Hoboken: John Wiley & Sons, 2006), 65.

the primary purpose of which is to obtain enough detailed information to create a final business case. Now that planning was complete, the team could finalize four key sections of the business plan:

- 6.0—High-level project plan
- 11.0—Risks and recommended mitigating actions
- 12.0—Overview of costs
- 14.0—Cost/benefit analysis.

Project Plan

The high-level Gantt chart shown as Figure 9.3 was the best estimate the team had at the time that they developed the initial business case. As a result of the work done in Chapter 13, they now had a more detailed and accurate schedule. While the detailed Gantt chart shown as Figure 13.6 was valuable and would be included in an appendix, the team knew that the business case was best served by a summary version of the plan. One advantage of using computer software for project scheduling is that it simplifies generation of Gantt charts, allowing the team to transform Figure 13.6 into a high-level schedule simply by selecting only summary tasks. Figure 15.1 illustrates the summary schedule for the cafeteria project. This

ID	❶	Task Name	Duration	Start	Finish	December	January	February	March	April	May
1		**Project Management**	**96 days**	**Mon 12/20/10**	**Mon 5/2/11**						
2		Project Plan	48 days	Wed 12/20/10	Wed 2/23/11						
10		**Floor Plan**	**10 days**	**Thu 2/24/11**	**Wed 3/9/11**						
14		**Food Service**	**43 days**	**Thu 2/24/11**	**Mon 4/25/11**						
22		**Furnishings**	**28 days**	**Thu 3/10/11**	**Mon 4/18/11**						
23		Wall Coverings	16 days	Thu 3/10/11	Thu 3/31/11						
28		Floor Coverings	18 days	Thu 3/10/11	Mon 4/4/11						
33		Food Preparation Equipment	28 days	Thu 3/10/11	Mon 4/18/11						
38		Food Serving Equipment	23 days	Thu 3/10/11	Mon 4/11/11						
43		Dishes and Utensils	24 days	Thu 3/10/11	Tue 4/12/11						
48		Seating	20 days	Thu 3/10/11	Wed 4/6/11						

Project: WWC Cafeteria	Task	Summary	Rolled Up Progress
	Split	Rolled Up Task	External Tasks
	Progress	Rolled Up Split	Project Summary
	Milestone ◆	Rolled Up Milestone ◇	

Page 1

Figure 15.1 Summary Gantt chart for cafeteria project.

chart and summary charts for the other two main projects would be included in the business case, replacing Figure 9.3.

Risks

As Chapter 8 indicated, risk assessment is not a one-time event but should continue throughout the project. The reason for this is simple, well stated by DeMarco and Lister: "Risk management sets up projects for success."* The project team recognized that their initial risk assessment might have been incomplete and that, furthermore, new risks would appear as the project continued. They also knew that ignoring risks was a recipe for failure. As a result, they continued searching for possible problems and developing methods for dealing with them.

Jim felt so strongly about the need for risk management that he added a new standard item to each meeting agenda: review of risks. Jonathan Talbot, who had assumed responsibility for updating the FMEA created as Figure 8.2, soon gained the nickname Risk Czar.

The FMEA became a living document and was updated whenever new risks were identified. Although the FMEA was part of the project documentation and was accessible by all concerned parties, it was important that everyone involved in the approval process understood the risks the project faced. Accordingly, the latest version of the FMEA replaced the preliminary one and formed part of the final business case.

Overview of Costs

The costs outlined in the preliminary business case are normally rough order of magnitude (ROM) or "ballpark" estimates, designed to give the review committee enough information to determine whether it would be worth the time and effort required to conduct the Planning phase and develop accurate cost estimates. Now that the Planning phase was almost complete and a detailed project plan had been developed through the WBS, the team was ready to create a more definitive cost model. The revised costs, like the revised schedule, would be critical inputs to the executive committee's review of the project.

There are a number of different methods for developing cost estimates. The key characteristics of four of the most common are outlined on Table 15.1. The team considered each of those techniques. Analogous estimates, they decided, were not appropriate for them, since neither GWC nor IW had relocated their headquarters. Although they could obtain relocation costs from other companies and estimates

---

* Tom DeMarco and Timothy Lister, *Waltzing with Bears: Managing Risk on Software Projects* (New York: Dorset House, 2003), 31.

Table 15.1   Cost Estimating Techniques

Name	Description	Cost to Develop	Accuracy of Estimate
Analogous (top-down)	Actual costs from similar projects are used as the foundation for the estimate. If it cost $100,000 to build and equip a conference room, and this one is three quarters the size, the analogous estimate would be $75,000.	Low	Lower than others
Parametric	A mathematical model is applied to characteristics of the project (parameters). For example, the cost of building a house may be based on dollars per square foot, where square feet is the parameter.	Medium	Varies, based on the accuracy of the original cost and whether other factors are involved
Bottom-Up	The estimates for individual tasks are summed, creating a total for the entire project.	High	Higher than some others, but depends on the accuracy of each individual estimate
Simulation (normally used only on large or complex projects)	A model, typically computer generated, simulates the costs based on factors entered by the team. Monte Carlo is one popular type of simulation in which random number generators are used to determine the value of each unknown variable (in this case, cost), repeating the exercise multiple times to provide multiple scenarios.	Varies	Higher than most others

from moving and relo companies, they did not believe that those costs would have enough accuracy for their needs.

When considering use of parametric estimating, the team realized that GWC had renovated a portion of its corporate headquarters and that they could possibly use the cost per square foot as a rough estimate of the interior renovations. However, they were concerned that labor and material costs in Colorado would differ substantially from their historical costs in New Jersey. As a result, they decided not to take this approach. They also dismissed simulation, believing that their project was not sufficiently complex to warrant the cost of the software involved. That left bottom-up, unless they could find other techniques that were more applicable.

DeFuria proposes an estimating technique he calls functional.* In functional estimates, each department or contractor provides estimates for the work it will perform. Although the team knew that they would ultimately need estimates from the various contractors and that those estimates would form an important part of the overall project budget, they were not yet ready to obtain those estimates. As a result, they decided not to employ functional estimating.

Richman introduces the concept of the rolling wave estimate, in which the detail for the next phase is developed when the current one is complete.† Although the team saw the merit of this approach, they believed it was most effective on a long project and did not consider it appropriate for the WWC headquarters project. That left them with bottom-up.

As indicated on Table 15.1, bottom-up estimates have a high degree of accuracy, since they are developed once the WBS has been established and the individual tasks have been identified. Costs are typically based on two factors: the effort involved (labor) and non-labor-related costs.

Companies with interdepartmental chargeback systems normally have an hourly labor rate for each department. If that exists, it can be used to create the cost estimate. If the company has not established standard billing rates, it will be necessary to determine them. When calculating labor costs, it is important to use what are known as fully loaded or burdened costs rather than simply converting salary into an hourly rate. In addition to wages, fully loaded costs include other employer-paid items, including benefits such as vacation and holiday pay, 401(k), insurance premiums, and payroll-related taxes.

Depending on company policy, each department may have a single blended billing rate for all its employees, or there may be separate rates for each individual or for groups of employees. Although individual rates present a more accurate picture of the true cost, they add complexity to the calculation, since they require the team to have already determined which person will be assigned to each WBS task. Both IW and GWC used a single rate for each department.

---

* Guy L. DeFuria, *Project Management Recipes for Success* (Boca Raton: Auerbach, 2009), 64.
† Larry Richman, *Project Management Step-by-Step* (New York: AMACOM, 2002), 83.

While labor is often the largest cost, other expenses should not be ignored. Non-labor-related costs include materials, permits, travel, and computer usage.

Cost/Benefit Analysis

Although the preliminary cost/benefit analysis performed for the first iteration of the business case was sufficient to obtain approval to proceed with the Planning phase, most companies demand a more complete, detailed analysis before they will grant approval to implement the project. In most companies, this cost/benefit analysis includes a calculation of Return on Investment (ROI). ROI goes beyond the question, "How much will this project cost?" by putting that cost in perspective against the proposed benefits. The ROI calculation seeks to answer the question, "Does it make sense to invest this much money on this particular project?"

There are three primary steps involved before ROI can be calculated:

1. Calculate the costs of the proposed solution.
2. Calculate the costs of the current situation.
3. Quantify the benefits of the proposed solution.

Step 1: Calculate the Costs of the Proposed Solution

Although the costs of implementing the project were identified in the previous step, they are not the only costs needed for a cost/benefit analysis. Because cost/benefit analysis extends over a number of years, a more accurate calculation includes not only the initial outlay but also the ongoing costs. This is the total cost. Calculating the total cost is important for two reasons. First, it is the true representation of the project's costs, which can—and probably will—be used to evaluate this project's merits compared to others. Secondly, since it is unlikely that first-year benefits will exceed the initial costs, the subsequent years' costs are needed to calculate the break-even period.

The initial costs of the WWC headquarters building included renovations to the former Bluebell Industries building (5,000) and relocation of employees (4,000). (Note that all costs are shown in thousands.) There would, however, be additional costs once the relocation was complete, namely, the cost of maintaining the building. WWC was leasing the building and would, during the first calendar year, owe half a year's lease payments (750) as well as six months of utility bills (60). The total cost for the first year would thus be 9,810. This is shown on Figure 15.2 as the Year 1 proposed cost. Subsequent years' costs included the lease and utility payments, increased by an inflationary factor.

	Costs		Benefits								
Year	Costs of Proposed Solution	Costs of Current Solution	Cost Reduction	Other Benefits	Total Benefits	Annual ROI	Cumulative Proposed Costs	Cumulative Costs of Current Solution	Cumulative Benefits	Cumulative ROI
1	9810	7840	−1970	0	−1970	−120	9810	7840	−1970	−120
2	1620	8154	6534	250	6784	319	11430	15994	4814	−58
3	1685	8480	6795	0	6795	303	13115	24473	11609	−11
4	1752	8819	7067	0	7067	303	14867	33292	18675	26
5	1822	9172	7349	0	7349	303	16689	42464	26025	56

Figure 15.2   Return on Investment (ROI) calculation.

Step 2: Calculate the Costs of the Current Situation

To present a complete picture of the costs, it is essential to identify the costs of the current solution. While the costs identified in Step 1 may appear high, it is important to understand that the current situation is not free. It is also important to be able to compare those costs, which represent the cost of doing nothing, with the costs of the proposed solution. Both current and proposed costs are used to calculate ROI.

For the WWC headquarters project, the costs of the current situation included the GWC building lease (1,800), the IW building lease (750), GWC utilities (150), and IW utilities (140). The single largest cost, however, were the salaries and benefits of the fifty employees whose positions would be eliminated as a result of the merger (5,000). As shown on Figure 15.2, these costs were adjusted each year by the same inflationary factor that was used for ongoing costs of the proposed solution.

Step 3: Quantify the Benefits of the Proposed Solution

As discussed in Chapter 9, costs are only a part of the total picture. Benefits are the reason the project was initiated. Although they knew that benefits are typically grouped into four categories—cost reduction, cost avoidance, quality improvement, and new features/increased functionality—when they drafted the initial business case, the team had already determined that cost reduction would be the primary benefit. Wanting to ensure that they had not missed anything, they reevaluated each category to determine whether there might be other benefits.

- *Cost Reduction*—For the WWC headquarters project, the primary cost reductions came from the consolidation of two buildings into one, resulting in lower lease payments and utility bills, and a reduction in staff. When they calculated the savings from the staff reduction, the team knew it was important to use fully loaded salaries and to include an annual inflation factor. The annual inflation factor was also applied to the utility bills.
- *Cost Avoidance*—As they worked through the Planning phase, the team identified an opportunity for cost avoidance. GWC's current building required an upgrade of its electrical system, which was avoided as a result of the move. The cost of $250,000 was thus avoided in the second year of the project.
- *Quality Improvement*—Although they believed that the modern building with its environmentally safe paint and carpets would improve the quality of the workspace, the team was unable to quantify that quality improvement. Instead, they listed it as a benefit but assigned no dollar value to it.
- *New Features/Increased Functionality*–According to the preliminary plan, the new WWC headquarters site would include basketball and tennis courts for the employees, neither of which had been available at the existing sites. Although the team believed that this had value, they were unable to assign a dollar amount to it. They did, however, list it as a benefit in the revised business case.

Even when cost reduction alone is sufficient to justify the project, it is helpful to include all categories of benefits to present a complete picture of the project and its benefits.

Return on Investment (ROI) Calculation

Since most companies are in the business of making a profit and will invest money only if there is a valid reason, ROI is an important calculation, especially to the Finance Department. The calculation is relatively simple, once the team has calculated costs and benefits. The basic equation is:

$$ROI = [(benefits - proposed\ costs)/proposed\ costs] \cdot 100$$

The costs represent the investment that the project team is asking the company to make. The benefits tell the review committee the reason that investment is a sound one. Because it is rare for a project to break even in the first year, ROI is normally calculated for several years until it becomes positive. As shown on Figure 15.2, the WWC headquarters project's ROI became positive in the fourth year.

When reviewing ROI, the Finance Department will typically ask for two additional calculations: payback period and Net Present Value (NPV). Payback period is the number of months or years until the cumulative benefits equal the cumulative costs. In other words, it is the time when ROI becomes positive. Figure 15.3 graphs the cumulative costs and benefits from the ROI calculation and can be used to demonstrate that the payback period is just over three years.

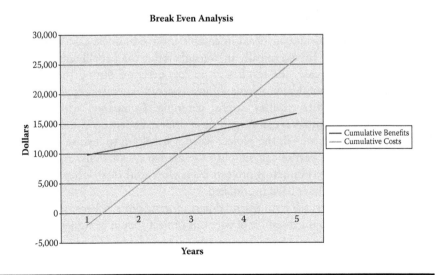

Figure 15.3   Break-even analysis.

Net Present Value recognizes that there is a value to the money that is being invested in this project. If it were not being spent on the project, it could be invested in something that would generate income. The percentage of income that the money would earn on the investment is referred to as the Internal Rate of Return (IRR). The NPV calculation discounts projected benefits by this rate, since the value of benefits is decreased by the fact that there will be a delay before they are achieved. This is commonly referred to as the time value of money. The basic premise is that a dollar received today is worth more than one received five years from now.

The equation to calculate Present Value (PV) is:

$$PV = FV \div (1 + I)^y$$

where FV is the future value of the benefit, I is the interest rate or IRR, and y is the number of years until the benefit will be realized.

Net Present Value includes costs in the equation:

$$NPV = PV \text{ benefits} - PV \text{ costs}$$

NPV can be calculated using free online calculators or with a simple Microsoft Excel function.

The team members had all the information they needed to update the business case. Once that was complete, they followed the approval process outlined in Chapter 8 to gain approval of the project and receive funding to continue.

What Can Go Wrong?

The most common mistake involved in completing the business case is the failure to include some costs. This is typically an oversight rather than a deliberate attempt to hide costs. In either case, the result will be cost overruns during the Execution phase and potential political problems if those overruns are substantial.

Identifying all costs requires careful planning. Companies with PMOs or good records of past projects can benefit from prior experiences. Whether or not a PMO exists, this is a time in the project when it is helpful to involve the Finance Department. Their expertise can simplify the needed calculations, and—because they are accustomed to evaluating projects from a financial view—they may be able to identify costs that have been overlooked.

A revised business case is an essential part of most projects because it provides an accurate answer to the question of why this project should be undertaken.

THE EXECUTION AND CONTROL PHASE, PART I: MORE PLANNING

V

The project is now entering the Execution and Control phase, the part of the project where all the planning that has taken place in the previous two phases is transformed into the reality of an active project. This is the stage where the project team increases in size, and where, if not properly managed, it can slip into panic. Avoiding panic is the reason that the Execution and Control phase begins with more planning and organization.

Chapter 11 outlined the four stages of team dynamics, pointing out that a team reaches the more productive stages of norming and performing only after it has established clearly defined roles, responsibilities, and processes—or what could be called ground rules. Those ground rules are the subject of Chapter 16.

Change is inevitable. No matter how well defined the project's requirements are, something will change during the project's life cycle. Chapter 17 is devoted to the change management process, discussing how to establish a formal process that will ensure that change is constructive rather than destructive to the project.

It is not only the project team that may panic. So, too, may customers and other stakeholders. Recognizing that possibility, Chapter 18 explains how a carefully planned and executed communication plan can help prevent panic.

Chapter 16

Ground Rules

At this stage of the project, the team has conducted extensive planning to ensure the project's success and is typically anxious to begin executing that plan. It is, however, important to do some additional planning, in part to avoid the possibility of the team's slipping into panic as the reality of the project's magnitude becomes apparent. Although the previous planning has been focused on the project, these planning steps are designed to increase the team's probability for success. Chapter 11 outlined the four stages of team dynamics, pointing out that a team reaches the more productive stages of norming and performing only after it has established clearly defined roles, responsibilities, and processes—or what could be called ground rules. This chapter discusses those ground rules.

The Need for a Rulebook

Projects experience problems. That is a simple fact of project management. The problems include scope creep, schedule and budget overrun, unproductive or unmotivated team members, and errors in execution. Two techniques for avoiding these problems are to first establish procedures that the team will use throughout the project execution and then to ensure that they are followed.

In describing the components of successful change as discussed in Chapter 2, William Bridges outlined the Four Ps. The third of those Ps was Plan/Processes. Although the plan was established in the previous phase of the project, now it is time to define the processes the team will follow. The goal is to ensure consistency throughout the project, leaving nothing to chance or individual interpretation. These procedures can be considered the ground rules under which the team operates, and—like all important aspects of the project—they should be written, communicated to the team, and easily accessible throughout the life of the project. Without formal, clearly understood rules and procedures, the project runs the risk of evolving into panic.

Ironically, although development of a rulebook is a technique for improving the team's efficiency, it created the first major disagreement on the WWC project. Both Lori Woods and Roy Morgan objected to the formality of it, insisting it was a waste of time. "We've managed projects before, and we never needed a rulebook," they told Jim. The problem, Jim realized as he continued asking questions to determine the root cause, was not the rulebook but the fact that it would be written. IW's teams had rules and procedures; they were simply not as institutionalized as GWC's. The root cause of the disagreement was the difference in corporate cultures between GWC and IW. Because IW was a much less formal company, its employees were accustomed to handling many aspects of project management verbally rather than in writing. When he was unable to convince Lori and Roy of the need for—and value of—a written rulebook, Jim had no choice but to become a benevolent dictator, telling them that because he was the project manager and the person with the ultimate responsibility for the project's success, the team would develop and use a formal rulebook.

What Is Included?

There are two primary categories of items to be included in the rulebook: standards and expectations. Standards are, as the name implies, rules that are to be followed. If the overall project plan is the road map, these are the traffic regulations that ensure that travelers make their way safely to their final destination. Included are:

- *Status Reports*—Although some companies, including IW, do not require formal status reports, believing that updates to the project schedule are sufficient, regular written status reports benefit both the employee creating them and the manager. Reporting status is not an exercise in bureaucracy. Instead, it forces the employee who is reporting to reflect on what happened, what will happen, and—most importantly—what might hamper progress. Like other forms of risk reporting, the regular identification of potential problems is an important part of minimizing their impact. Status reports are important, and their format and frequency should be clearly defined. Figure 16.1 provides a sample status report template that includes three sections: progress, problems encountered during the reporting period, and plans for the next period.
- *Other Documentation*—Although status reports are important, since they help keep the project on track, projects normally require other, more permanent types of documentation. When developing standards for them, the team should include the following:

Name:	Period Ending:
Progress	
WBS#	Description
Problems	
WBS#	Description
Plans for Next Period	
WBS#	Description

Figure 16.1   Status report.

- *Identification of types of documentation to be provided.* Will there be additional design documents, user manuals, training materials, or other documents? The WWC project documentation included blueprints, floor plans, and supplier bids.
- *Content of each type of documentation.* All items that are expected to be included in each form of documentation should be listed, along with a table of contents, showing the correct order. When the WWC team issued the RFP to food service suppliers, they specified the order and

format of the response, knowing that the consistency would reduce the time required to review and evaluate responses.

- *Format.* If a specific format is required—and, for consistency, it should be—the standards should indicate that. Formats may include the word processing or other program to be used to create the documentation and the specific version of that program as well as type fonts, margin sizes, etc., if those are important to the company.
- *Examples.* Since it is possible to have multiple interpretations of the level of detail required if all that is provided is a table of contents, the team should develop a sample of each type of documentation, showing the desired contents and format. In addition to increasing consistency, these samples are designed to reduce confusion, which will in turn reduce the time required to create the documentation.

■ *Filing System*—All that documentation needs to be stored, and—more importantly—it needs to be easily retrieved. The rulebook should include a description of the filing system that will be used, what will be included, where documents will be stored, who can access them, and how updates are performed and by whom.

■ *Walk-Throughs and Reviews*—Peer reviews are an important part of most projects. The frequency of those reviews and the format that will be employed (informal meeting, formal presentation, electronic round-robin review of documents) should be clearly identified.

■ *Other Standards*—Depending on the type of project, there may be a need for other types of standards. Creation of a software program, for example, should include standards for:

- *The programming language and version of the language to be used.* If multiple languages are allowed, there should be a clear definition of when each is used.
- *Naming conventions.* This includes data element as well as program and file names.
- *Identification and use of reusable components.* Since one of the objectives of a software project, for example, is normally to deliver the software at the lowest possible cost and in the shortest possible schedule, reuse of code is important. The project team should define which types of modules will form part of a reusable code library as well as when and how they will be reused.

Expectations

In addition to standards, it is important to outline the project manager's expectations of the team. Normally, those expectations include more than coming to work each day and performing assigned tasks. Two other expectations are problem and opportunity reporting, the two sides of what DeFuria calls risks.

Chapter 10 pointed out the importance of building trust among team members, focusing on the trust that the team members must have in the manager. Trust needs to be bidirectional. Just as team members need to know that they will not become scapegoats if they deliver unwanted news, the manager needs to trust that employees will report problems when they occur. If the manager has established an environment of shooting the messenger, problems will not be reported, and they may fester. Similarly, if the manager has not explicitly asked for potential problems to be identified, they may not.

Jim knew that, which is why he created a "rules of the road" document similar to the code of conduct used for meetings (Figure 6.1). His rules of the road included:

- The only dumb question is the one you do not ask.
- Problems are to be reported, not ignored.
- Messengers are rewarded, not shot.

Problems are not the only items that should be reported. So should opportunities for improvement. It is the team members, the people who are closest to the work being done, who are often able to identify ways to improve the project, to streamline a process, or to reduce costs. There should be no question that this information needs to be reported as soon as it is discovered, but if the manager does not make these expectations explicit, important opportunities may be lost.

Realizing that, Jim gained approval for what he called the bounty system, whereby team members who identified opportunities for improvement were awarded small gifts (t-shirts, mugs, and similar items) simply for reporting the opportunity. If their recommendations were implemented, they were entered into a drawing for the grand prize: a weekend for two at one of the Colorado ski resorts.

Who Is Responsible?

Responsibility for establishing the ground rules lies with the project manager. If a Project Management Office (PMO) exists, many of the ground rules may have already been developed. In that case, the project manager's primary responsibility becomes communication. If there is no PMO or rulebook from an earlier project, the project manager will need to create one. Ideally, members of the team will participate in the development of the rulebook to ensure that no elements are forgotten and that the standards and procedures are realistic. In either case, the project manager should review the proposed ground rules with the entire team before finalizing them. This gives the team the opportunity to express concerns and provide suggestions for improvement. Once the ground rules have been finalized, they should be made available to the team in written format so that they can be accessed whenever needed.

What Can Go Wrong?

The most common mistake is skipping this step entirely. Some project managers, pressured to begin work, believe that a set of ground rules is a nice-to-have feature rather than an essential one. The step is not unnecessary overhead. Instead, it is an important part of building a productive team and increasing the probability of success. It should not be overlooked.

Chapter 17

The Change Management Process

As Chapter 2 discussed, change is an intrinsic part of project management, since projects, by definition, are designed to implement one or more changes. Unfortunately for the project team, there are more changes involved than the ones they are creating. The simple fact is, change to a project's scope is almost inevitable. It is a rare project where none of the requirements are modified during the Execution and Control phase. That is why Morris and Sember point out that planning and execution are not one-time events in a project but are, rather, cyclical during the project's life.* As shown on Figure 17.1, Initiation/Definition and Closeout may occur once, but Planning and Execution are often repeated multiple times, thanks to changes in requirements.

Most often, modifications are initiated by the customer. That was the case at WWC, where two months into the project, the executive committee requested a private dining room located next to the cafeteria. Though both GWC and IW's executives were accustomed to having meals catered by the in-house food service and served in conference rooms, the newly formed group wanted the ability to offer more formal meals to visiting customers and the board of directors. Since the floor plans were complete and materials had been ordered, implementing this request would clearly impact both cost and schedule. But, since the request had come from senior management, the team knew there was a high probability that the work would need to be done.

---

* Rich A. Morris and Brette McWhorter Sember, *Project Management That Works* (New York: AMACOM, 2008), 53.

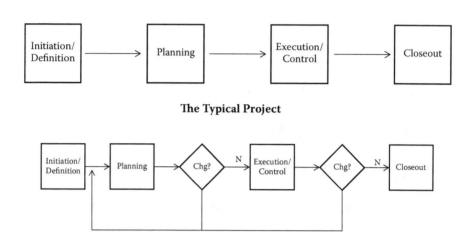

Figure 17.1   Effect of change on a project life cycle.

It is also possible that the project team itself may request a change when they discover that a feature cannot be implemented as requested or that there may be a better way to accomplish an objective. In these instances, although the project team becomes the customer/requestor, the process remains the same.

Change will occur. The question is, will it be managed? Without a formal change management process, the project runs the risk of becoming derailed with schedule and budget overruns, disappointed customers, and panicked team members. It is also possible that spurious requests for modifications may be implemented, creating a negative impact on the project. The WWC team knew that a formal change process reduces the possibility of these pitfalls and instituted a hybrid of the ones GWC and IW had used in the past.

There are three primary components to an effective change management system: the request form, the process, and the review board.

The Request Form

Requests for changes can and will come to the project team in a variety of ways: e-mail notes, phone calls, casual conversations in the hallway, occasionally a formal memo. The problem with these methods is that there is no consistency or, in Six Sigma terms, there is too much variation. Not only do casual conversations lend themselves to misunderstandings, but it is also unlikely that all the necessary information will be included, even in a memo or e-mail message. A standard request form ensures that all needed information is provided, thus saving both the team and the requestor the time required for follow-up calls and messages.

Although there are as many different forms as there are companies, when complete, each should include answers to the following questions:

- What is being requested?
- Why is this important?
- How much will it cost and/or how much will it delay the schedule?
- Is the work approved?

The answers to the first two questions are provided by the requestor, while the project team answers the third, and the review board makes the decision to approve or reject the request. The form that the WWC team used is shown as Figure 17.2. In this case, the "request" section is completed by the person asking for the change, while the remainder of the form is used by the project team.

Although most of the fields are self-explanatory, several may benefit from clarification.

- *Type* (in Request section)—These radio buttons allow the requestor to categorize the reason for the request. A correction is designed to fix problems in the initial specifications, while an addition asks for new functionality. Mandates may come from either outside regulatory agencies or the company's senior management. In either case, as their name suggests, they are not optional. Although Frank Seely classified the separate dining room request as an addition, it was closer to a mandate.
- *Triage* allows the project team to indicate the action taken after the initial impact assessment was completed. Like Type, these are radio buttons, meaning that only one may be selected. The first is used for minor changes. Although the limits shown on Figure 17.2 are arbitrary, it is beneficial for the project team to have a threshold for small requests, allowing them to be incorporated into the project without major review. The second option is cancellation by the requestor. Normally this occurs as a result of the cost and schedule impact; however, it is also possible that the requestor may have had second thoughts about the work and may simply withdraw the request. The third option, and the one that typically applies to the majority of requests, is that the work must be approved by the steering committee/review board discussed below.

The team estimated the impact of the dining room request to be $25,000 and two weeks' schedule delay. Frank, speaking for the executive committee, believed that was a reasonable cost and time frame and agreed that the request should be forwarded to the review board.

Scope Change Request		SCR#
		Date Received
Request		
Requestor Name		Date of Request
Requestor Department		Date Required
Description of Change Requested		Type: O Correction O Addition O Mandate
Impact		
Cost	Estimated By	Date
Schedule	Estimated By	Date
Requestor Notified	By	Date
Triage		
O No impact on schedule, cost less than 1% of project; proceed; requestor notified		Date
O Requestor withdrew request: O Cost O Schedule		Date
O Requires CCB review; next meeting date: _____; requestor notified		Date
Decision		
CCB Meeting		Date
O Include in first release O Delay until _____ O Do not implement		
Requestor Notified		Date
Implementation		
WBS Modified	By	Date
Schedule Modified	By	Date
Project Specifications Modified	By	Date
Budget Modified	By	Date
Work Assigned	By	Date
Work Completed	By	Date

Figure 17.2 Scope change request.

The Process

Creation of a scope change request form implies the presence of a process. To ensure that everyone affected understands the process and his or her role in it, it is helpful to document the process and review it with both the team and all stakeholders. The Six Sigma tool of choice for this documentation is the process map, specifically the functional process map. Since multiple groups are involved in change management, the use of a functional process map clearly delineates individual responsibilities and where hand-offs occur. Figure 17.3 provides an example of a functional process map for scope change based on the change request form shown as Figure 17.2. Appendix C describes the process of creating a functional process map.

The Review Board

If it is an axiom that change occurs, it is another that not all requested modifications should be implemented. Although it is possible for the project team to make the determination of which requests are the most critical, they should not. Not only might the team not have the correct perspective—its focus is, after all, completing the project as quickly as possible—but excluding customers from the process sends the message that customers are not an integral part of the project. The company does not need to have adopted Six Sigma principles to know that that is the wrong message.

The solution is to develop a steering committee or what some companies call a Change Control Board (CCB). The CCB is a specialized team, a group of customers with a vested interest in a specific project. Its role is to review and prioritize individual requests for modifications to the project. Because it serves as the "voice of the customer," it is important to have the right customers as members of the team.

The CCB is typically convened by the project's champion, and that individual may serve as the facilitator or leader, although it is customary for the project manager to lead the board. Each major customer department should be represented on the board. Although the champion normally issues invitations to customer department heads, in large organizations it is common for department heads to delegate their responsibility and for lower-ranking staff to serve as members of the CCB. This is not a problem, so long as the individuals chosen have the authority to speak for their departments.

As with all teams, it is important that the members of the CCB have the right attributes. The characteristics shown on Table 5.2 are as important for the CCB as they were for the project's initial stages. It is also important that the team members be knowledgeable about the project's proposed functionality and its impact on their departments.

The CCB should meet on a regular schedule throughout the project's life. While the frequency will vary depending on the length of the project, with shorter projects requiring more frequent meetings, a rule of thumb is that the CCB should meet no less frequently than monthly. The reason for this is that if customers' requests

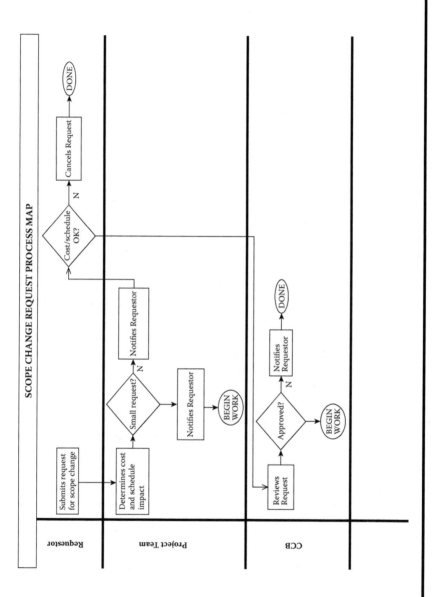

Figure 17.3 Scope change request process map.

remain in the queue without a decision for an extended period, customers may believe that they have fallen prey to the black hole syndrome, where requests are lost, never to be found again. As both Figures 17.2 and 17.3 show, the CCB's decisions should be communicated to the requestor as soon as they have been made.

No one was surprised when the WWC CCB approved the request for the separate dining room.

Who Is Responsible?

There are two aspects to this question: the initial planning and the ongoing operation, and the answers frequently differ. Project managers have the ultimate responsibility for developing the change management process. Whether they do the actual work or delegate it, they are the ones who need to ensure that the process is established and communicated to the team and all stakeholders. They are not, however, the ones who are typically in charge of the day-to-day implementation.

Depending on the project's organization, requests for modifications may be channeled to any team member, with the recipient being responsible for logging in the request and forwarding it to the correct person for impact estimation. While this approach is feasible, it takes time away from the individual team member's assigned tasks and may result in schedule slippage. Particularly on large projects, it is helpful to establish a single point of contact for all scope change requests. That person receives all requests, logs them, assigns them for estimation, tracks their status, serves as a member of the CCB, and is responsible for all status-related communication with the requestor. The advantage of centralizing the responsibility is efficiency. A single person trained in specific responsibilities can be more effective than multiple individuals trying to juggle this responsibility with many others. Geraldine Kelly volunteered for this role on the WWC project, pointing out that her customer service background meant that she was accustomed to dealing with people and defusing potentially volatile situations.

Regardless of who is responsible for tracking requests, it is important that everyone on the team understands the need for the change management process and that each request form is updated at every stage of implementation. Scope change requests become an important component of the overall project documentation and can be of benefit to future project teams.

What Can Go Wrong?

Even when a change management process has been instituted, there are potential problems.

- *Circumventing the System*—This is particularly common when customers have a good working relationship with individual team members. "It's only a small request," a customer will say. "Can't you take care of it for me?" And, unless the process is fully ingrained in the team's culture, the work may be done outside the system. The possibilities for error are numerous. Verbal requests, as noted above, can easily result in a misunderstanding of requirements and the implementation of a solution that does not meet the customer's needs. Furthermore, without the rigor of a formal review, it is possible that a modification may inadvertently impact another portion of the project. To reduce the likelihood of this occurring, the project manager must ensure that everyone on the project—including customers—understands the importance of the process.

■ *An Unwieldy Process*—Although the change management process is established to prevent problems, if it is perceived as bureaucratic, customers will be more likely to try to circumvent the system. When developing the process, the team should make every effort to ensure that the process provides value. This can be done by streamlining the process, having the CCB meet electronically if there are no critical issues that would require discussion, and expanding the definition of the "free pass" requests, those small enough to be implemented without formal review.

The importance of change management to the overall project success cannot be overstated.

Chapter 18

The Communication Plan

There is a reason the *Project Management Book of Knowledge* (*PMBOK*) lists communication as one of the nine knowledge areas for a project manager. Quite simply, it is an essential part of any successful project. Why? Spinoza said, "Nature abhors a vacuum.*" So too do people, particularly those involved in change. They want to know what is happening, when, why, and to whom.

It is important for project teams to understand that there will always be communication about a major project. The question is whether the information disseminated will be accurate or a product of the rumor mill. That is why communication, like the project itself, must be managed. Unless the project team takes ownership of communication, the information being circulated may be misleading or even totally wrong.

Whether it is called the rumor mill or the grapevine, informal communication is active in most companies, seeking to fill the vacuum. That was certainly the case at both GWC's and IW's current headquarters. Faced with what would be major life changes—either layoffs or relocation to another state—employees were nervous and quick to spread the latest news, whether or not it had any basis in reality. Jim had faced the problem at the beginning of the project, when rumors were contributing to wild enthusiasm, and he knew it was in everyone's best interests to preempt rumors by providing clear, consistent, targeted, and ongoing communication.

The rumor mill is expensive, distracting the team and requiring team members to spend unscheduled time in correcting it. The information spread through the grapevine is frequently inaccurate, based only on speculation or grains of truth. This means that instead of simply communicating facts, the project team becomes

---

* Benedict Spinoza, *Ethics*, cited in *Bartlett's Familiar Quotations* (Boston: Little, Brown, 1980), 308.

involved in damage control, denying the misinformation and then presenting the facts. This frequently requires more than twice the amount of time that would have been involved in straight forward communication. A properly planned and executed communication plan is another case of prior planning preventing poor performance, because it can prevent—or at least greatly reduce—the rumor mill and its effects.

Communication is typically categorized as formal and informal. Since most project teams use both types, it is important to understand the differences and the uses of each. While informal communications are normally verbal, formal communication can be either written (memos, e-mails, updates to websites) or verbal (speeches, teleconferences, meetings). The primary distinction between the two classifications is that formal communications are planned, whereas informal ones are not. Both have their uses and advantages.

Formal Communication

The majority of official communication about a project is typically formal and may be delivered in a number of different ways. Table 18.1 shows some of the communication mechanisms that are often used and their target audiences.

Table 18.1 Communication Mechanisms

Communication Mechanism	Target Audience	Uses
Memos	Managers	Explain details of specific decisions, plans, etc.
Posters	Customers	Outline key points and progress
Newsletters	All stakeholders	Review progress and plans, share success stories
Web page	All stakeholders with Internet access	Provide summary of project. May include the same information as posters and newsletters
Town hall and departmental meetings	All stakeholders (either together or in separate groups)	Provide status (typically through a formal presentation), encourage two-way communication
Briefings	Senior management	Provide status (typically through a formal presentation), respond to questions and concerns

When designing formal communications, the team needs to consider whether to make them "push" or "pull." Communications that are "pushed" are delivered to the target audience without any need for action on their part, whereas "pulled" communications require the recipient to do something to obtain the information. In general, it is preferable to push communications during a project, since that ensures that the audience receives them. Meetings, briefings, memos, newsletters, and posters are examples of pushed communications, while web pages typically require pulling. If key information is contained on the web page, it is advantageous to send an e-mail alert to all stakeholders, announcing the update.

In the case of a major change, particularly one that involves staff changes, it is frequently desirable to develop a written communication plan. The purposes of a formal plan are to:

- Ensure that the right people are involved
- Develop a common message
- Identify the correct timing for delivery of the message

In other words, a communication plan outlines *what* will be communicated, *by whom*, and *when*.

The contents of a communication plan include the key messages, a schedule of events, and a list of frequently asked questions (FAQs) and answers. All of these are prepared in advance and reviewed with the individuals who will deliver the messages prior to the kickoff of the project. This helps increase the consistency of the information being delivered.

- *Key Messages*—Particularly when sweeping changes are planned, it is essential to ensure that everyone affected understands the major elements, the Five Ws (who, what, where, when, and why). The message should focus on:
  - What changes are being planned?
  - Why is the change needed?
  - When will it happen?
  - Who will be affected?
  - Where will it happen? In many cases, the "where" aspect is of less importance, although in the case of the GWC/IW merger and for companies that are combining previously decentralized groups, it is a critical component of the message.
- When developing the key messages, it is important to keep them simple. Details will be presented in subsequent communications, and, as noted in an earlier chapter, different audiences may receive different pieces of information. The key messages, however, should be communicated to everyone at the project's initiation and should be repeated regularly until they have become incorporated into a shared vision.

■ *Schedule*—This is not the overall project schedule but rather one for project communications. The reason for developing a communication schedule is that it is important to know who will communicate what, to whom, and when. This aspect of the project needs to be managed as carefully as any other. Building commitment begins by getting buy-in from advocates and agents at an early stage. These groups may be included in "preannouncement" meetings so that they are prepared for the reactions when the general announcement is made. Table 18.2 illustrates a sample communication plan schedule.

■ *FAQs*—Any announcement of change will elicit a number of questions. In order to ensure that messages are not "lost in the translation," it is helpful to have a brainstorming session to outline all possible questions that may be raised and to develop answers for them. Putting both the questions and the answers in writing helps to prepare the person who will actually deliver the message and increases consistency. Some companies prepare a frequently asked questions (FAQ) document and distribute it to the affected groups. Others simply give the document to those who will be delivering the messages.

Although a communication plan is not necessary, it embodies the Five Ps (prior planning prevents poor performance) and helps increase the project's chances of success, particularly when the project is a lengthy one or involves major change, as in the case of the GWC/IW merger.

Who Is Responsible?

The responsibility for developing the communication plan and schedule normally falls on the project manager. Depending on the company and the project, a member of the Public Relations or Internal Communications departments may be involved. If such a department does not exist internally, the project manager may want to consider the use of an outside consultant. Even though there is an additional cost for consultants, there is also value, particularly for large, controversial, and complex projects. Communications professionals have expertise in framing and delivering messages for a variety of audiences and can help the team ensure that it does not inadvertently create more problems with poorly chosen words and ill-timed messages.

Although use of public relations consultants is optional, if staff reductions or other major personnel changes are anticipated, it is critical that the Law and Human Resource departments be active participants. Not only do they have needed expertise, but, like communications professionals, they can provide guidance on the best way to present sensitive subjects. Law and HR should be included in the development and review of all materials related to staffing, and HR should participate in the actual delivery of the message. As Table 4.1 illustrates, members of the Law, Human Resources, and Communications departments were part of the core WWC team.

Table 18.2 Communication Plan Schedule

Date	Audience	Medium	Key Messages	Accountability
12/1: 2 p.m.	Department heads	Meeting (travelers to dial in)	Overview of project Impact on employees Timing Overview of communications process Next steps: Schedule meetings with HR reps to review process for RIF and relo	Project Champion
12/2–12/6	HR reps	Memo Meeting with HR reps (dept. heads to use memo as basis for discussion with their HR reps)	Overview of project Impact on employees RIF selection criteria Relo policy (severance available if employee chooses not to move) Timing Overview of communications plan	Department Heads
12/8	Affected departments (all employees)	Meeting	Overview of project Vision and reason for project Impact on employees 　Some layoffs 　Enhanced severance 　Relo is voluntary Communications plan Weekly updates of project status Send questions to central e-mail box Answers posted weekly	Department Heads

Internal Team Communications

The communications discussed above are designed for all stakeholders. Although team members are also recipients of those communications, they have additional needs. Because of this, the project manager needs to establish a plan for internal team communications.

Just as it is important to divide the overall project schedule into tasks with short durations so that progress can be measured on a regular basis, so too is it important to establish a schedule for frequent communication among team members. That communication has two primary purposes:

- Reporting progress and identifying problems before they become too complex to resolve
- Keeping the team members involved and motivated

On a large project, like the WWC headquarters building, although there is an overall team that may be comprised of hundreds of people, as shown on Figure 11.1 there are normally smaller work teams. The most frequent communication (daily or weekly) is at the work unit level, and if the team is colocated, the preferred method of communicating is in-person meetings. Other types of communication and their recommended frequency are outlined on Table 18.3.

Informal Communications

Informal communications are often nicknamed the "water cooler" communications, since they tend to be *ad hoc*. While those conversations are important to helping employees feel involved, they can also result in feeding the rumor mill, since employees may misinterpret what they have heard and repeat incorrect information. A more effective informal communication mechanism is the Rumor Control Session (RCS).

During a period of major change, the champion or project manager schedules regular RCSs with each of the affected departments as well as the project team. (Typically these are held weekly.) Attendance is optional, there are no planned messages to be delivered, and the leader makes no speeches. Instead, he or she may begin the session by asking, "What's the latest rumor?" and either confirming or denying it. The leader also responds to questions. An honest "I don't know" or "I can't tell you that yet" is a valid answer; silence is not, since the objective of an RCS is to allay fears and give employees a chance to gripe.

When dealing with the change that every project involves, it is important to understand that resistance is often because the employee feels a loss of control. Whether it is real or not, the employee's perception is critical. The project team members are agents of change and may not be able to restore any real control, but

Table 18.3 Routine Team Communications

Frequency	Medium	Participants	Purpose
Daily	Meeting or telecon	Work unit	Team members report progress, problems, and plans so that the team can attempt to resolve problems internally.
Weekly	Meeting or telecon	Unit team leaders	Team leaders report their teams' progress, problems, and plans so that all units are aware of problems and that any needed coordination is scheduled.
Weekly	Meeting or telecon	Work unit	Unit team leaders report summaries of other teams' progress, problems, and plans to their own teams so that all team members are kept aware of the overall project.
Monthly	Newsletter or memo	All teams	Document reports overall progress of project, focusing on positive aspects and benefits to be derived. Besides providing information, the document is designed to be motivational.
Quarterly	Meeting or telecon	All teams	Champion addresses entire team, amplifying the monthly newsletters and providing an opportunity for team members to have their questions answered.

they can help mitigate the sense of loss by keeping all affected people informed of progress and including them in decision-making meetings. This helps build commitment, which in turn fosters more successful change.

Exception Reporting

In addition to formal and informal, there is a third type of communication: exception reporting. Although it is not scheduled, it should be planned. Just as change is inevitable, so too are problems. That is why it is important to have a standard process for reporting problems and a plan for escalating them when they cannot be resolved within a work unit.

If the project manager has not instituted regular team meetings, the problem section of team members' weekly status reports is often the first indication of a potential problem. Depending on the nature and severity of the problem, this may be too late. The WWC team established the following procedure for exception reporting.

1. Any time a problem will impact the project budget or schedule, the person discovering the problem must notify his or her supervisor/manager immediately.
2. If the supervisor determines that the problem can be resolved within the work unit, no escalation is required, but the problem and its resolution must be reported on the discovering person's next status report.
3. If the problem cannot be resolved within the work unit or involves another work unit, the supervisor must escalate it to the next level of the project hierarchy within half a day of discovering that the problem cannot be resolved internally.
4. If the problem cannot be resolved within the project team, the project manager must notify the champion immediately.

Although there are a number of possible communication methods for exception reporting, the general rule is that the greater the severity of the problem, the greater the need to report in person or via the phone rather than leaving e-mail or voice mail. The reasons for this approach are:

■ It is more personal, and thus more likely to result in faster resolution. It is, after all, more difficult to ignore a person in one's office than an e-mail message.
■ The person delivering the message knows that it has been received. Voice mail and e-mail messages might not be retrieved for hours or even days.
■ The personal approach allows for questions, discussions, and possible resolution.

Exception reporting is a critical type of communication and, like the others, should have a well-planned and clearly communicated process.

What Can Go Wrong?

The most common problem associated with communication plans is that they are either nonexistent or inadequate. Other problems include:

■ *The message is garbled.* It is possible that even with a formal communication plan, the message that is actually delivered is not the one that was intended. Although this may occur with written communications, it is more common when messages are being delivered verbally. To avoid this problem, the project manager needs to ensure that all key points are written and that the person presenting them uses the official wording. It is also important to select the correct messenger. No matter how gifted a public speaker he or she may be, an employee with a tendency to ad lib and provide editorial comments is not the ideal person to deliver a critical message.

■ *Recipients are skeptical.* Unfortunately, there is no panacea for this. Mistrust and skepticism are normal reactions, particularly when the message is an unpleasant one. The primary solution is to establish trust, and that occurs when the skeptics see that the project team members' actions match their words.

Projects will always involve communication. It is the manager's responsibility to ensure that that communication is accurate, frequent, and properly targeted—in other words, managed.

THE EXECUTION AND CONTROL PHASE, PART II: MAKING IT HAPPEN

The next stage of the project is the one where what many consider the "real work" begins. This is where all the planning turns into reality. During this phase, the project manager's responsibility changes from planning to ensuring that the project proceeds according to the plan that has resulted from the previous work. This phase is appropriately named—Execution and Control—because there are two primary aspects to it. While others are involved in the actual execution, the project manager controls.

Figure 1.1 illustrated the three primary project constraints: time, scope, and resources (cost). Chapter 19 outlines methods for monitoring progress on all three fronts and correcting problems as they occur.

Some pundits claim that there is a fourth project constraint—namely, quality. Chapter 20 addresses this subject, explaining the difference between quality assurance and quality control. It also introduces the concept of controlling a project with metrics, scorecards, and a control plan.

The project may have been executed flawlessly, but if internal customers are not prepared for the changes that they are responsible for implementing, the project will not be a success. Chapter 21 discusses organizational readiness, including the development of training programs.

Though few project managers want to admit that they have more than a passing acquaintance with Murphy, the reality is that his famous law of "If anything can go wrong, it will" can impact a project. Chapter 22 discusses potential pitfalls and ways to avoid or, if that is not possible, to mitigate them.

Chapter 19

Monitoring the Project

As the project enters the next phase of execution, the project manager's responsibility changes from planning and leading to monitoring and controlling. As shown on Figure 1.1, there are three primary project constraints: time, scope, and resources (costs), which form a triangle. It is the project manager's responsibility to monitor progress on all three, ensuring that the triangle remains in balance and does not begin to resemble the disconnected triangle shown as Figure 1.2. Controlling the triangle, although conceptually simple, is one of the most challenging responsibilities a project manager faces, because scope, schedule, and budget rarely remain constant throughout a project's life cycle.

Scope

Scope creep is something many project managers dread. Creep refers to those small changes that, taken individually, appear insignificant, but when combined have a major impact on the scope and, therefore, the schedule. Scope creep occurs most commonly when someone on the project team—anyone from the champion to the person actually doing the work—agrees to make a change without following a formal change management process. Work is slipped into the schedule without considering the full implications.

Chapter 17, which outlines the change management process, emphasizes the importance of following it rigorously. This is one instance when Whitten's "benevolent dictatorship"* should be employed, with the emphasis on the second word.

---

* Neal Whitten, *Neal Whitten's No-Nonsense Advice for Successful Projects* (Vienna, VA: Management Concepts, 2005), 8.

Avoiding scope creep—and the unwelcome budget and schedule overrun surprises that frequently accompany it—is the primary reason for instituting and enforcing a formal change management process. If the process is a good one and if it is followed, there should be no surprises. All changes to scope will be documented, reviewed, and if they are approved, the budget and schedule will be modified to reflect the extra time and cost associated with them. And, in a well-managed project, those changes will be communicated to everyone affected so that there are no unrealistic expectations, no disillusionment, and no panic.

Even in a benevolent dictatorship, the best way to ensure that the change management process is followed rather than being ignored or circumvented is to have a fully performing team—that is, a team that has reached the fourth stage of team development as outlined in Chapter 11. If that team is built on a solid foundation of trust—not just trust of the project manager but also trust among the team members—everyone will recognize the dangers of uncontrolled modifications to scope, and they will not occur. As discussed previously, the key to establishing trust is frequent, honest communication.

Although the project team cannot control the number or magnitude of change requests, it can ensure that those requests are managed and that scope creep is not permitted.

Schedule

The second challenge project managers face is monitoring and controlling the schedule. Lewis states, "One of the primary features that distinguishes project management from general management is the special attention to scheduling."* It is not enough to spend significant time establishing the schedule during the Planning phase. Once that schedule has been developed and work begins, the project manager is responsible for monitoring the schedule and ensuring that it does not slip.

Monitoring is the first step. In addition to reviewing team members' status reports, the project manager should track the schedule. If the precept of establishing Work Breakdown Structure (WBS) tasks with durations less than or equal to forty hours has been followed, and if deliverables are carefully reviewed to ensure that tasks declared complete are in fact complete, the project manager should be able to determine whether the project is on schedule and, if it is not, to take immediate corrective action to ensure that no further slippage occurs.

Schedule slip occurs for a number of reasons, including:

■ *Estimates were unrealistic.* This is most likely to occur if the people who will actually perform the work were not involved in developing the estimate or

---

* James P. Lewis, *Fundamentals of Project Management* (New York: AMACOM, 1997), 49.

if the team members assigned to a task lack the experience and expertise to perform it.

■ *Some necessary tasks were not included in the original plan.* Again, this is often the result of not including the right individuals in the development of the Work Breakdown Structure and the time and cost estimates.

■ *The team is not working the planned number of hours.* A frequent cause of this problem is that team members are being shared with other projects or other responsibilities. This was the case on the WWC project. Although Dustin Monroe and Lori Woods were supposed to be devoting all of their time to the project, both of their departments had lost staff when employees who did not want to relocate to Colorado found other jobs, leaving Dustin and Lori to fill the gaps. In their book, *Project Rescue: Avoiding a Project Management Disaster,* Sanjiv Purba and Joseph Zucchero advise project managers to ask a number of questions to determine whether their projects are heading for disaster. These include, "Is each team member working only on the specifically assigned tasks in the plan?"*

Whenever the schedule slips, the project manager needs to take corrective action. This includes determining the cause of the slippage, updating the schedule with revised dates, and informing all stakeholders of the change. If the cause is unrealistic time estimates or missing tasks, the WBS and project plan should be modified to reflect the changes. For slippage caused by an inexperienced staff member, the project manager should determine whether another person can assist or mentor the individual to prevent future slippage. If the problem is caused by team members having conflicting priorities, the project manager needs to resolve those conflicts, either by having the employee reassigned to the project fulltime or adjusting the schedule to reflect a smaller number of available hours.

Corrective actions may be needed, but the project manager's goal should be to keep schedule slippage from occurring. One of the most effective ways of doing this is to establish an environment of frequent communication. Status reports and daily team meetings help identify problems before they become major ones. In addition, if the team is colocated with the manager, Management by Walking Around is a powerful tool for learning exactly what is going on and for fostering an environment of trust. Team members who know that their manager takes an active and genuine interest in their work are often more productive than those whose managers are less involved in day-to-day work.

Although many stakeholders believe that the project schedule is fixed once it has been established and published, the reality is that it may need to be adjusted as the project proceeds. Whitten recommends refining estimates at each major

---

* Sanjiv Purba and Joseph J. Zucchero, *Project Rescue: Avoiding a Project Management Disaster* (Emeryville: McGraw-Hill/Osborne, 2004), 104.

milestone.* The theory behind this approach, which is sometimes called "rolling wave" estimation, is that the experience derived from the execution of one phase of the project helps establish more realistic estimates of the work required for the next phase. Estimates are frequently revised at toll or stage gates, with the new cost and schedule being major components of the decision whether or not to proceed with the remaining phases of the project.

Other Schedule Challenges

It is possible that a project may be on schedule but face a major scheduling challenge, such as the need to compress it and complete the project ahead of the original schedule. This occurs for a variety of reasons, including the fear that a competitor may be developing a similar product and the company's desire to be the first to market. Other reasons for wanting to shorten a project schedule include new regulations that mandate the changes and internal corporate politics. Whatever the reason, the result is the same: the project manager needs to find a way to deliver the same scope in a shorter time frame. This is often referred to as project crashing.

Project Crashing

Figure 1.2 shows that the project constraints triangle is out of balance, since the time leg has been shortened. Since it has been decreed that scope will remain fixed, there is only one component that can be modified. Resources must be increased to keep the triangle in balance, with all legs touching. As is true whenever the overall schedule must be compressed, when faced when the need to crash a project, the manager must first focus on the critical path. Since that is the longest leg of the schedule, if changes are made to other legs without shortening the critical path, the project will not be completed in less time than originally scheduled.

The goal of project crashing is to identify activities where adding more resources will shorten the duration. It is important to note that when a project is crashed, costs, which are one component of resources, normally increase along with the team size. While it is true that there may be no apparent increase in costs if existing employees work unpaid overtime as a result of the schedule compression, burnout may occur, and there is a high cost to that.

Although the WWC team had been given July 1 as a target date for the project, before they received approval for the business case, Frank Seely was informed that the two companies believed they would receive approval for the merger prior to July 1. As a result, Isabelle Crumpton, the new CEO, wanted to know if it was possible to complete the building renovations a month or so early and, if so, how much extra it would cost.

---

* Whitten, *Neal Whitten's No-Nonsense Advice*, 132.

The team pulled out their high-level Gantt chart for the overall WWC headquarters building project (Figure 9.3) and began to brainstorm. They soon realized that the logical place to consider crashing was in the planning section, since all other tasks are dependent on that. Although they had no additional staff available to assign to any of the tasks, they admitted that they could hire contractors to assist with several of the activities. While this would increase the cost, since the contractors' billing rates were double the fully loaded internal cost, it might shorten the schedule.

The team proposed the following:

- Double the resources on Task 6, Finalize Customer Requirements. This would shorten the task duration from eight to five days. Note that the time was not halved, despite doubling of resources, since the team realized that additional coordination would be needed.
- Double the resources on Task 7, Develop WBS. This also shortened the duration from eight to five days.
- Triple the resources on Task 9, Draft Project Specification, shortening the duration from fifteen to six days.

In addition, the team used a technique sometimes called fast-tracking and considered which tasks might be begun in parallel rather than being done serially. Although they ran the risk that there might be some rework required, they decided that Task 10, Calculate Costs and Benefits, could begin as soon as the WBS was completed (Task 7) rather than waiting for the completion of specifications (Task 9). As shown on Figure 19.1, these revisions reduced the duration of the planning phase from fifty-two to twenty-six days and shortened the overall project by more than a month.

Budget

Cost control is an important element of project management and is the reason why large and lengthy projects often have a person with an accounting background responsible for recording and monitoring costs. That person is responsible for ensuring that employees submit time sheets on a regular basis so that internal labor costs can be calculated and that all other costs, such as contractor bills and materials, are tracked. Although the person may be responsible for tracking costs, it is the project manager's responsibility to review all costs and ensure that they, like scope and schedule, remain within bounds.

Earned Value Analysis

A simple method of monitoring costs is to compare the amount actually spent against the budget. Although this provides a basic measurement, it does not consider

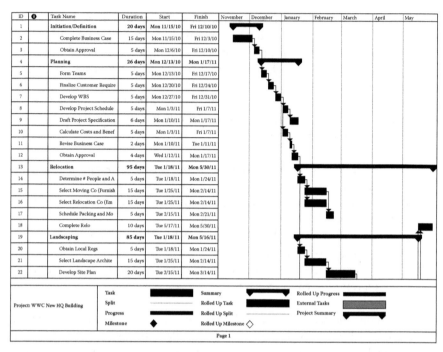

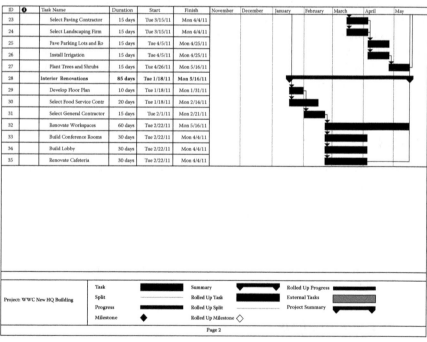

Figure 19.1   High-level Gantt chart after project crashing.

whether or not a task is complete and may, therefore, be misleading. A more sophisticated technique for determining how well a project is performing is Earned Value Analysis (EVA). This uses budget and actual cost data for each WBS task not only to evaluate that activity but also to estimate the overall progress of the project.

There are a number of calculations in EVA, most of which are based on three pieces of information:

■ The budget—This is the cost that the original plan allocated for a specific task. It is referred to as Budgeted Cost of Work Scheduled (BCWS) and represents the total cost expected to be incurred for the task when it is complete.
■ The actual cost—This is the amount actually spent on the task as of the reporting period. It is referred to as Actual Cost of Work Performed (ACWP). As its name implies, it may or may not be the total that will ultimately be spent on the task.
■ Percentage complete—This reflects how much of the task has been completed at the time of the report.

The key formulas associated with EVA are shown on Table 19.1.

EVA allows the project manager to evaluate the project in terms of both cost and schedule. Budgeted Cost of Work Performed (BCWP) or Earned Value (EV) reflects the amount that should have been spent on this task to complete the amount of work that has been done. It is a simple calculation, the multiplication of percentage complete by the budget (BCWS). BWCP can then be used to determine whether the task is on budget. This is done by calculating the variance. Cost Variance (CV) indicates the difference between the amount that should have been spent (BCWP) and the amount that has actually been spent (ACWP) and is

Table 19.1 Earned Value Analysis Terms and Formulas

Acronym	Description	Formula
BCWP or EV	Budgeted cost of work performed or earned value	BCWP = BCWS × percent complete
CV	Cost variance	CV = BCWP − ACWP
SV	Schedule variance	SV = BCWP − BCWS
CPI	Cost performance index	CPI = BCWP/ACWP
SPI	Schedule performance index	SPI = BCWP/BCWS
EAC	Estimate at completion	EAC = total original budgeted cost/CPI
SAC	Schedule at completion	SAC = total original time scheduled (weeks, months, etc.)/SPI

calculated by subtracting ACWP from BCWP. If the cost variance is negative, the task cost more than was planned.

BCWP can also be used to determine whether the task is on schedule. Schedule Variance (SV) is the calculation of the difference between the amount that was scheduled to have been spent for the task when it is fully complete (BCWS) and the amount that should have been spent on the work that was actually completed (BCWP). BCWS is subtracted from BCWP. If the schedule variance is negative, the task took longer to accomplish than was planned.

Because some managers prefer ratios rather than absolute variances, EVA provides for them. The budgeted cost of work performed can be used to calculate performance indices. These are ratios rather than simple variances and are calculated by dividing BCWP by actual cost of work performed to determine the Cost Performance Index (CPI) or by the budgeted cost of work scheduled to determine the Schedule Performance Index (SPI). In either case, an index of less than 1 indicates that the project is underperforming. If CPI is less than 1, the project is over budget. If SPI is less than 1, the project is behind schedule.

Besides indicating current performance, CPI and SPI can be applied to the overall project cost and time estimates to determine the budget Estimate at Completion (EAC) or the Schedule at Completion (SAC). Each of these calculations is the result of dividing the original budget or schedule by the appropriate index.

Figure 19.2 shows the various EVA calculations applied to the Planning phase of the WWC headquarters building project shown on Figure 19.1. When using EVA, it is important not to micro-manage. If Jim were to focus exclusively on Task 9, which is both behind schedule and over budget, he might believe his project was in more trouble than it actually was. Although the spreadsheet calculates CPI, SPI, EAC, and SAC at the task level, the most meaningful calculations are those gained by aggregating all experiences to date. While it is important to determine how an individual task is performing against expectations (the CV and SV for that task), since corrective actions can only be taken at the task level, it is difficult to extrapolate overall project performance from a single task. That is the reason that the indices and "at completion" estimates are of more value when applied to the whole project rather than a single task.

Responsibility

Although the overall responsibility for monitoring the project rests with the project manager, except on small projects managers may want to delegate some of that responsibility. As Chapter 17 pointed out, it is often helpful to have a single point of contact for receiving and tracking scope change requests. Similarly, it may be beneficial to have a person with an accounting or finance background responsible for monitoring the budget and providing reports to the project manager.

Task #	Task Description	BCWS	ACWP	% Compl	BCWP	CV	SV	CPI	SPI	EAC*	SAC**
5	Form Teams	5000	4900	100	5000	100	0	1.02	1.00	3,920,000	24
6	Finalize Customer Requirements	8000	10000	100	8000	−2000	0	0.80	1.00	5,000,000	24
7	Develop WBS	8000	11000	100	8000	−3000	0	0.73	1.00	5,500,000	24
8	Develop Project Schedule	5000	5200	100	5000	−200	0	0.96	1.00	4,160,000	24
9	Draft Project Specifications	15000	14500	72	10800	−3700	−4200	0.74	0.72	5,370,370	33.33
10	Calculate Costs and Benefits	5000	4500	80	4000	−500	−1000	0.89	0.80	4,500,000	30
11	Revise Business Case										
12	Obtain Approval										
	Total-to-Date	46000	50100		40800	−9300	−5200	0.81	0.89	4,911,765	27.06
*	Original budget = 4,000,000										
**	Original schedule = 24 weeks										

Figure 19.2 Earned Value Analysis (EVA) for WWC headquarters building.

What Can Go Wrong?

Two problems project managers may experience in monitoring the project are the "hidden factory" and the "90 percent syndrome."

"Hidden factory" is a term some companies use to describe the informal detection and correction of defects. While it is most often used in a manufacturing environment and represents errors that are corrected before they reach Quality Control and can be reported, the hidden factory may also be present in a project. If team members discover that their task specifications are ambiguous, they may either make assumptions about what should be done or they may contact the customer directly to obtain the needed information. While these approaches may resolve the problem, they mask the fact that there was an underlying error—namely, incomplete specifications. If the correction is done without the project manager's knowledge, several problems may result. First, the specifications remain incorrect. Since they form part of the project's repository, this is undesirable. Secondly, since the effort involved was not reflected in the original schedule, it is likely that there will be schedule slip. And, thirdly, future projects are unable to learn from the lesson of incomplete specs, since the problem was not reported.

Although there is no guaranteed way to prevent a hidden factory, establishing and enforcing formal processes for change control and having open communications within the team can reduce the likelihood of one.

The "90 percent syndrome" reflects the fact that some tasks reach 90 percent completion but never appear to move beyond that. It occurs most often with team members whose lack of experience leads them to underestimate the amount of work remaining. The potential problem is that the project manager will accept the 90 percent estimate as accurate and will assume that the task is close to being completed, when the reality may be that it is only half done. Managers should be alert to the possibility of an inaccurate assessment and should question any task that remains at the same percentage complete for more than one week. While the apparent stagnation may have a valid cause, it should be questioned and, if needed, additional resources should be provided to help complete the task.

Monitoring and controlling are important aspects of a project manager's responsibility. Fortunately, simple techniques can help ensure that problems are identified before they become serious enough to destroy the project.

Chapter 20

Quality and Control

It is possible for a project to be completed on schedule and within budget and still not be considered a success. The reason is simple: quality. If the quality does not meet the customer's expectations, nothing else matters. Although many project managers focus heavily on schedule and budget, quality is sometimes relegated to a secondary role. However, it is such an important aspect of project management that Morris and Sember consider it one leg of what they call the "iron triangle," their version of the project constraints triangle shown as Figure 1.1 that has cost, schedule, and quality as its components.*

While it is arguable whether quality should replace scope as a primary project constraint, few would dispute the importance of quality, and certainly not a Six Sigma company with its emphasis on quality as the way to attain customer satisfaction. That is why quality measures form an integral part of every Six Sigma project and why they should be included in all projects, not simply those initiated by Six Sigma companies.

Quality Assurance vs. Quality Control

When discussing quality, it is important to distinguish between quality assurance and quality control. Classic quality control inspects products to find defects, then corrects them. Quality assurance, which had its origins in W. Edwards Deming's principles of quality, seeks to prevent those defects before they can occur and has as one of its precepts that quality assurance should be an integral

---

* Rick A. Morris and Brette McWhorter Sember, *Project Management That Works* (New York: AMACOM, 2008), 65.

Table 20.1   Comparison of Six Sigma Quality Assurance and Quality Control

	Action Taken	Action Is On	Effect Is	Effect Is On	Need to Repeat
Quality Control	Inspect	Product	Correction of error	1 product	Constantly
Six Sigma/ Quality Assurance	Analyze	Process	Prevention of defect	All products	None

part of the process, not a step that is tacked on at the end. The difference is analogous to the difference between fire fighting and fire prevention. Six Sigma, which is an extension of Deming's quality movement, focuses on the process rather than the product, analyzing the process to determine what is causing the problem, then changing it to ensure that product defects are not created. As shown on Table 20.1, the effect of prevention is widespread and permanent. It also results in lower costs, because the earlier a problem is found and corrected, the less costly that problem becomes.

Although projects are by their nature unique—unlike a manufacturing process, which is (or should be) consistent and unchanging—project management itself can benefit from the rigor of quality assurance. Prevention of errors is the reason for a formal project management methodology, which helps ensure that no critical tasks are omitted, and for the establishment of a project management office, which provides experience and expertise gained on previous projects to assist each team with its unique challenges.

The reality is, a project requires both defect prevention and correction, because it is unrealistic to expect that there will be no errors. Defect prevention, aka quality assurance, begins with careful planning, peer review of all documents, and development of a Failure Modes and Effects Analysis (FMEA) to identify potential risks and determine ways to mitigate them.

Defect correction involves inspecting or testing every aspect of the project's deliverables, followed by correcting any errors that were detected. This is classic quality control. The project team should, however, take one additional step. It should consider each defect that was identified as an opportunity to prevent future ones. Rather than simply correcting a problem, each should be evaluated to determine the cause and whether the same error might occur elsewhere in the project. If that possibility exists, corrective actions should be undertaken immediately to prevent the problem from occurring. An error log similar to the one shown as Figure 20.1 provides valuable information to the project team and can benefit future projects.

				Prepared By	Harry Parr
Project Name	WWC Headquarters				
WBS Task	308 - Report time in cafeteria line			Date	3/15/2011

Error	Type of Error			Root Cause					Phase Error Was Introduced				
	Erroneous Logic	Missing Logic	Standards Violated	Ambiguous Reqmts	Carelessness	Design Defects	Incomplete Reqmts	Lack of Training	Coding	Program Design	Technical Design	Functional Design	Requirements Definition
Requirement to ensure that tray chip has been reset was not incorporated into module		1			1				1				
Requirement to validate checkout line was hard coded rather than using standard table			1					1	1				
Requirement for tracking trays that are removed from cafeteria is missing		1					1						1
Totals	0	2	1	0	1	0	1	1	2	0	0	0	1

Figure 20.1 Error log.

Responsibility for Quality Control

Although the project manager, as always, has the ultimate responsibility for the quality of the project's deliverables, testing and inspection is normally a multistage task, with immediate responsibility at lower levels in the project team. The first review is typically an internal one, conducted by team members, with the second testing done by customers. While both the peer review and the customer inspection are essential, particularly for complex projects and those involving computer software, the importance of having independent professional testers involved in the process cannot be overemphasized.

Both team members and customers test with the objective of proving that everything works as expected. This is their natural bias. Professional testers, on the other hand, have as their objective proving that the product *does not* work. This is a critical distinction. Professional testers are the ones who will stress the limits, who will ignore normal boundaries and enter what should be impossible combinations of data. They are the ones who have the tenacity to test every field on every screen. Because they have no pride of authorship in the product, they are willing to uncover every possible flaw. They are, in short, a valuable resource for creating a defect-free product.

The Four Elements of Control

The fact that the third phase of a project is called Execution and *Control* indicates how important the issue of control is. As DeFuria states, "The purpose of all control is to keep variance within acceptable limits."[*] But, to do that, the project team needs to be able to determine how great that variance is and, as a corollary, what has caused it. This is why Kerzner points out that there are three aspects to control: measuring, evaluating, and correcting.[†] Although he is correct, there is one additional element that needs to be included: reporting. For a project manager, control involves all four responsibilities, beginning with measurement.

Measurement

As a Six Sigma company, GWC had a lot of experience with measurement. Measurement is, after all, the second phase of any Six Sigma project. When he convened a meeting to identify key measurements, Jim Wang told the WWC team that GWC measured everything. He was quick to point out, though, that that was an exaggeration and that one of the Six Sigma tenets was to measure only what you value. A family discussing its vacation trip would be unlikely to cite the number of times the RV's wheels revolved. Instead, they might mention the number of miles they had traveled that day. Although both could be measured, only the latter had value to them.

---

[*] Guy L. DeFuria, *Project Management Recipes for Success* (Boca Raton: Auerbach, 2009), 172

[†] Harold Kerzner, *Project Management: A Systems Approach to Planning, Scheduling, and Controlling*, 9th ed. (Hoboken: John Wiley & Sons, 2006), 193.

Just as requirements can be evaluated using the SMART system, Jim explained that an acronym can be used to describe characteristics of good measurements. Measurements should RAVE. That is they should be:

- *Relevant*—For the WWC headquarters building project, there would be no relevance to measuring the number of pallets of sod delivered or the average length of the fluorescent bulbs installed in conference rooms. Neither could be directly translated into the customers' requirement for energy efficiency.
- *Adequate to detect changes*—If the length of time employees spent in line in the cafeteria were measured in days rather than minutes, it would be impossible to determine whether the new cafeteria met the requirement of spending no more than five minutes in line. A smaller unit of measure was needed.
- *Valid and consistent from time to time*—Since the team knew that schedule fidelity was an important element to measure, when it first proposed measuring the number of days spent on each task, it envisioned a simple calculation: date task was completed minus date task began. The team soon realized that that was neither valid nor consistent, since it did not account for nonworking days like weekends or holidays.
- *Easy*—Although there might have been value in measuring the net cost of the cafeteria on a weekly basis, the company's existing financial systems had a monthly reporting cycle. Using the existing system was easier (and less expensive) than creating a new one, yet it still met the objective of determining cost performance.

In reviewing customers' requirements, the team decided that four items were the most important to measure during the life of the project: budget, schedule, speed of processing scope change requests, and errors. Other measurements that would indicate whether or not the project had met its objectives would be instituted once the project was complete. For the cafeteria, those measurements would include the net monthly cost of the cafeteria, the number of injuries sustained there, the average time in line, and overall customer satisfaction with the menu and services.

The team also knew the value of developing metrics rather than simply measurements. The distinction is that a measurement is a single dimension, capacity, or quantity, whereas a metric is a value calculated from multiple measurements. In most cases, a metric is of more value, because it puts the measurement into a context, just as Earned Value Analysis (EVA) puts spending-to-date into context with the percentage of work completed.

Using the example of the project budget, dollars spent-to-date (or Actual Cost of Work Performed [ACWP] in EVA terminology) is a measurement. Without a context, it is of little meaning, since there is no way of evaluating whether the amount spent was what was expected. In contrast, Cost Variance (CV) is by definition a metric, since it is calculated using two measurements: ACWP and BCWP (Budgeted Cost of Work Performed). It is also a more useful piece of information for the project team and everyone associated with it than simple dollars spent, since it compares the actual expenditure to the amount that should have been spent.

Because any metrics that are developed will be used to determine the success of the project, it is essential that the team use only reliable measurements. As part of their Six Sigma program, GWC had developed a metric reliability assessment spreadsheet to help determine which metrics would be most valid. The spreadsheet includes an evaluation of both the data being collected and the person who will collect that data, since the goal is to have repeatable, reproducible, objective measurements.

When Jim saw several team members' confused expressions, he realized that it was time for a couple definitions. He explained that if the same person measures the same item more than once and has the same results, the measurement is *repeatable*. It is *reproducible* if a different person measures the same item and reports the same results as the first person. An *objective* measurement does not require any evaluation by the rater or inspector. It is simply observed and reported. Length of time in line is objective; quality of food served in the cafeteria is not.

Appendix E details the use of a metric reliability assessment matrix. The one the team developed for the four key metrics for the WWC headquarters building project is shown as Figure 20.2. While a metric reliability assessment may appear to be overkill on many projects, the reality is that it is a useful tool, since it helps identify weaknesses in measurements. As Figure 20.2 shows, although budget and schedule fidelity are typically more important measures of the project's success than the speed with which scope change requests are processed, their reliability is lower.

Evaluation

Lori Woods was clearly unhappy. "What's the point of all this?" she demanded. "I've led a lot of projects, and I never developed metrics."

Jim should not have been surprised. Lori had complained about what she called his unnecessary bureaucracy more than once. The problem, Jim knew, was not simply the use of standard procedures. The underlying cause of Lori's complaints was the difference in corporate culture between GWC and IW. As a long-term IW employee, Lori was accustomed to operating in an informal environment where project performance was reported verbally and metrics were rarely developed. Though he had held several one-on-one discussions with Lori, today's outburst told Jim she still was not convinced of the value of standard processes for managing projects.

It was Dustin Monroe, Lori's peer, who explained that metrics were input to the second aspect to control: evaluation. Dustin agreed with Lori that there is no point in taking measurements and developing metrics if no action will be taken based on them. That is the reason for the precept of "measure what you value"; however, it is not enough to simply measure. The purpose of establishing metrics is to facilitate monitoring of the project. The metrics chosen should track the project's vital signs,

Project:	WWC Headquarters Building							
Prepared By:	Geraldine Kelly							
Date Prepared:	January 10, 2011							
Metric	Measurement	Collector	Data Reliability	Data Repeatability	Collection Delays	Collector Availability	Total Metric Reliability	Comments
Budget fidelity (CV) *Calculation = (BCWS * %Complete) - ACWP*	Actual cost of work performed (ACWP)	Finance Department	10	7	4	10	31	Outside materials costs are entered only monthly
	Budgeted cost of work scheduled (BCWS)	Project Team	7	10	10	10	37	Established as part of WBS; accuracy dependent on individual experience
	% complete	Individual Team Member Responsible for Work	4	10	4	7	25	Accuracy dependent on individual
Average			7	9	6	9	31	
Schedule fidelity (SV) *Calculation = (BCWS * %Complete) - BCWS*	Budgeted cost of work scheduled (BCWS)	Project Team	7	10	10	10	37	Established as part of WBS; accuracy dependent on individual experience
	% complete	Individual Team Member Responsible for Work	4	10	4	7	25	Accuracy dependent on individual
Average			5.5	10	7	8.5	31	

Figure 20.2   Metric reliability assessment spreadsheet.

% Scope change requests processed within 24 hours of receipt	Calculation = (changes with requestor notified / all changes received) * 100	Count of all scope change requests received	Team Member Responsible for Scope Change Requests	10	10	10	40	Data taken from change request database; accuracy dependent on timely entry of data
		Count of scope change requests with requestor notified of impact	Team Member Responsible for Scope Change Requests	10	10	10	40	Data taken from change request database; accuracy dependent on timely entry of data; metrics are calculated weekly
Average				**10**	**10**	**10**	**40**	
% Rework caused by specification errors	Calculation = (rework caused by specification errors / total rework) * 100	Total increased effort due to rework	Team Lead	7	7	4	22	
		Rework caused by specification errors	Team Lead	7	7	4	22	Requires accuracy in categorizing error
Average				**7**	**7**	**4**	**22**	

Figure 20.2 (Continued)

much as blood pressure and cholesterol readings are used to monitor a person's health. And, just as a physician takes specific action when presented with elevated blood pressure, the project manager should have a plan for dealing with variances.

That plan begins with the determination of acceptable variance levels. Although every project manager hopes that the project will remain on schedule and within budget, the reality is that some variances will occur. As was true when calculating EVA and the related indices, the key is to avoid overreacting to individual variation but rather to focus on trends, attempting to correct them before they become major problem areas. Instead of responding to each variance as it occurs, the project manager can benefit from the development of a control plan as part of the Execution and Control phase. Because it should be created at the same time that metrics are identified, the control plan was one of the items on the measurement meeting agenda.

A control plan, as shown on Table 20.2, lists each metric and assigns an acceptable variance level to it. Variances below this threshold are considered normal and will not be addressed. This is consistent with most manufacturing processes that establish a tolerance range for results rather than expect the process to operate at a single level. In manufacturing terms, upper and lower specification limits are established by the customer, and any product that is within those limits is acceptable. Variances equal to or greater than the threshold must be addressed. That is why an action plan is developed, showing what will be done each time an unacceptable variance is encountered.

The advantage of a formal control plan is that it eliminates the need for judgment calls each time a problem is identified, thus saving time and ensuring consistency throughout the life of the project. It should also be noted that by having a standard process that has been communicated to all team members, individual employees do not feel as if they are being singled out unfairly if their work exceeds a variance threshold. This helps maintain a productive relationship between the project manager and team members.

Correction

As Chapter 19 pointed out, it is important to implement corrective actions whenever problems are uncovered. The actions shown on the control plan are the first step in correcting the underlying problem; however, it is likely that additional actions will be required. Chapter 19 discussed methods of dealing with the most common problem, schedule slippage.

Reporting

Not only is it important to actually use the metrics that the team develops, but it is equally important to report those metrics to the team and other stakeholders. Although there are a number of techniques for reporting, the WWC team used a scorecard. As shown on Figure 20.3, the scorecard is a single page, showing each of the four key

Table 20.2 Control Plan

Metric	Variance Threshold	Action Plan
Budget fidelity (individual work unit level)	≤ 3%	If under budget: 1. Determine whether percent complete estimate is correct. 2. If estimate appears to be too high, revise estimate and recalculate. If over budget: 1. Determine cause. 2. Search for ways to reduce costs on other tasks to bring overall budget into desired range.
Schedule fidelity (individual work unit level)	≤ 5%	If ahead of schedule: 1. Determine whether percent complete estimate is correct. 2. If estimate appears to be too high, revise estimate and recalculate. If behind schedule: 1. Determine cause. 2. If task is not yet complete, determine whether adding staff can bring it back onto schedule. 3. If task is complete, search for ways to reduce time on dependent tasks to bring overall project back onto schedule.
% Scope change requests processed within 24 hours of receipt (total for week)	≥ 96%	1. Determine cause. 2. Implement procedure to prevent recurrence.
% Rework caused by specification errors (total for week)	≤ 7%	1. Analyze each request to determine whether there is a common cause. 2. If there is a common cause, notify the PMO so that other projects can be aware of it.

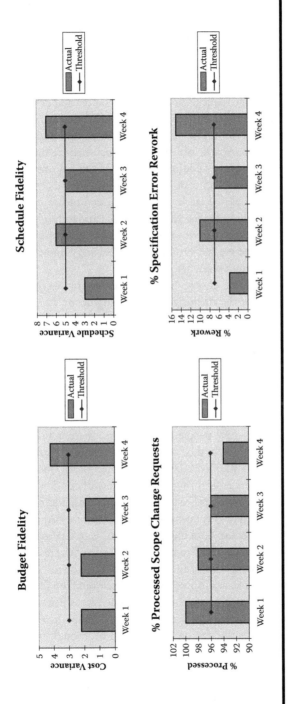

Figure 20.3 Scorecard.

metrics graphed against the established goals. The scorecard is created at the end of each week and is posted on the project's website no later than noon the following Monday.

After they developed the scorecard, the team realized that it could be confusing, since there was no indication of whether the threshold represented the highest or the lowest acceptable value. In the case of budget fidelity, schedule fidelity, and percent rework, the goal was to remain below the threshold, whereas the greater the percentage of scope change requests processed, the better. For consistency, the team revised the scope change request metric to calculate *unprocessed* requests. By doing that, all thresholds shown on the scorecard represented upper specification limits.

In addition to the scorecard, the WWC project website had a page showing traffic light (red, yellow, green) coding for each of the key metrics. Designed to give casual browsers a quick indication of the project's status, the page shows the four key metrics with a colored circle next to it. Green indicates that the variance has been below the threshold for the past four weeks and requires no action. Yellow indicates caution. While the current week's variance is below the threshold, at least one of the previous three weeks' variance exceeded it. Variances that exceed the threshold during the current week are coded red.

The methods that teams choose to track and report project status will vary. What is important is that the tracking and reporting occur.

What Can Go Wrong?

Two common problems associated with the quality and control aspect of this project phase are incomplete testing and time wasted on the wrong measurements.

- *Incomplete Testing*—Few people enjoy testing. There is little glory associated with uncovering errors, and, if testing or inspection is done by peers, there is the possibility for strained relationships among team members. As a result, many team members rush through their review of another's work rather than subjecting it to a comprehensive test. This is one reason errors escape detection and why the finished project does not meet the customer's quality requirements. The single most effective cure for this problem is to use professional testers or trained quality assurance staff to perform the bulk of the testing. Although this may appear to represent an additional cost, it frees the rest of the project team to work on other tasks and is likely to improve overall quality.

- *Time Wasted on Wrong Measurements*—Some teams become enamored with measurement for the sake of measurement, perhaps in the mistaken belief that if they collect sufficient data, there will be enough positive results that stakeholders will not notice the areas where the project has not met expectations. Metric overload accomplishes nothing but wasting time. It is the project manager's responsibility to apply the KISS principle and measure only the few items that have the greatest impact on the project.

Chapter 21

Organizational Readiness

A project is successful if and only if its customers are satisfied. Even though those customers, or someone within their chain of command, may have initiated the project, satisfying them is not always easy. The reason is simple: by definition, a project creates change. As Chapter 2 pointed out, change is difficult, particularly for what Conner calls "targets," the people who will be directly impacted by the change.

Schwalbe claims, "Organizational issues are often the most difficult part of working on and managing projects."* Richman agrees, citing knowledge of the organization as a key project management skill.† Knowledge of the organization involves more than reading a company's organization chart. It means understanding the corporate culture. How formal is the company? Is the organization hierarchical or matrix based? What are the average age and tenure of the employees? How high is annual employee turnover? Are promotions normally made from within or through outside hiring? The answers to these and dozens of other questions define a company's culture.

From the project manager's perspective, one of the most critical questions is how the company perceives change. Does it welcome innovation, or is change merely tolerated? If the company has been in existence for a long time, has a stable product line, and has survived without mergers and restructurings, it may be less comfortable with change than a young company with a rapidly evolving product line that has recently gone from being privately held to becoming a publicly traded corporation.

Jim knew that among the major challenges he faced were the cultural differences between GWC and IW. Within the team itself, he received the most resistance from

---

* Kathy Schwalbe, *Information Technology Project Management* (Cambridge, MA: Course Technology, 2000), 30.
† Larry Richman, *Project Management Step-by-Step* (New York: AMACOM, 2002), 31.

the IW staff, who were unaccustomed to the Six Sigma–based processes he used for managing a project. Customers were different. Though IW was the younger company, it had had few organizational changes during its existence and was less receptive to change than the GWC staff, who had endured numerous reorganizations and were accustomed to being agents of change thanks to their Six Sigma training. While neither organization welcomed the merger, especially since it would be accompanied by layoffs and relocation, the GWC staff approached it with resignation rather than outright hostility.

Even within a single company, culture may vary by department. The Information Technology Department may be less traditional than Finance, and Marketing may value innovation more than Facilities and Services. Understanding the overall culture and the subculture of the group most impacted by the project is important, because it helps identify the most effective methodologies for easing customers' transition through the changes the project will effect.

The key to success is the "no surprises" doctrine. Although it is normally understood that there should be no surprises for the customers when the project is complete, the same rule should be in effect throughout the life of the project. Three elements contribute to creating an environment devoid of surprises: involvement, communication, and training. While the techniques used will vary based on the corporate culture, the precepts remain constant: keep customers involved, communicate with them regularly, and ensure that they are fully trained.

Involvement

Although customers, or at least a group of customers, are involved in the early stages of the project while requirements are being gathered, they often have little contact with the team during the execution phase. The result is that they may feel like outsiders rather than an important component of the project. This can create serious problems. There are two typical reactions: apathy and panic. While apathy, in which customers no longer care about the outcome of the project, is undesirable, panic is more dangerous. When customers experience panic, they may be convinced that the project will never be completed or, if it is, that it will not meet their needs. Panicked customers can be as irrational as people in the first stage of the SARAH model, escalating their concerns and demanding changes in the project team—in short, creating more work and stress for the project manager.

One way to prevent these problems, or at least reduce the likelihood of their occurring, is to ensure that customers understand their role in the project. "Part," another term for role, is one of Bridges' elements of successful change, the Four Ps that were discussed in Chapter 2. If customers understand the overall plan (another of the Four Ps), they will also understand when they will be involved and what is happening while they are not active participants. This can help avoid panic. So too can frequent communication.

Communication

It is impossible to overestimate the importance of communication in establishing and maintaining a productive relationship with customers. Frequent targeted communication helps them feel involved, even when they are not taking an active role. Because they are aware of what progress is being made, they are less likely to panic, and their interest in the outcome of the project remains elevated.

The two adjectives—*frequent* and *targeted*—are critical. Communication should be frequent, ideally regularly scheduled, so that customers have no need to resort to the rumor mill for information about the project. It should also be targeted—that is, appropriate for and of interest to the recipients. Although a report of budget fidelity would be valuable to the Finance Department, the employees who are facing relocation would be more interested in the project's schedule.

Table 18.1 lists basic communications techniques, all of which can be valuable. The ones that will have greatest applicability to an individual project will depend on both the nature and length of the project and the corporate culture. The WWC team had several heated discussions over the most appropriate format for their progress reports. IW had a casual open-door culture and wanted to develop a cartoon character as the spokesperson for the project. This character, whom they called Moving Moe, would appear on everything from the team's website to the posters that would be hung in both companies' cafeterias and meeting rooms. The GWC team members knew that their employees, accustomed to a more formal environment, would not be amused by Moving Moe and might view the use of a cartoon character as a trivialization of the relocation.

Although the team discussed the possibility of having different communications mechanisms for the two companies, they quickly realized that that approach was undesirable, since it merely continued the distinction between them. The resolution was to make the text as light-hearted as possible to appeal to the IW staff but to eliminate Moe in recognition of GWC's more serious communication style.

Training

Training is the third component of a successful customer project experience. It can be viewed as a specialized type of communication. While other forms of communication stressed what was going to happen (the picture in Bridges' terminology) and how the project would unfold (the plan), training addresses how customers will use or interact with the end result.

The amount and type of training provided varies based on the project. Implementation of a new general ledger system will require more formal training than WWC's move to a new headquarters building. One thing remains constant: every project should include some form of training, although it may be nothing more than a memo. Table 21.1 provides a comparison of formal training methods.

Table 21.1   Comparison of Training Methods

Training Method	Advantages	Disadvantages
Computer-Based (CBT)	Self-paced; good for both quick and slow learners.	No interaction with other students.
	Flexible scheduling allows student to train at most productive time of day; no need to wait until a class is available.	Scheduling time to train may be difficult because of job commitments.
	May be less expensive than classroom, particularly if only a few people need to be trained.	May require special software.
Instructor-Led Classroom	Encourages interaction with other students and with instructor.	Pacing may not be ideal for all participants.
	Content can be modified during delivery to meet students' needs.	Time away from workplace may create conflicts with job assignments.
	Scheduled class ensures that training takes place.	
Instructor-Led Online	Semi-flexible scheduling allows students to read material at their most productive times.	Flexibility is not as great as CBT. (Classes are held within specific time frames, and assignments are due on a specified schedule.)
	Online chats encourage interaction with other students and with instructor.	Body language and other interpersonal cues are not available. This may decrease the instructor's ability to gauge participants' rate of learning.
	May be less expensive than classroom, particularly if only a few people need to be trained.	
	Normally requires no special software.	

Just as it was important to create a communication plan (Table 18.2), for large and complex projects where different categories of customers require different types of training, it is helpful to create a training plan that identifies the types of training to be provided as well as the target audiences. Table 21.2 shows the format of one training plan. The plan should be developed in conjunction with key customers to ensure that it will meet their needs. Like other project documents, it should undergo a formal review and approval process. Once approved, the plan serves as a primary input to the development of a training schedule.

Just as it was important to select the correct spokespersons for the project, it is important to ensure that whoever will deliver training has the skill set to do that effectively. Although using in-house staff as trainers is normally the lowest cost option, it may not be the best. When selecting in-house staff, it is essential to realize that not everyone is comfortable teaching in a classroom environment. Simply understanding the material does not qualify a person to be a facilitator. Some people who are very effective as one-on-one mentors fail in a classroom setting because it takes them out of their comfort zone and requires presentation skills they do not have.

If using outside trainers, the team should check references and ideally audit a course to be certain that the facilitators can communicate effectively. This is another case where corporate culture plays a role. Employees accustomed to formal training where they do little more than watch PowerPoint slides and take notes may not react well if the instructor uses a more participative approach.

When determining what type of training would be needed, the WWC team realized their customers' training needs fell into two different categories: familiarity with the new building and an understanding of the relocation process. Because they wanted everyone who was moving to Bluebell to feel comfortable with the building from the first day, they developed brochures showing a picture of the exterior, a site design that indicated the location of entrances and parking lots, and an interior floor plan. This was laminated and distributed to everyone, whether or not they would be part of the new company. Although the team could have reduced costs by providing the information electronically, they realized that employees would benefit from having a floor plan that they could carry with them for the first few weeks until they became familiar with their new office space. They also decided that the brochure should be available to all current employees, rather than further demoralize those whose jobs were being eliminated by excluding them from the planning process.

To address employees' need for information about the actual relocation, the team posted the company's relo policy online, developed a poster showing the URL for the policy, and hung the posters in all common areas. In addition, they scheduled weekly town hall meetings with representatives from both Human Resources and the Facilities and Services departments and established a forum for submitting questions anonymously.

Table 21.2 Training Plan Overview

Course Name or Brief Description of Training	Length (Hours)	Prerequisites	Target Participants[a]	Training Method[b]	Trainer[c]	Participant Materials[d]	Other Training Materials[e]

[a] *Target participants:* Category of customers to be trained (managers, professionals, administrative staff, etc.)
[b] *Training method:* CBT, classroom, online
[c] *Trainer:* Name of organization providing trainers; if in-house and instructor is known, use name
[d] *Participant materials:* List of all materials that will be provided to participants
[e] *Other training materials:* List of other materials that trainer will require to conduct the class

Training is critical. In many cases, it will be the customers' first experience with the product the project has produced, and first impressions matter. Developing appropriate training and having the correct trainer help ensure that the experience is positive.

What Can Go Wrong?

The two most common problems encountered in this portion of the project are lack of communication and inadequate or poor training.

- *Communication*—Although most project managers recognize the need to communicate within the team and to keep the champion informed, customers are sometimes short-changed. The solution need not be expensive or time consuming. Even simple communications like weekly e-mails that provide project updates are valuable, helping to ensure that customers do not believe the project has fallen into the black hole.
- *Training*—It can be argued that poor training is worse than none at all, because it gives customers an unfavorable introduction to the product. Effective training is training that is targeted to customers' needs and comfort zones and delivered by skilled trainers. Since a project's success is measured by how well the end result is received, this is not a place to skimp.

Chapter 22

When Murphy's Law Takes Effect
Possible Problems and Ways to Avoid Them

It is a fact of life: even the best-run projects face problems. That is the reason books like Purba and Zucchero's *Project Rescue: Avoiding a Project Management Disaster* exist. As the title suggests, the project manager's goal is to avoid a disaster, and avoidance begins with an understanding of what may occur and when. That is why each of the previous chapters of this book has included a "What Can Go Wrong?" section.

Once the project enters the Execution and Control phase, problems tend to become more obvious. There are two reasons for this: Execution and Control is normally the longest phase of a project, and it is the one that involves the most people. While it is an exaggeration to say that people equal problems, the reality is that many problems are people related. Each of the potential problems discussed below has people at its root.

Interpersonal Conflict

In a lengthy project or one that involves major change, it is likely that conflict will arise, both within the team and between the team and others, including customers. Add to that equation contractors, if they are used, and the opportunities for conflict increase. If multiple firms are providing contracting services, the situation becomes more complex with the possibility that there will be disagreements between them.

Conflict may be major; it may be minor. It cannot be prevented, but it can be—and must be—managed.

Meredith and Mantel divide conflict into a series of categories, including schedule, priorities, labor, technology, procedures, cost, and personality.* It is significant to note that labor and personality relate directly to personnel, and that, with the exclusion of technology and cost, the other conflicts would not exist if there were not individuals involved. That is why it is critical to the success of a project to know how to resolve interpersonal conflicts.

Richman[†] identifies five techniques for dealing with conflict:

- Problem solving, sometimes called confrontation
- Compromise
- Smoothing
- Forcing
- Withdrawal

Each has its value. While confrontation, the second term used to describe problem solving, may sound combative, the reality is that this technique is designed to resolve problems by having both sides address the underlying problem and reach a resolution. It is the most direct of the five techniques and one of the most likely to have a positive outcome.

Compromise involves bargaining, with the two sides searching for a resolution that will achieve at least some of their objectives. It should be noted that, although this is typically referred to as a win–win solution, neither party may be completely satisfied by the resolution.

In smoothing, the mediator seeks to minimize the conflict by identifying the points both sides have in common while avoiding the areas of disagreement. While this technique may result in less hostility, it frequently does not address the underlying issue and may be considered a delaying tactic.

When mediators force an issue, they impose their solution on both parties. The classic win–lose situation, this approach to conflict has the potential to backfire, with the losing side refusing to cooperate in the resolution. It may, however, be the only possible solution if other techniques have failed.

In withdrawal, the problem is simply ignored rather than being addressed and resolved. Although this is normally the least desirable approach to conflict, since it accomplishes nothing, it may be appropriate if the project manager/mediator determines that the conflict is trivial and will disappear without intervention.

A different approach to dealing with conflict is to determine the nature of the specific point of contention and then choose the resolution technique best suited to it.

---

* Jack R. Meredith and Samuel J. Mantel Jr., *Project Management: A Managerial Approach*, 6th ed. (Hoboken: John Wiley & Sons, 2006), 301.
† Larry Richman, *Project Management Step-by-Step* (New York: AMACOM, 2002), 218–19.

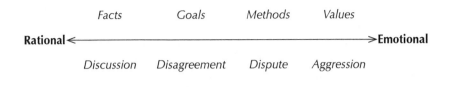

Figure 22.1 Conflict continuum.

This is sometimes referred to as the conflict continuum. As shown on Figure 22.1, conflict can be described as rational or emotional, with various steps between the two extremes. The items on top of the arrow represent the nature of the conflict, while those below it show the progression of the conflict itself.

The premise of the conflict continuum is that as conflict moves from the rational to the emotional side of the continuum, it becomes more difficult to resolve, and the reactions, shown below the arrow, become more extreme. Conflicts over facts are normally relatively simple to settle, whereas issues related to an individual's values are often nonnegotiable. Conflicts that are based on values cannot be easily resolved and should in most cases not be discussed or debated in a work environment.

Some disagreements, such as the value of low-VOC (volatile organic compounds) paint for the WWC headquarters, are easily settled. Others, such as the initial decision to merge the two companies and lay off a substantial portion of the headquarters staff, may never be resolved. The difference between them is their position on the conflict continuum. One has as its underlying nature a fact, the other a value. Disputes that revolve around facts like the question about paint are more easily resolved than those that are based on personal values, like the staff layoff issue. The reason is that factual questions relate to a person's rational side. A person's opinion can be changed by demonstrating a fact.

When Sarah Alexander, the Finance Department representative on the team, questioned the additional cost for the low-VOC paint, Roy Morgan was able to resolve the dispute by pointing out that that paint produces lower fumes, substantially fewer toxins, and results in both cleaner air and a room that can be occupied more quickly. When she understood the facts, Sarah realized that over time the paint might actually save the company money through reduced employee illness, and even if it did not, the other benefits were worth the extra cost. In contrast, values such as the importance of lifetime employment are intrinsic to the individual and will not be easily changed.

When faced with conflict, the person who is attempting to mediate should use the conflict continuum to identify the nature of the conflict. If it is caused by a disagreement over facts, it should be relatively easy to resolve by understanding the question and determining the correct answer. Facts are unambiguous. Once identified, the discussion will normally end.

If the nature of the conflict is not factual, the objective should be to move the dispute toward the rational end of the continuum by finding common ground. For example, if the disagreement is over the right way to accomplish a task (method), the dispute may be resolved by getting both parties to agree on the goal they are trying to accomplish. Once they understand that they have the same goal, they can agree to disagree on the best method of reaching that goal.

In some cases, it may be necessary to go all the way back to facts to obtain agreement. In the case of the merger and related layoffs, the fact may be that eliminating x corporate headquarters jobs through the merger will save the company y million dollars, preventing the closing of two plants with $3x$ employees. While the person's value (saving jobs) has not changed, the facts presented illustrate that the proposed merger will actually save more jobs than it will eliminate. Knowing the facts may resolve the conflict.

Change of Players

While its frequency is less than interpersonal conflict, loss of staff can have a greater effect on the project. Although it is less likely on short-term projects, it is almost an axiom that a large, lengthy project will have staff turnover. That is why, as mentioned in Chapter 8, DeMarco and Lister include employee turnover as one of the five core risks to a project.* Murphy's law says that this turnover will occur at the worst possible time, crippling the project at least temporarily.

There is virtually no way to prevent staff from leaving. "Stay bonuses," which promise payment if critical team members remain for the length of the project, may have some effect, but unless they are offered to everyone on the team, they may have the unwanted result of demoralizing those who are not included, thus creating more problems than they solve.

The best approach for dealing with potential staff turnover is to consider it a risk, include it in the risk assessment Failure Modes and Effects Analysis (FMEA) (Figure 8.2), and create a succession plan for mitigation. While this is the ideal situation, few project teams, including the WWC headquarters team, focus on loss of staff at the initial stages of the project. When brainstorming risks, they are more likely to consider problems in finding qualified team members and contractors than the possibility that key contributors may leave before the project is complete. This is a mistake, because it means that when staff turnover occurs, as it did on Jim Wang's project, the project manager must deal with it on an emergency basis rather than having prepared for it.

Jim felt as if he had been blindsided the day Roy Morgan announced his resignation. Though Roy's official reason was that his family did not want to leave California, speculation was rampant that he had been angered when he was not selected to lead the headquarters project and, believing that his career

---

* Tom DeMarco and Timothy Lister, *Waltzing with Bears: Managing Risk on Software Projects* (New York: Dorset House, 2003), 102.

was stalled if not dead, he had begun his job search. The reasons did not matter; what did was that Jim had a vacancy in his organization, and he had no simple options.

Jim had considered the possibility that Lori, who had been vocal in her discontent, might leave, but he had thought that quiet, hard-working Roy was as content as anyone on the project. Too late, Jim realized that he should have followed DeMarco and Lister's advice and recognized staff turnover as a risk. He had no plan, and after reviewing the team's composition and workload, he realized he could not reassign anyone. Jim's only recourse was to assume Roy's responsibilities in addition to his own.

Whether planned in advance or devised when it occurs, the strategy for dealing with staff turnover typically varies depending on the function of the person who needs to be replaced.

- *Team Members (worker bees)*—These are the arms and legs of the project, the people who are doing the majority of the work. While they are not interchangeable, it may be possible to compensate for the loss of one by having remaining staff work overtime, employing contractors, or recruiting other in-house staff to the project. Each of these approaches has a cost. Overtime can create burnout; contractors normally cost more than in-house staff and may result in budget overruns; in-house staff may not have the needed skills and may require mentoring by other team members. Whatever approach is taken, the project manager should review the schedule carefully when a team member leaves. In many cases, loss of staff will create a delay. If a delay is anticipated, the schedule should be revised and the new target dates communicated to all stakeholders. In most cases, it is a mistake to expect to be able to maintain the original schedule, even if new staff is hired.
- *Project Leaders*—Losing a project leader is normally more serious than the loss of a worker bee. The three approaches suggested for replacing team members can be considered possible solutions for the loss of a project leader; however, there are additional caveats. It is unlikely that asking other project leaders to work overtime will be an effective resolution, since one of the expectations of a project leader is that the individual will be available while the team members are working. Adding nights and weekends to the project leader's workload does not address that issue, and the project runs the risk of more serious problems if a single project leader is spread too thin and unable to handle either the originally scheduled work or the new responsibilities. This proved to be the case when Jim assumed Roy's responsibilities. He soon discovered himself overworked and close to burnout. Concerned by the possibility of losing Jim as well as Roy, Frank volunteered to chair many of the meetings Jim (in his role as overall project manager) had previously led. Jim also decided to compartmentalize his time, arranging to handle Roy's former team's work during

the mornings and his original responsibilities in the afternoons. Although this was not an ideal situation, it helped relieve the pressure on Jim.

While it is possible to hire contractors to serve as project leaders, the risk is higher than reassigning in-house staff, since outsiders are not familiar with the corporate culture and may inadvertently create additional problems. The sensitivity of the merger and related planned layoffs was the primary reason Jim did not attempt to fill Roy's position with a contractor.

Reassigning in-house staff, ideally promoting someone who is already on the project team, is often the least risky approach, although it creates a ripple effect, since the person who is being promoted will need to be replaced. As was true in the case of team member turnover, it is important to reassess the project and potentially revise the reschedule when a project leader must be replaced.

■ *Project Manager*—Loss of the project manager almost always creates serious problems and results in schedule slippage. This is because the project manager is the keystone to the project and is frequently the only person who understands the entire project. Loss of a project manager affects all aspects of the project, including relations with customers and within the team.

It should be noted that a change in the project manager may be either voluntary or involuntary. While the official name of this phase is Execution and Control, for a poorly run project, this is the panic stage. If a project is in trouble, senior management or the project's champion may believe that the way to turn the project around is to replace the project manager. Similarly, project managers may believe that failure will destroy their career at the company and may choose to leave, deserting what they believe to be a sinking ship. In either case, the effect on the project will be significant. While there is no prevention, because of the project manager's importance to the overall project, a succession plan should be part of the initial FMEA.

■ *Champion*—Occasionally the champion will leave the company or be reassigned during the life of the project. While it may appear that the project can and should continue without interruption, since all the "doers" are still in place, whether or not this is the correct approach depends on the state of the project and the time until completion. If the project is on schedule and close to completion (within three months of the scheduled end date), it may be appropriate to continue without a new champion. If, however, there are more than three months until the project's scheduled end date or the project is encountering problems that may result in delays or budget overruns, or if there are tollgates to pass, the project manager should take three steps:

1. Request a replacement champion.
2. Brief the replacement on the project.
3. Gain formal commitment from the new champion to continue the project.

In simplest terms, the project manager is returning to the Initiation/Definition phase and is once again seeking approval for the project. Failing to do this means that the project has no champion, and, as discussed in Chapter 5, an effective, engaged, and enthusiastic champion is one key to project success.

Change of Priorities

Although it is less likely on a short project, a change of corporate priorities can occur at any time, resulting in what was previously viewed as a critical project being superseded in importance by a new one. The consequences of the priority shift will vary, depending on the company and the project itself. Possibilities include the following.

- The project may continue, but some staff may be reassigned. In this case, it is essential to review and revise the schedule.
- The project may have a temporary hiatus. If this is proposed, the project manager should ensure that the champion understands the problems that may result. Not only will there be a loss of momentum, meaning that the team will need a start-up phase when the project is resumed, but some team members may be permanently reassigned. If a hiatus occurs, it will be necessary to review and revise the schedule before the project can resume.

In either case, it is likely that both the team and customers will become discouraged. This is normal, since the project has, in effect, been demoted, and no one enjoys a demotion. Even if the project manager cannot reverse the change in priorities, it is possible to mitigate the negative effects through communication. In this case, the project manager becomes a cheerleader, reminding everyone of why the project was important enough to be initiated and reassuring them that the work will be completed, albeit not on the original schedule. As is always true, it is essential that the project manager be honest with team members and customers at the same time that he or she presents the project in the best possible light.

Lack of Enthusiasm

While priority changes come from outside the project, lack of enthusiasm is an internal problem. It is most common on projects of long duration when team members feel as if they are on a treadmill, running faster and faster but never reaching the end. Unlike many of the problems addressed in this chapter, this one can be prevented. Two techniques are particularly effective: scheduling and communication. Tasks with short durations and clearly defined deliverables give team members a sense of completion and help prevent the treadmill effect. Just as importantly, the project manager should continue to remind everyone on the team of the Four Ps (purpose, picture, plan, and part). Understanding how each person's work fits into the overall picture and what part each person is expected to perform helps keep enthusiasm high.

Lack of Funding

Occasionally project funding is reduced or eliminated, even though the project itself is showing no sign of failure. In that case, while the project cannot continue as scheduled, the project manager may want to attempt to overturn the decision and get funding reinstated. This is one time when it is essential to enlist allies—namely, the project's champion and key customers. The champion has (or should have) the clout to approach the highest levels of the company to determine why the decision was made and to potentially have it reversed. Since customers are the reason the project was undertaken in the first place, they are logical candidates to fight for its survival. If the need that triggered the project still exists, key customers should be willing to add their voices and influences to the champion's. There is no guarantee that even the most persuasive of champions and customers can achieve the goal of reinstating funding, but project managers who believe in their projects will try.

Other Problems

The most common other problems, scope creep and schedule slippage, were discussed in Chapter 19. In addition to these potential problems, the project manager needs to be alert for symptoms that something is wrong. Purba and Zucchero provide a list of telltale symptoms of a project in trouble, including the absence of problem reporting.* They point out that problems are normal on a project, and if none is reported, it is possible that the team either does not understand the full requirements or is deliberately suppressing bad news. Morris and Sember's list of signs of a failing project includes a lack of team involvement.† This is similar to the lack of enthusiasm discussed above but is more extreme, verging on apathy. In both cases, the project manager should be aware that the project is not proceeding as expected and should intervene to determine the underlying cause of the symptoms and correct the problem before it has a substantial effect on the project.

The bottom line is, it is the project manager's responsibility to attempt to resolve all problems, even those that appear to be outside his or her control. Murphy cannot be allowed to join the project team.

---

* Sanjiv Purba and Joseph J. Zucchero, *Project Rescue: Avoiding a Project Management Disaster* (Emeryville: McGraw-Hill/Osborne, 2004), 16.
† Rick A. Morris and Brette McWhorter Sember, *Project Management That Works* (New York: AMACOM, 2008), 42–43.

THE CLOSEOUT PHASE

With the Execution and Control phase complete, the project might appear to be over. It is not. There is one more phase, Closeout, or—in facetious terms—"punishment of the innocent and reward of nonparticipants." Chapter 23 discusses the final steps in a well-run project, providing techniques to ensure that the project is remembered as well managed and successful.

Chapter 23

The Final Steps

The project has reached its scheduled end; the last task is complete; the customer has signed off on the final deliverable. The project is over. Or is it? While some projects, notably those that are managed in a haphazard manner, might end at this point, a well-managed project has a fourth phase: Closeout.

This final phase has a number of purposes:

- Ensure the orderly completion of all tasks
- Document successes and failures
- Provide for sustainability
- Recognize and formally release the team

Because these activities, while important, are sometimes forgotten, DeFuria recommends including the related tasks in the project schedule so that closeout becomes a continuation of the Execution phase.*

Completion of All Tasks

Although at this point it might appear that the project is over simply because the tasks in the Work Breakdown Structure (WBS) and schedule are complete, there is still more work to be done. The Closeout phase is often considered cleanup. Painters have not finished their work when the last wall has its final coat of color. Homeowners would agree that their effort is not complete until the scaffolding

---

* Guy L. DeFuria, *Project Management Recipes for Success* (Boca Raton, FL: Auerbach, 2009), 233.

and drop cloths have been removed, the rollers and roller trays cleaned, and everything put away. So too a project is not finished until all aspects of the work are closed.

Richman provides a project closure checklist that includes, among other items, finances, documentation, and resources.*

- *Finances*—Although the team may have been released and assigned to other projects, the project manager's work is not complete until the final accounting is done and a report is submitted to the champion, the primary customers, and other key stakeholders. Typically there is a time lag of weeks, sometimes months, before this can be achieved. Invoices, particularly from outside contractors, may not be received and paid until weeks after the project's official completion date, and internal chargebacks may have similar delays, since many are generated on a monthly basis. It is nonetheless important that the final accounting be performed, since the project and therefore the project manager's performance will be evaluated on budget fidelity as well as the cost savings or other benefits that are realized. The project finance officer, if one exists, or the project manager should ensure that all costs are reflected in the final report. In addition, the project charter (Figure 6.2) should be updated with the total cost.
- *Documentation*—Few people enjoy producing documentation, especially after the project is over; however, documentation remains long after the team has been disbanded, and its quality and completeness can be viewed as a reflection of both the project manager and the project itself. All project documentation should be reviewed and, if needed, updated with end-of-project information. This includes the various WBS documents and the project schedule. The results of the next step, the evaluation of the project's successes and failures, should also be added to the formal documentation. Companies with Project Management Offices (PMOs) will normally require this, but even if the company does not have a formal PMO, documentation should become part of the corporate archives, because it can provide valuable information for future project teams.
- *Resources*—People are typically the most important resource on a project, which is why their recognition and release are discussed separately; however, in addition to human resources, most projects utilize other resources. In the case of the WWC team, these included the use of a trailer at the new building site. Once the project is complete, those resources should be formally released. This is usually done by sending a memo, a copy of which forms part of the official documentation, to the appropriate department.

---

* Larry Richman, *Project Management Step-by-Step* (New York: AMACOM, 2002), 204.

Project Evaluation

The project evaluation, which is sometimes referred to as the postmortem, is designed to document lessons learned by the team. Its primary purpose is to provide guidance to future project teams, helping them understand what worked well and what could have been improved so that they can build on this team's success and learn from their problems. While there is a natural hesitancy to discuss problems, particularly when it is known that everything will become part of the formal project documentation, a postmortem is an essential step.

The evaluation should be conducted from two different perspectives: the project team's and the customer's. Although any of the techniques shown on Table 6.4 can be used to evaluate the project, brainstorming and the related nominal group technique are the most commonly used methods for obtaining the team's assessment. When Jim Wang convened the WWC postmortem meeting, he began by asking each member to list the three things the team did best. These were categorized, discussed, and eventually distilled into a prioritized list of successes. That activity was followed by a similar one identifying the three areas that needed the most improvement. By beginning with successes rather than failures and then ending with a recapitulation of the successes, Jim kept the team focused on the positive aspects of their work.

Surveys similar to the one shown as Figure 23.1 are commonly used to elicit customers' opinions. While the simplicity of checking a box to indicate a rating is appealing to both the survey respondents and those who compile the results, it is also helpful to allow for comments. Comments give the respondent the opportunity to vent anger or express appreciation, both of which are helpful to the project team. Figure 23.1 provides a single comment box, while other surveys allow for comments related to each category.

An alternative approach for obtaining customer feedback is to conduct focus groups. As Table 6.4 points out, the disadvantage of a focus group is that some individuals may not be comfortable expressing opinions in a group setting. If focus groups are used, the facilitator should be careful in the selection of participants. Recognizing the tension between former IW and GWC employees and the differences in the two companies' cultures, the WWC team conducted separate sessions for each group. They realized that IW employees' tendency to be more outspoken might intimidate GWC staff and wanted to avoid potential unpleasantness.

While the primary focus in the postmortem is on the overall project, it is also important to evaluate each team member's performance and to provide appraisals to all employees as well as their managers. Even if this is not a formal performance evaluation, the information should become part of the employee's regular appraisal. Besides being an effective way to recognize accomplishments, another benefit of staff assessment is the prevention of "punishment of the innocent and reward of nonparticipants."

Project Name:

We recently completed a project for you. Please let us know how well we met your needs.

Category	Ranking (check one)					
	Excellent	Very Good	Satisfactory	Fair	Poor	N/A
QUALITY OF WORK How well did our work meet your requirements?						
ON-TIME DELIVERY Did we complete the work when we promised we would?						
DEFECTS Was our work defect free?						
PERFORMANCE TO BUDGET Was our work completed within budget?						
ISSUE RESOLUTION If problems occurred, how well did we resolve them?						

Figure 23.1 Customer satisfaction survey.

PERSONNEL ASSIGNED How would you rate the staff assigned to your project?				
COMMUNICATION Did we keep you adequately informed about our progress?				
OVERALL SATISFACTION How would you rate the quality of service we provided?				
COMMENTS				

Would you like a follow-up call to discuss your ratings? _____ (Yes) _____ (No)

If yes, please complete the following:

Name	
Phone	
Best time to be called	

Figure 23.1   (Continued)

Although individual contractors should not receive formal performance appraisals, since that could create the impression of co-employment, it is appropriate for the project manager to hold a "what worked/what didn't" discussion with each of the contracting firms. The firm's overall performance should be noted in the project documentation to provide future teams with facts for their own contractor selection process.

Sustainability

The project may have accomplished all of its goals, but—depending on the nature of the project itself—Closeout may be only the beginning. In describing a typical life cycle, Kemp includes three phases following the project close: production and maintenance, obsolescence, and decommissioning.* The addition of these phases reflects the fact that for projects such as development of computer software or upgrading of an assembly line, unlike a one-time event such as Johnny's birthday party, once the initial work is done, there is a transition from development into production. The project, which by definition was unique and finite, has ended, but it is replaced by the ongoing, repetitive work of the production state. The WWC headquarters project had both a one-time component, the relocation of employees from California and New Jersey to Colorado, and ongoing aspects. For this team, the production state was the day-to-day running of the building. The ease with which employees settled into their new offices, the efficiency of the cafeteria, and the savings the company derived from the environmentally sound building techniques were the ultimate measure of the project team's success.

Whenever a project has an ongoing component, the project manager is responsible for ensuring that there is a formal transition from development to production. It is likely that different individuals will be responsible for the running of the system or the operation of the building. Rather than simply walk away once the project is complete, the team should work with the groups that will be responsible for the continuing operation, ensuring that they have the information they need to be successful.

One of the keys to long-term success is effective maintenance. Whether it is computer software or a new piece of equipment on the assembly line, the people who have to keep it running should be involved as early as possible in the project so that they understand why the final product was designed the way it is and how to tweak or overhaul it to keep it running smoothly.

Chapter 21 discussed the importance of providing training for everyone who will be impacted by the project. Depending on the project, this may not be a

---

* Sid Kemp, *Project Management Demystified* (New York: McGraw-Hill, 2004), 66–68.

one-time event. It may also be necessary to plan for future training. Staff turnover during the life of the system or product may later require some people to receive all the training that was given initially. In addition, it may be desirable to provide refresher training for those who were trained as part of the project implementation. Although the WWC team did not envision a need for ongoing training, many other projects will benefit from it.

The considerations for training replacement staff are the same as those for the initial training, with one exception. Since it is likely that there will be only a few people who need training at any one time, it may not be cost effective to conduct classroom training. The team may want to consider alternative approaches, including developing a computer-based training (CBT) course and supplementing that with mentoring by more experienced staff.

Refresher training is different from initial training but can be equally critical to the project's success. Anyone who has done training knows the depressing statistics of how little participants retain from a class, no matter how well delivered it is. To increase customers' knowledge of the system or product, it is important to provide continuing education. This can be done in a variety of ways.

- *Refresher Courses*—The team may want to offer the initial training, one section at a time. Covering only one aspect of the system or product in any one session allows employees to select the functionality they feel least comfortable with and does not require a major commitment of time. It is, after all, easier to leave the workplace for a half day than for the three to five days that may have been involved in initial training.
- *Newsletters*—In addition to touting the successes of the project, a regular newsletter can provide a "Did You Know?" column, focusing on different ways to use the system or product. In some cases, this may be nothing more than a reiteration of the material that was covered in class. In others, it may be an introduction of a more advanced function that was not included in the original training. As with other forms of communication, the newsletter can be delivered in either paper or electronic format, depending on the company's culture and user preferences.
- *Lunch and Learn*—If the team wants to demonstrate specific functionality or teach users new techniques but does not want to develop or conduct a full course, a classroom environment may be preferable to a newsletter. Some companies have established monthly "Lunch and Learn" sessions in which users are invited to bring their lunch to a classroom and learn a new aspect of the system or product. The advantage of this approach is that it does not require employees to schedule time away from their jobs. It may also encourage camaraderie and sharing among customers.

Training may not be the only aspect to sustainability. The original project description for the WWC headquarters building project was "Provide office space for 150 employees, including ten executives; create five meeting rooms and a cafeteria that will accommodate 100 people; reduce total building operating costs (defined as water and power) by 25 percent from Bluebell Industries' costs for the prior year." While the first two clauses of that definition represent one-time efforts whose success can be measured at the completion of the project, the reduction of operating costs is an ongoing goal. At the conclusion of the Execution and Control phase, the project team had no proof that its efforts had indeed reduced operating costs. Only the passage of time and careful measurements would determine whether the project met that goal.

The WWC project is not unique. Many projects' cost/benefit analysis and ultimate justification are based on cost reductions in future years. For all of these, it is important to develop a process for measuring and communicating the project's success in meeting those goals. The WWC team knew that the key was effective metrics. As they did in Chapter 20, they determined which items to measure. Although overall operating costs were important, because of seasonal fluctuations and the fact that they had only annual costs from Bluebell Industries, they could report on cost reductions only once a year. They would, of course, track cost information and provide annual reports, but overall operating cost would not be their primary metric. Instead, they focused on the goals for the cafeteria and developed a scorecard similar to the one shown as Figure 20.3 to report the progress on four items: net monthly cost, number of injuries, average time in line, and customer satisfaction. This scorecard was created monthly and posted on the project website. In addition, posters showing the results on a quarterly basis were displayed at the entrance to the cafeteria.

Reporting results is important; however, it is not enough. It is also essential to determine what actions should be taken if the expected results are not attained. This is done through the development of a control plan, a tool that Jim learned to use during his Six Sigma training. As illustrated on Figure 23.2, the control plan lists each metric, shows how it is developed, the expected results, and what is to be done if the goals are not achieved. The answer to "What do we do if there's a problem?" is a reaction plan. In some cases, the reaction plan is a simple one. In others, where a more complex process is invoked, reference is made to another document. A sample reaction plan is shown as Figure 23.3.

While some teams may question the need for the formality of a control plan and one or more reaction plans, there is a reason why establishing them is important: they reduce variation. As discussed previously, one of the tenets of Six Sigma is the need to reduce variation, since that reduces costs and increases quality. If a control plan exists, when a problem occurs, everyone involved knows how to react to it. This translates into faster resolution of problems and more satisfied customers. In other words, a control plan is an example of the Five Ps in action.

Project	WWC Cafeteria					
Metric	What's Being Measured?	What Are the Expected Results?	How Are We Measuring?			What if There's a Problem?
			Measurement/Control Technique	Sample Size	Sample Frequency	Reaction Plan
Average Time in Line	Tray has embedded chip; system tracks time removed from stack to time exiting checkout	Maximum time ≤ 5 minutes	System calculates elapsed time, flags if 50% of trays within a 10 minute interval exceed limit	n/a; all trays are measured	Continuous	WWC-408
Net Monthly Cost	Total operating cost of cafeteria (cost center 98001) and total operating revenue	Net operating cost ≤ $5,000	Finance Department calculates cost as part of the monthly closing process	n/a	Monthly	Notify director of F&S
Customer Satisfaction	Customer satisfaction on five key elements using score of 1 - 5	Overall satisfaction ≥ 4; no elements < 2	Survey results are scanned into system; system calculates averages	n/a; all surveys are tabulated	Daily	Notify director of F&S
Number of Injuries	Number of accidents that result in injuries requiring visit to Medical Department	< 1 per quarter	Medical Department reports injuries at end of each month	n/a; all injuries are reported	N/A	Notify director of F&S and director of HS&E

Figure 23.2 Control plan.

Worldwide Widget Company Standard Operating Procedure

Procedure Number	WWC-408		Revision Number: 0
Procedure Name	Reaction to Excessive Time in Line Alert		
Date Issued	12/01/10		
Date Revised	N/A		
Primary Responsibility	F&S Cafeteria Supervisor		
Out of Spec Condition	> 50% of trays used within 10 minutes exceeded the 5 minute maximum for time in line		
Identified By	Cafeteria Tray Tracking System		
Probable Cause	*What to Check*		*Corrective Action*
Large Group of Customers	Summary screen shows customer count in five minute intervals.		If greater than 30, System capacity has been exceeded. Implement discount procedure (check-out clerks to provide all customers with 5% discount coupons for next visit). If > 20 and < 30, Verify that all check-out stations are operational (check-out screen indicates status).
Serving Station Delays	Visually check number of customers in line at each station.		If > 5 at any station, Determine whether there are equipment problems; if detected, offer customer 5% discount coupon to choose another line. Determine whether all ingredients are available; if not, notify Replenishment assistant to reorder, and give customer 5% discount coupon for inconvenience.

Figure 23.3   Reaction plan

Team Recognition and Release

The project manager's final responsibility is to ensure that the facetious punishment of the innocent and reward of nonparticipants does not occur. Instead, this is the time to recognize the team's accomplishments and officially disband it. The team has been working together for some time. If the project manager has been successful, they have reached the fourth stage of team development and are fully performing. And, although there may have been disagreements and personality conflicts, at this point most teams have developed a sense of camaraderie. While they are naturally eager for the project to be completed, there is also a sense of impending loss, for many of them will not work together again. Recognizing this as a natural human reaction, the project manager should ensure that the project ends with a formal celebration of all that the team has accomplished. Similar to graduation exercises, this provides the opportunity for the team to reflect on what they have done together at the same time that they look forward to the future.

Both IW and GWC had a history of celebratory events that included team lunches and trips to sporting or cultural events. While IW had reserved these events for the culmination of a project, GWC had a policy of organizing celebrations when major project milestones were met for projects that exceeded six months in duration. Within both companies, it was a tradition that at the conclusion of projects, the sponsoring department would hold a departmental meeting to recognize the team's accomplishments. Depending on the size and cost savings generated by the project, team members might receive a plaque or a certificate citing their accomplishments. Large-scale projects frequently included monetary awards as part of their celebration step. In all cases, the project's conclusion was highlighted in the company's quarterly newsletter and on its internal website.

The headquarters team celebration had two parts. The first was a team dinner at one of Denver's finest restaurants. In addition to the team and the champion, both Isabelle Crumpton and George Webster attended to thank the team for their successful completion of the work. That was followed by a meeting of all headquarters staff in—where else?—the new cafeteria. During the meeting, both Isabelle and George delivered public accolades to the team and announced that each team member would receive an extra week's vacation and that Frank had been promoted to senior vice president because of the project's success.

What Can Go Wrong?

The two most common problems associated with the Closeout phase are failure to recognize team members' accomplishments and failure to ensure the project's sustainability.

- *Team Recognition*—It is human nature to want one's accomplishments to be recognized, yet all too often project managers forget that congratulations and thanks are key to employees' self-esteem and that managers who compliment their staff are the ones who gain a reputation for being fair. DeFuria recommends going beyond the team members themselves and sending letters of appreciation to the functional managers who provided staff to the project. As he points out, this is a good political move and may make it easier to obtain staff for the next project.*

■ *Project Sustainability*—It is understandable that project managers are eager to complete a project and begin the next one, but failure to ensure the sustainability of the current one can be a fatal mistake. A project manager's reputation depends not just on the successful completion of all primary tasks but also on the long-term success of the product produced. Planning for ongoing measurement of achievements and communication of the results is an essential part of being a project manager.

Project management is complex and involves a variety of skills. As they work to plan and execute a project, managers must surmount obstacles at the same time that they juggle the myriad tasks of scheduling work, motivating staff, communicating with customers, and balancing budgets. It is a challenging job, but with the correct tools and techniques, the probability of success is greatly increased. Prior planning does prevent poor performance.

---

* DeFuria, *Project Management Recipes for Success*, 242.

APPENDICES

Appendix A:
List of Acronyms

Acronym	Meaning
ACWP	Actual Cost of Work Performed, a component of Earned Value Analysis
ADM	Arrow Diagram Method, a method of project scheduling
BCWP	Budgeted Cost of Work Performed, a component of Earned Value Analysis; also referred to as Earned Value (EV)
BCWS	Budgeted Cost of Work Scheduled, a component of Earned Value Analysis
CBT	Computer-Based Training
CCB	Change Control Board
CMM	Capability Maturity Model, the five-level definition of software process maturity
COE	Center of Excellence
COPQ	Cost of Poor Quality, the cost of defects or problems, including inspection, rework, and reporting
CPAF	Cost Plus Award Fee, a type of contract
CPFF	Cost Plus Fixed Fee, a type of contract
CPI	Cost Performance Index, a component of Earned Value Analysis
CPIF	Cost Plus Incentive Fee, a type of contract
CPM	Critical Path Method, a method of project scheduling

Acronym	Meaning
CSF	Critical Success Factor, the things that must go right if a project is to meet its objectives
CV	Cost Variation, a component of Earned Value Analysis
DFSS	Design for Six Sigma
EAC	Estimate at Completion, a component of Earned Value Analysis
EF	Early Finish, a component used to calculate project slack
ES	Early Start, a component used to calculate project slack
EV	Earned Value, a component of Earned Value Analysis; also referred to as Budgeted Cost of Work Performed (BCWP)
EVA	Earned Value Analysis, a method of measuring project performance
FAQs	Frequently Asked Questions, normally a document that is part of the project's formal communications
FF	Finish-to-Finish, a network diagram dependency relationship.
FFP	Firm Fixed Price, a type of contract
Five Ps	Prior Planning Prevents Poor Performance
Five Ws	Who, What, Where, When, Why
FMEA	Failure Modes and Effects Analysis, a tool used to document and prioritize risks
Four Ps	Components of successful change: purpose, picture, plan, part
FPIF	Fixed Price with Incentive Fee, a type of contract
FS	Finish-to-Start, a network diagram dependency relationship
FV	Future Value, used in Present Value calculations
GERT	Graphical Evaluation and Review Technique, a method of project scheduling
GRACE	Items to be reviewed at the start of each meeting: Goals, Roles, Agenda, Code of Conduct, Expectations
HS&E	Health, Safety, and Environment
IRR	Internal Rate of Return; the interest rate the company uses to calculate Net Present Value

Acronym	Meaning
IT	Information Technology
KISS	Keep It Simple, Stupid; the basic principle for communication
LF	Late Finish, a component used to calculate project slack
LS	Late Start, a component used to calculate project slack
MSA	Master Services Agreement; the primary contract specifying the terms and conditions under which a company and a contractor will do business
NPV	Net Present Value; a calculation used to determine the value over time of the money invested in a project
PARIS	The roles shown on a responsibility matrix: Participant, Accountable, Review Required, Input Required, Sign-off Required; a variation of a RACI matrix
PDM	Precedence Diagram Method, a method of project scheduling
PERT	Program Evaluation and Review Technique, a method of project scheduling
PMBOK	Project Management Book of Knowledge
PMO	Project Management Office
PMP	Project Management Professional, certification given by the Project Management Institute
PV	Present Value, a calculation used to determine how much future benefits would be worth if they were delivered today
QFD	Quality Function Deployment, a complex matrix relating requirements (what's) and the functions or features that will be used to satisfy them (how's)
RACI	The roles shown on a responsibility matrix: Responsible, Accountable, Consult, Inform
RAVE	Characteristics of measurements: Relevant, Adequate to detect changes, Valid and consistent from one time to the next, Easy
RCS	Rumor Control Session, an informal communication method designed to help employees cope with impending change
RFP	Request for Proposal, a formal request that a potential supplier present a proposal for goods or services to the requesting company

Acronym	*Meaning*
RIF	Reduction in Force, layoff
ROI	Return on Investment
ROM	Rough Order of Magnitude, a preliminary estimate of costs or time, a "guesstimate"
RPN	Risk Priority Number, a column on the FMEA, representing the degree of risk a particular potential problem poses to the project
SAC	Schedule at Completion, a component of Earned Value Analysis
SEI	Software Engineering Institute, the division of Carnegie Mellon University that developed the Capability Maturity Model (CMM)
SMART	Characteristics of a problem statement or requirement: Specific, Measurable, Attainable, Relevant, Time bound
SOW	Statement of Work; typically an amendment to an MSA, identifying the specific work to be performed by a contractor but not the overall Ts and Cs
SPI	Schedule Performance Index, a component of Earned Value Analysis
SS	Start-to-Start, a network diagram dependency relationship
SV	Schedule Variance, a component of Earned Value Analysis
SWOT	Strengths, Weaknesses, Opportunities and Threats; an analysis typically used to evaluate a project during strategic planning
Ts and Cs	Terms and Conditions; normally applies to contracts and refers to the non-pricing-related elements
WBS	Work Breakdown Structure, a hierarchal list of all tasks to be completed as part of the project

Appendix B: The Project Charter

The charter is the single most important document in a project, since it is used to establish the project and provides a summary of key information. While other forms are optional, all projects should have a charter. Figure B.1 shows a sample charter. The remainder of this appendix outlines the use of the charter and explains how to complete each field.

Who creates it? Although the project's champion may begin to complete some of the basic fields, it is normally the project manager or a designated recorder/scribe who is responsible for creating the charter.

When is it created? Key fields are completed during the team's first meeting. Others are added at later stages in the project.

Who is responsible for updating the form? The project manager has continuing responsibility for the accuracy and completeness of the charter.

How often is it updated? Whenever information shown on the form changes, the charter should be updated.

Who can view the data? At a minimum, the charter should be available to all team members and affected customers (although some companies may insist that financial information be removed before distributing it to external customers). Ideally, the charter should be available to anyone within the organization.

Summary					
Project Name		Total Financial Impact			
Team Leader		Champion			
Start Date		Target Completion Date			
Project Description					
Departments Impacted					
Processes Impacted					
Benefits					
	Units	Current	Goal	Actual Achieved	Projected Date
Cost Reduction					
Increased Sales					
Customer Sat					
Other Benefits					
Team Membership					
Name	Role		Department		% Time
Support Required					
Training Required					
Other Support Required					
Schedule					
Milestone/Deliverable	Target Date	Owner	Estimated Cost	Comments	
Critical Success Factors and Risks					
Critical Success Factors					
Risks					
Approvals					
Role/Title	Name		Date		
Revision History					
Revision Number	Authors		Date		

Figure B.1   Project charter.

Field	*How to Complete It*
Summary Section	This section serves to document key descriptive information about the project.
Project Name	Enter the project's name. This is one of the key fields that should be entered at the team's first meeting.
Total Financial Impact	Enter the net financial effect of the project; that is, the anticipated cost savings minus any costs incurred during the project. It is unlikely that this information will be available at the early stages of the project, but the impact should be documented as soon as it is estimated.
Team Leader	Enter the name of the person who has been designated the team leader/project manager. This information should be available and entered at the first team meeting.
Champion	Enter the name of the project champion. This information should be available and entered at the first team meeting.
Start Date	Enter the date that the project was initiated. Depending on the company's preference, this can be either the date that the team was chartered or the date of the first team meeting. The start date should be entered at the first team meeting.
Target Completion Date	Enter the date that the execution phase of the project is expected to be completed. Although this field is subject to revision as the project progresses through the various phases, it should be entered as soon as it is projected.
Project Description	Enter a brief description of the project, including a summary of anticipated benefits. Once the formal problem and goal statements are developed, they should be added to this field.
Departments Impacted	List all departments whose employees will be affected by the results of the project.
Processes Impacted	List all processes that will be changed as a result of the project.

Field	How to Complete It
Benefits Section	The purpose of this section is to quantify the projected benefits of the project. Although three potential benefit categories have been listed, it is likely that a project will have other benefits. These should be described and quantified on separate lines. When "Other Benefits" are quantified, it is important to replace the words "Other Benefits" with the specific benefit to be achieved.
Benefits—Units	All entries in the benefits section should have the unit of measure specified in this field. Increased sales unit of measure might be "tons," if the company's product were sold in tons, while customer satisfaction units might be "scale of 1 to 5."
Benefits—Current	Enter the current or baseline level of this item.
Benefits—Goal	Enter the projected level for this item once the process improvements have been implemented.
Benefits—Actual Achieved	Enter the level that was actually achieved once the process improvements were implemented. This column will not be completed until the Control phase of the project.
Benefits—Projected Date	Enter the date at which the benefits are anticipated to have been realized.
Team Membership Section	This section identifies the people who will serve on the team, their roles, and the percentage of time they are expected to devote to the project.
Name	Enter the team member's name.
Role	Enter his or her role on the team. At a minimum, Team Leader should be identified with all other participants being listed as Team Members.
Department	Enter the team member's department or, if he or she is an external customer, his or her company affiliation.
% Time	Enter the percentage of time the team member is expected to spend on the project. It should be noted that this is an average, and that at certain phases of the project, participation may be at a higher or lower level.

Field	*How to Complete It*
Support Required Section	This section allows the team to clearly identify support requirements other than team members' time and the costs associated with each milestone/deliverable below.
Training Required	Enter the type of training that will be required. If training must be completed by a specific date, it is helpful to note that, as well as any costs that will be incurred.
Other Support Required	If the project team will need other types of support, such as contiguous workspace or access to specific network drives, enter that information, along with the date that the support is needed.
Schedule Section	This section serves as a high-level project plan, showing—at a minimum—the dates on which each of the project phases is targeted to be completed. Longer projects may divide phases into smaller milestones and may document the schedule for completion of specific deliverables on the charter.
Milestone/ Deliverable	Enter the name of the milestone or deliverable.
Target Date	Enter the date on which the milestone or deliverable is expected to be completed.
Owner	Enter the name of the person with overall responsibility for the milestone or deliverable. This may not always be the team leader.
Estimated Cost	If there will be costs in addition to team members' time, enter them here. Costs may include travel expenses. Items listed in the "Support Required" section should not be repeated here.
Comments	This field can be used to indicate the completion of a milestone or to document the reasons for a changed target date.
Critical Success Factor and Risk Section	The purpose of this section is to identify the CSFs and risks that the project faces.
Critical Success Factors	Enter the events that must occur if the project is to be successful.

Field	How to Complete It
Risks	Enter the potential reasons that the project may not be successful.
Approval Section	The approval section serves to document the review and approval of the project charter. Approvals of other project documents are recorded on the individual deliverables.
Role/Title	If the approver is the project champion or sponsor, enter the role; otherwise, enter the individual's title.
Name	Enter the reviewer's name.
Date	Enter the date on which the reviewer approved the project charter.
Revision History Section	The purpose of this section is to document when changes were made to the project charter and by whom.
Revision Number	Enter the revision number. Normally revisions are given sequential whole numbers.
Authors	Enter the name of the persons who actually revised the document. This may or may not be the person who instigated the change to the document.
Date	Enter the date on which the revision was made.

Appendix C: The Functional Process Map

Process maps are tools used to provide pictorial representations of the sequence of steps in a process. While other maps depict only the tasks or steps, the functional process map clearly illustrates which department or function is responsible for each step. Figure C.1 shows the format of a functional process map. The remainder of this appendix outlines the use of a map and explains how to complete each field.

Who creates it? Anyone on the project team may be responsible for creation of a functional process map.

When is it created? The initial process map is typically created during the Initiation/Definition phase of a project. This is often referred to as the "as is" process. Maps showing the proposed revisions to the process, the "to be" state, are developed at the end of this phase.

Who is responsible for updating the form? The individual who created the initial map should assume responsibility for its updates.

How often is it updated? Whenever the team uncovers new steps or dependencies, or if the process changes, the map should be updated.

Who can view the data? At a minimum, the map should be available to all team members and affected customers. Ideally, it should be available to anyone within the organization.

Functional Process Map

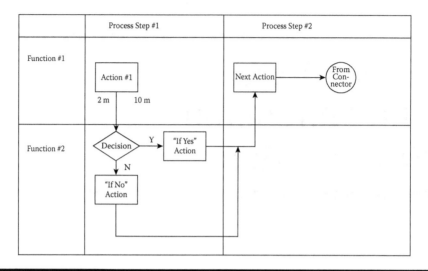

Figure C.1 Functional process map.

Mapping Conventions

Rectangles represent actions.

Diamonds indicate a decision point. Each diamond will have two lines exiting from it, one representing the action taken if the answer to the question is positive, and the other showing the result of a negative response.

Circles represent connectors from one page to the next. The corresponding "from" and "to" connectors will have the same number.

Lines with arrowheads illustrate the directional flow of tasks and decisions.

Field	How to Complete It
Process Step #1, Process Step #2	Enter the names of the individual process steps being charted along the top of the map. Examples are "Order Entry" and "Packing." If there is only one step, this information may be omitted.
Function #1, Function #2	Enter the names of the departments or the functions within departments that have responsibility for tasks. "Customer" or "Supplier" may be used as function names.

Field	*How to Complete It*
Action #1	1. Enter the first step in the process, using a verb/object construct; e.g., "Enter customer name and number." The position of the action box indicates which department or function has primary responsibility for it. In this example, Function #1 initiates Action #1.
	2. Draw a line exiting from the action and pointing to the next action or decision. Depending on where the next action box will be placed on the map, the exit line should come from either the right side or the bottom of the action box. In this case, since the next activity is a decision to be made by Function #2, the line exits from the bottom and points to a diamond within Function #2.
	3. If the team has identified the minimum and maximum time required for the action, these can be indicated below the box. The minimum time is shown to the left, the maximum to the right. In this case, the range of times for Action #1 is from two to ten minutes.
Decision	1. Enter the question that requires a decision, using an abbreviated question format; e.g., "Customer in database?"
	2. Draw two exit lines, one from the right side of the diamond, the other from the bottom.
	3. Label the line to the right "yes" or "y," the one from the bottom "no" or "n."
"If Yes" Action	Following the rules shown for Action #1, enter the action to be performed if the answer to the decision was "yes." In this example, the responsibility for this action is with Function #1.

Field	*How to Complete It*
"If No" Action	Following the rules shown for Action #1, enter the action to be performed if the answer to the decision was "no." In this example, the responsibility for this action is with Function #1.
Next Action	Following the rules shown for Action #1, enter the next action to be performed. In this example, the responsibility for this action is with Function #2.
Connector	Because the next action will be shown on another page, a connector is needed. Enter a unique number in the circle. The next page will begin with a connector with the same number.

Appendix D: The Failure Modes and Effects Analysis (FMEA)

The Failure Modes and Effects Analysis spreadsheet (FMEA) is used to identify the risks in a project, to quantify the effects on customers if those risks became reality, and to establish mitigation plans for high-risk items. Figure D.1 shows the format of an FMEA. The remainder of this appendix outlines the use of the spreadsheet and explains how to complete each field.

> *Who creates it?* Anyone on the project team may be responsible for creation of an FMEA.
>
> *When is it created?* A preliminary risk assessment often occurs at the beginning of a project when the champion is evaluating whether or not a project is feasible. Once a project has been initiated, an FMEA is typically created at the end of the Initiation/Definition phase, with highlights included in the business case.
>
> *Who is responsible for updating the form?* Anyone on the team can assume responsibility for the updates.
>
> *How often is it updated?* The FMEA should be updated when the actions outlined in the Action Plan section are completed. Additionally, since it is a "living" document, the FMEA should be reviewed periodically as part of the Execution and Control phase to determine whether there are any new potential failure modes.
>
> *Who can view the data?* The FMEA is often included in the briefing given to senior management when seeking approval for the project. As a key project document, it should be made available to all team members and to interested customers.

249

| Project Name: | | Date Prepared: | | Revision Number: |
| Prepared By: | | Revised By: | | Revision Date: |

| | What Could Happen? | | Why and How Often? | | What Will We Do? | Action Plan | | | |
Project Phase	Potential Failure Mode	Potential Failure Effects / S E V	Potential Causes / O C C	R P N	Proposed Action (Avoidance, Containment, Mitigation, Evasion)	Actions Recommended	Resp.	Target Date	Date Completed/ Comments

Figure D.1 Failure Modes and Effects Analysis (FMEA).

Field	*How to Complete It*
Project Name	Enter the project's name.
Prepared By	Enter the name of the person completing the initial version of the FMEA.
Date Prepared	Enter the date the initial version was created.
Revised By	For all subsequent versions of the FMEA, enter the name of the person who documented this revision. This may or may not be the person who was responsible for the change being documented.
Revision Number	Enter the revision number. Normally revisions are given sequential whole numbers.
Revision Date	Enter the date on which the revision was made.
Project Phase	Enter the name of the project phase during which the risk might occur. If the FMEA is being created after the Work Breakdown Structure (WBS) has been developed, include the task number.
"What Could Happen?" Section	This section describes the possible failures and their effect on customer requirements.
Potential Failure Mode	Describe ways in which the project might fail. Each potential failure should be listed in a separate row.
Potential Failure Effects	Describe the impact that the failure would have on customer requirements.
Severity	Quantify the impact of a failure on the customer's requirements. To provide clear distinctions among potential failures, a scale of 1-4-7-10 is recommended.
"Why and How Often?" Section	This section quantifies potential causes and the frequency with which the failure occurs.

Field	How to Complete It
Potential Causes	List possible causes of the failure. If there are multiple causes for a single failure, each should be shown in a separate row.
Frequency of Occurrence (OCC)	Quantify the frequency with which this possible cause might occur, resulting in failure. Use a scale of 1-4-7-10.
Risk Priority Number (RPN)	This is a calculated field, the result of multiplying Severity and Occurrence. Failure modes with high RPNs should have corresponding corrective action plans developed.
"What Will We Do?" Section	This section describes the proposed action to be taken and the probability that it may not detect/prevent the failure.
Proposed Action	Categorize the proposed action as avoidance, containment, mitigation or evasion. If the action is either containment or mitigation, provide an explanation of the reserve to be maintained (containment) or the actions to be undertaken (mitigation).
"Action Plan" Section	This section describes the actions that will be taken to mitigate high-risk items.
Actions Recommended	Describe the action that will be taken to reduce the occurrence or the failure probability.
Responsible Person	Enter the name of the person responsible for completing the action.
Target Date	Enter the date that the corrective action is to be completed.
Date Completed/Comments	Enter the date the action was completed and any explanatory notes.

Appendix E: Metric Reliability Assessment Spreadsheet

The metric reliability assessment spreadsheet helps a team determine which metrics will have the most validity. Figure E.1 shows the format of the metric reliability assessment spreadsheet. The remainder of this appendix outlines the use of the spreadsheet and explains how to complete each field.

Who creates it? Anyone on the project team may be responsible for creation of a metric reliability assessment spreadsheet.

When is it created? Metric assessment typically occurs at the beginning of the Execution and Control phase when the team begins to establish its key metrics.

Who is responsible for updating the form? The form is rarely updated; however, anyone on the team can assume responsibility for the updates.

How often is it updated? Rarely. Once metrics have been established, there is no need to revise the spreadsheet.

Who can view the data? All team members and interested customers should have access to the information.

Project:										
Prepared By:										
Date Prepared:										
Metric	Measurement	Collector	Data Reliability	Data Repeatability	Collection Delays	Collector Availability	Total Metric Reliability	Comments		
Averages										

Figure E.1 Metric reliability assessment spreadsheet.

Field	How to Complete It
Project Name	Enter the name of the project for which metrics are being developed.
Prepared By	Enter the name of the person completing the assessment spreadsheet.
Date Prepared	Enter the date the assessment was completed.
Metric	Enter the proposed metric.
Measurement	Enter each of the measurements that form part of a metric.
Collector	Enter either the name of the person who will take the measurement or the person's job title/function.
Data Reliability	Quantify the objectivity of the data: • 1 = subjective, no historical basis • 4 = based on individual estimate • 7 = based on direct observation • 10 = obtained directly from an objective source; e.g., computer system, time stamp
Data Repeatability	Quantify the degree to which the measurement is repeatable among collectors: • 1 = subjective • 4 = based on data specific to the collector; e.g., operator's wrist watch • 7 = transcribed from printed source • 10 = obtained directly from an objective source; e.g., computer system, time stamp
Collection Delays	Quantify the delays in obtaining the data: • 1 = Request for measurement waits in a queue or inbox and is addressed sporadically • 4 = Request for measurement is processed at regular intervals but less frequently than daily • 7 = Request for measurement is processed at regular intervals more frequently than daily but not immediately • 10 = Request is processed immediately

Field	*How to Complete It*
Collector Availability	Quantify the degree to which the collector is involved in other activities and unable to take measurements: • 1 = Higher priority activities require >75 percent of time • 4 = Higher priority activities require >50 but <75 percent of time • 7 = Higher priority activities require >25 but < 50 percent of time • 10 = This is the collector's highest priority or the data comes from an automated source
Total Metric Reliability	This is a calculated field, the result of summing the four previous fields.
Comments	Enter any information about the individual measurements that may explain low reliability scores.
Averages	This is a calculated field, the result of averaging each of the numeric fields. It is useful in pointing out areas for improvement.

Appendix F:
Suggested Reading

Berkun, Scott. *The Art of Project Management*. Sebastopol, CA: O'Reilly Media, 2005.

Bridges, William. *Managing Transitions*. Cambridge, MA: Perseus, 2003.

Carnegie Mellon University Software Engineering Institute. *The Capability Maturity Model*. New York: Addison-Wesley, 1995.

Chowdhury, Subir. *Design for Six Sigma*. Chicago: Dearborn Trade, 2005.

Chowdhury, Subir. *The Power of Six Sigma*. Chicago: Dearborn Trade, 2001.

Conner, Daryl R. *Managing at the Speed of Change*. New York: Villard, 1992.

DeFuria, Guy L. *Project Management Recipes for Success*. Boca Raton, FL: Auerbach, 2009.

DeMarco, Tom, and Timothy Lister. *Waltzing with Bears: Managing Risk on Software Projects*. New York: Dorset House, 2003.

Harry, Mikel, and Richard Schroeder. *Six Sigma: The Breakthrough Management Strategy Revolutionizing the World's Top Corporations*. New York: Doubleday, 2000.

Hersey, Paul, and Kenneth H. Blanchard. *Management of Organizational Behavior*. Englewood Cliffs: Prentice Hall, 1988.

Johnson, Spencer. *Who Moved My Cheese?* New York: G. Putnam's Sons, 1998.

Jones, Richard. *Project Management Survival*. London: Kogan Page, 2007.

Kanter, Rosabeth Moss. *The Change Masters*. New York: Simon and Schuster, 1983.

Kemp, Sid. *Project Management Demystified*. New York: McGraw-Hill, 2004.

Kerzner, Harold. *Project Management: A Systems Approach to Planning, Scheduling and Controlling*, 9th ed. Hoboken: John Wiley & Sons, 2006.

Lewis, James P. *Fundamentals of Project Management*. New York: AMACOM, 1997.

Meredith, Jack R., and Samuel J. Mantel Jr. *Project Management: A Managerial Approach*, 6th ed. Hoboken: John Wiley & Sons, 2006.

Mintzer, Rich. *The Everything Project Management Book*. Avon, MA: Adams Media, 2002.

Morris, Rick A., and Brette McWhorter Sember. *Project Management That Works*. New York: AMACOM, 2008.

Orr, Alan D. *Advanced Project Management*. London: Kogan Page, 2004.

Pande, Peter, and Larry Holpp. *What Is Six Sigma?* New York: McGraw-Hill, 2002.

Project Management Institute. *A Guide to the Project Management Body of Knowledge*, 3rd ed. (*PMBOK Guide*). Newtown Square: PMI, 2004.

Purba, Sanjiv, and Joseph J. Zucchero. *Project Rescue: Avoiding a Project Management Disaster.* New York: McGraw-Hill/Osborne, 2004.

Richman, Larry. *Project Management Step-by-Step.* New York: AMACOM, 2002.

Schwalbe, Kathy. *Information Technology Project Management.* Cambridge, MA: Course Technology, 2000.

Tayntor, Christine B. "The Outsourcing Contract, Part 1: The Process," *Information Management: Strategy, Systems and Technologies.* Boca Raton, FL: Auerbach, 2003.

Tayntor, Christine B., "The Outsourcing Contract, Part 2: Terms and Conditions," *Information Management: Strategy, Systems and Technologies.* Boca Raton, FL: Auerbach, 2003.

Tayntor, Christine B. "A Practical Guide to Staff Augmentation and Outsourcing," *Information Management: Strategy, Systems and Technologies.* Boca Raton, FL: Auerbach, 2000.

Whitten, Neal. *Neal Whitten's No-Nonsense Advice for Successful Projects.* Vienna, VA: Management Concepts, 2005.

Index

259